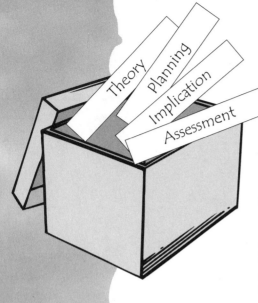

Theory Planning Implication Assessment

Early Childhood Curriculum

Incorporating Multiple Intelligences, Developmentally Appropriate Practice, and Play

Rae Ann Hirsh

Early Childhood and Elementary Consultant
Pittsburgh, Pennsylvania

PEARSON
and

Boston   New York   San Francisco
Mexico City   Montreal   Toronto   London   Madrid   Munich   Paris
Hong Kong   Singapore   Tokyo   Cape Town   Sydney

Series Editor: Traci Mueller
Marketing Manager: Elizabeth Fogarty
Composition and Prepress Buyer: Linda Cox
Manufacturing Manager: Andrew Turso
Cover Administrator: Kristina Mose-Libon
Designer: Karen Mason
Editorial-Production Coordinator: Mary Beth Finch
Editorial-Production Service: Stratford Publishing Services
Electronic Composition: Stratford Publishing Services

For related titles and support materials, visit our online catalog at www.ablongman.com.

Between the time Website information is gathered and then published, it is not unusual for some sites to have closed. Also, the transcription of URLs can result in typographical errors. The publisher would appreciate notification where these errors occur so that they may be corrected in subsequent editions.

Library of Congress Cataloging-in-Publication Data
Library of Congress Cataloging-in-Publication Data not available at press time.

ISBN: 0-205-37629-0

Printed in the United States of America

10   9   8   7   6   5   4   3   2   1   08   07   06   05   04   03

We live in a time where change is needed and
necessary for our children to thrive.

This text is dedicated to my children,
Victoria and Gabrielle,
and to the children they will grow up with.
May all children realize their unique and
wonderful strengths and use those strengths to create
an outstanding community rooted in respect,
intelligence, strength, and understanding.

For my dad,
without his loving support, encouragement, interest, and
drive for excellence, this text would not be possible.

For my mom,
who showed me as a child how unique and special my
strengths were and who allowed me to be me.

For Rachel and A.J.,
so that your children will grow up in a world that
respects the unique strengths and interests
of your children.

For my wonderful husband, Gary,
who has been my biggest supporter.
Without him, this book would not be possible.

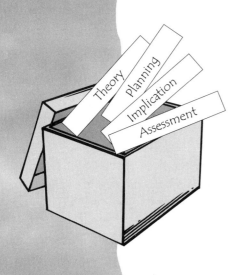

Contents

3 Traditional Intelligences 37

4 Talent or Intelligence? 75

5   The Personal Intelligences   112

6 Additional Intelligences   134

PHASE 2   PLANNING   150

7 Facilitating the Intelligence with Activities and Projects   150

8 Play   179

9 Planning Spaces and Time   227

PHASE 3   CURRICULAR IMPLICATIONS   253

10 Curricular Implications   253

PHASE 4   ASSESSMENT   272

11 Assessment   272

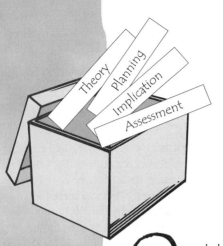

Preface

Our children are our most precious resource. The children you teach today will have an impact on generations to come. The early years of development are the most critical. It is in the early years of life that crucial brain connections are made and a foundation for intelligence is formed. You, as an early childhood teacher, are a powerful individual. The bonds you form and the environment you create will have an impact, not only on the child you teach today, but on the relationships that child will have in the future. It is absolutely necessary to make those years the best possible. This is done through:

- creating an early childhood curriculum that recognizes the many potentials that exist for children,
- respecting developmentally appropriate practice,
- creating an environment where children can construct knowledge,
- utilizing assessment as a curricular tool (instead of an end product),
- respecting the cultural, familial, and special needs of each child,
- and recognizing the unique strengths and challenges each child possesses.

This text will address these important curricular issues through a framework suggested by the National Association for the Education of Young Children (NAEYC). NAEYC explains that curriculum develops in four phases: theoretical, planning, implementation, and assessment. This text will present meaningful theory, planning concerns, implementation strategies, and assessment techniques and materials. In order to help you track your own professional growth, journal questions will be integrated throughout the text.

Introduction to the Curriculum Journal

Most early childhood texts provide questions at the end of each chapter. This text is different. Reflective questions, activities, and experiences are planned throughout the text. The questions do not necessarily have a right or a wrong answer. Instead, they invite you to thoroughly reflect on the content presented, in an ongoing journal. It is recommended that you purchase a blank journal to accompany this text. You can use the journal to complete the questions and activities. The journal will provide you an opportunity to see your own professional growth and development.

Acknowledgments

This book is heavily influenced by the multiple intelligence theory developed by Dr. Howard Gardner, application work of the theory developed by Dr. Thomas Armstrong, through years of early childhood classroom experience under the guidance of Susan Kessler-Buehl at Laural Learning center, and through work in elementary and special education classrooms under the guidance of Jim Buck at Washington Elementary School. There are many individuals who offered support, guidance, and review of this text. I'd like to take a moment to acknowledge their support.

TRACI MUELLER, her support, inspiration, and motivation were vital to the completion of this text. I thank her for her belief in me and in this project; **GARY HIRSH,** for countless hours of inspiration, support, review, and understanding; **BARBARA GEARY,** for her genuine response to the text from a teacher's perspective; **ALLEN GEARY,** for his generosity in sharing technology and interest in this text and for believing in me; **DR. ROBERTA SCHOMBURG,** for showing me what it means to be a professional in the early childhood field and for her support, encouragement, and review of the material in this text; **ANNETTE SANTELLA,** for providing me with a love of early childhood education through her support and guidance in the college classroom; **MARK GRGURICH AND THE STAFF AT ST. JOAN OF ARC ELEMENTARY SCHOOL IN LIBRARY, PA,** for allowing me to train them using strategies and techniques developed in this text; **JIM BUCK,** for showing me how students matter and for supporting the unique strengths and challenges students face; **MARIETTA DELLEFEMINE,** for her encouragement and support to write an early childhood text; **SUSAN KESSLER-BUEHL AND THE CHILDREN AT LAURAL LEARNING CENTER,** for allowing me to observe and photograph them; and to Sue Kessler-Buehl and Kathy Kessler, for providing me with a wonderful beginning in the field of early childhood education; **ANGELA GAUGHAN AND THE CHILDREN AT MOM'S HOUSE (NORTH SIDE),** for allowing me to observe and photograph them; **VICTORIA HIRSH,** for her enthusiasm for providing artwork and examples for this text. **DEB CONWAY,** without her support, motivation, and encouragement, this text would have never been completed. **BARBARA GEARY,** for her beautiful gift of putting theory into practice every day and for making the world a better place through teaching and caring for young children. I would also like to thank the following reviewers for their valuable insight and contribution to this text: **JUDITH LYNNE MCCONNELL,** Washburn University; **ROBERTA SCHOMBURG,** Carlow College; **ALAN M. WEBER,** Suffolk County Community College; **REY GOMEZ,** Arizona State University; and **JOLEEN VOSS-RODRIGUEZ,** Los Angeles Pierce College.

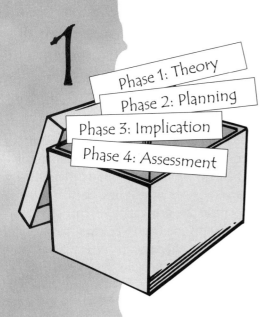

Phase 1: Theory

Phase 2: Planning

Phase 3: Implication

Phase 4: Assessment

Philosophy

Introduction

Victoria walks to the classroom with a large box. The box is heavy; she has trouble carrying it to the door. As she slowly reaches the door, she drops the box at the doorway and runs into the classroom with outstretched arms. On passing through the doorway, everything in the box is forgotten.

Gabrielle walks to the classroom with a large box. The box is heavy; she has trouble carrying it to the door. As she reaches the door, her teacher helps her to carry the box inside. Gabrielle is instructed to keep the box with her. She does not share everything that is in the box, nor does she keep the box completely closed. The box is never ignored. She accesses the contents of the box and adds to the box as needed throughout her time spent in the classroom.

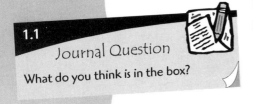

1.1

Journal Question

What do you think is in the box?

What's in the Box?

This text addresses the early childhood years between ages three and eight. Children, at these young ages, already have quite a heavy box. Inside this heavy box is everything the three- to eight-year-old child brings to the classroom. The "everything" involves a variety of feelings, emotions, people, and experiences. Figure 1.1 includes a sampling of the "everything" children bring in their box. Some of the contents were given to the child, some constructed by the child, and some were forced into the box. Each item has meaning and shapes the way the child will respond to the early childhood curriculum.

Children like Victoria don't really exist. It is nearly impossible to leave the box or empty it upon entering the classroom setting. Urie Bronfenbrenner (1979) explains that children do not develop without influence. The child exists in many systems of influence such as: family, siblings, culture, values, and laws. Interactions between the systems directly or indirectly influence the development of the child. The systems are contained in the child's box. Like Gabrielle, children bring a variety of people, thoughts, feelings, values, and ideas in their boxes. This is an important revelation for all teachers and should shape the structure for the early childhood curriculum. Children are different and each child presents different strengths, interests, and needs.

The student is not the only one who brings a heavy box into the classroom. The teacher brings a box as well. The teacher also brings many feelings, emotions, thoughts, ideas, experiences, and people in her box. Take a moment to look over the contents of the box in Figure 1.2.

FIGURE 1.1 │ What's in the Box?

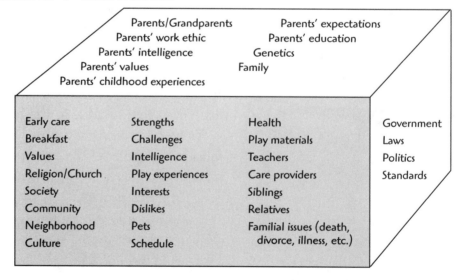

FIGURE 1.2 | The Early Childhood Teacher's Box

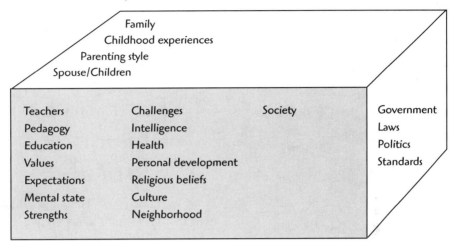

All teachers bring a unique box to the classroom. Education, parenting style, relationships, work ethic, family, and attitude of the teacher greatly influence the early childhood curriculum. The contents of the teacher's and the children's box together influence the structure of the early childhood curriculum.

It is important to recognize the many influences that affect the early childhood curriculum. What is written in a lesson plan is only a fraction of the contents of the curriculum. When researching information for this text, it was astounding to discover how many books address early childhood curriculum. Hundreds of methodologies were found, each claiming to have the answer as to how to reach all children. The methodologies ranged from a strict dictatorship to chaos theory. How can all of these different methodologies have the answer? The answer: they do and they don't. Each text might have contained a little truth as to how to reach a particular child, with a particular background, with a particular culture, with a particular need, on a particular day. One strategy might work for one child.

Obviously, however, more than one child is in the classroom. Recognizing the uniqueness and accepting the contents of each child's box will benefit both the teacher and the child. Understanding multiple methodologies and multiple strategies for teaching young children will bring a unique strength to the teacher's box. This text will draw

1.2

Journal Questions

Think about the box you bring to the classroom. Take a moment to write down the contents of your box. What beliefs do you hold regarding early childhood education? What has influenced your philosophy concerning early childhood curriculum? How were you raised? What school experiences had an impact on you?

1.3

Journal Questions

Define curriculum (include your beliefs about curriculum, the components of a curriculum, and who should be involved in the curriculum).

- What is the goal of early childhood curriculum?
- How does the curriculum help meet that goal?
- How does a philosophy influence the curriculum?
- How would you define developmentally appropriate practice?

upon the contents of each teacher's box, and will offer strategies for organizing and building upon the contents of the box that relate to teaching. Defining curriculum offers an appropriate starting point.

Defining Early Childhood Curriculum

What is curriculum? The early childhood curriculum extends far beyond objectives and assessment, far beyond the daily lesson plans. The curriculum begins as soon as the child enters the classroom and lasts until the child returns home. The curriculum involves each aspect of the child's day. A position statement from the National Association for the Education of Young Children and the National Association of Early Childhood Specialists in State Departments of Education (1991, p. 21) defines curriculum as "an organized framework that delineates the content that children are to learn, the processes through which children achieve the identified curricular goals, what teachers do to help children achieve these goals, and the context in which teaching and learning occur." Every experience, interaction, and part of the child's day can facilitate or hinder the achievement of curricular goals. Each part of the day contributes to the early childhood curriculum.

What is the organized framework intended to do? What is the purpose of the early childhood curriculum? Sue Bredekamp and Teresa Rosegrant (1999, p. 6) summarize the main goal of the early childhood curriculum: "The goal, then, of early education is to ensure that children acquire the foundation of healthy development and learning necessary to achieve their potential in the future . . ." The early childhood curriculum focuses on potential. This opens the curriculum to endless possibilities that are unique to each group of children. The focus on potential greatly influences what, why, and how the early childhood curriculum is implemented. It is not meant to drill facts and figures into the child's head; rather, it should allow the child to construct knowledge to reach their individual potential.

This text acquaints the early childhood teacher with the numerous potentials that exist for young children and gives the teacher tools to optimize the learning environment and interactions to facilitate the development of those potentials. These tools are important assets in the teacher's box.

 # Organization of the Early Childhood Curriculum

Curriculum development involves a process. Bredekamp and Rosegrant (1999) describe the process as having four phases: theoretical, planning, implementation, and assessment. This text is organized around the four phases of curricular development. The theoretical aspect of curriculum will examine intelligence, theory, and curricular content. The planning phase will incorporate activities, projects, scheduling, and environment. The implementation phase will incorporate implementation strategies for integrating multiple intelligences, play, and developmentally appropriate practice in the early childhood classroom. The assessment phase will incorporate appropriate assessment techniques, sample assessment tools, adult intelligence assessment, and a sample portfolio.

BOX 1.4 | *Reaching Early Childhood Potentials*

Potentials can be reached through:

■ Understanding intelligence (Gardner, 1991, 1993)

■ Creating a developmentally appropriate environment (Bredekamp & Copple, 1996; Bredekamp & Rosegrant, 1999)

■ Creating healthy relationships (Greenspan, 1997)

■ Facilitating appropriate play experiences

(Hughes, 1995; Schomburg, Tittnich, & Smith, 1986; Piaget, 1962)

■ Recognizing and utilizing appropriate assessment strategies (Gardner, 1991, 1993; Bredekamp & Rosegrant, 1992)

■ Respectfully planning activities, materials, room arrangement, and schedule (Gandini, Edwards, & Foreman, 1998; Katz, 1999)

Key concepts in curriculum development will be addressed in each of the four phases of early childhood curriculum development. The key concepts in curriculum development include intelligence, developmentally appropriate practice, healthy relationships, play, assessment, and planning. These key concepts are defined in order to provide an understanding for the framework utilized in this text.

Intelligence

Intelligence has been defined by many different people, across many different cultures, with many different motivations. It has been defined across disciplines as a potential (Gardner, 1999) and the early childhood curriculum focuses on *realizing potentials* (Bredekamp and Rosegrant, 1999). This text begins by concentrating on defining and understanding intelligence in order to understand what potentials young children can reach. Many definitions of intelligence were investigated in the research for this text. Howard Gardner's theory of multiple intelligences grasps and organizes the unlimited number of potentials that exist.

This text utilizes Howard Gardner's definition of intelligence, "a biopsychological potential to process information that can be activated in a cultural setting to solve problems or create products that are of value in a culture" (Gardner, 1999, p. 34). The success of intelligent behaviors contributes to the development and progress of a culture. Cultures look at many behaviors as intelligent and there are multiple ways of being intelligent. Looking at intelligence as a multiple entity challenges the restrictive way intelligence has been viewed traditionally. Linguistic and mathematical potentials are the traditional components of intelligent behavior. Gardner proposes that intelligence includes musical, personal, bodily, kinesthetic, spatial, and naturalist potentials in addition to the traditionally held linguistic and mathematical potentials.

Gardner (1993) initially proposed seven intelligences: musical, spatial, logical/mathematical, interpersonal, intrapersonal, bodily/kinesthetic, and linguistic. More recently, Gardner has accepted an eighth—naturalistic—and proposes that more may exist: existentialistic, spiritual, and perhaps, a moral intelligence (Gardner, 1999).

If the multiple potentials of a human being are not respected, the very essence of humanity is demeaned. What would the world be like without music, dance, empathy, mathematics, language, intuition, or geometry? These human characteristics are essential to life. They are essential to our humanity. The multiplicity of intelligence cannot be denied, ignored, or limited to a few sets of skills in very isolated disciplines. Intelligence cannot be confined to a test score. The multiple intelligence theory permits the success of all children by allowing their culture, life experience, and neurochemistry to consummate. After the consummation, the intelligence potential of each child can be realized through the curricular facilitation of each intelligence.

Intelligence is a potential (Gardner, 1993) and reaching that potential is the driving force of the early childhood curriculum (Bredekamp and Rosegrant, 1999). Understanding what potentials exist is a crucial task for the early childhood educator. Several chapters in this text are dedicated to the multiple potentials that exist, through a presentation of the multiple intelligence theory.

Developmentally Appropriate Practice

A developmentally appropriate environment provides an optimal way to help children reach their potential. The National Association for the Education of Young Children is considered a leader in early childhood curriculum. NAEYC describes developmentally appropriate practice as a decision process that educators go through in order to create suitable learning environments for young children (Bredekamp and Copple, 1996).

BOX 1.5 | *Defining the Process of Developmentally Appropriate Practice*

The process of developmentally appropriate practice is governed by three principles:

1. "What is known about child development and learning,
2. what is known about the strengths, interests, and needs of each individual child in the group,
3. and knowledge of the social and cultural contexts in which children live."

From *Developmentally Appropriate Practice in Early Childhood Programs, Revised* by Bredekamp and Copple, 1996

Developmentally appropriate practice means doing what's best for children based on what is known about them. The child's development, strengths, interests, and culture are respected in the classroom and serve as the focal point for the curriculum.

Children need opportunities for many different kinds of interactions with people and materials. Opportunities are created through child-initiated play experiences, teacher-directed activities, collaborated projects, and through interactions during the various scheduled times of the child's day. Each of these opportunities holds equal importance. It is critical to understand that developmentally appropriate practice supports all of these varied learning opportunities. The time and schedule for these opportunities will be determined by the three guiding principles mentioned in Boxed Feature 1.5. The following article reprinted from *Young Children* magazine illustrates a definition of developmentally appropriate practice.

The Impatient Gardener

A gardener plants eight tomato seeds in the ground. She carefully cultivates each plant, making sure it has enough room to grow, is not taken over by weeds, and that it has the right amount of sun, rain, and fertilizer. She recognizes that each plant is a little different and requires special attention.

By midsummer, she has eight tomato plants. Each one is unique, but all produce an abundance of tomatoes. The gardener is happy and satisfied with her crop. She knows that her tomatoes will produce fine seeds that will develop into another wonderful crop the next growing season.

An impatient gardener down the street plants 15 tomato seeds. She wants them to grow quickly so she gives them more water and fertilizer than they need. She constantly grumbles at her plants to grow faster. Because they are not growing fast enough, she figures her plants deserve the weeds that grow around them. By midsummer, a few of her plants survive, along with three medium-sized tomatoes. The rest are either burned by too much fertilizer, overwatered, or strangled by weeds. She wonders what went wrong. She gave them more than what they needed to grow.

Contemporary American society has become the impatient gardener. This society seems content in its mission to speed up childhood. The expectations and content of college education are experienced in most high schools. The expectations and content of high school curriculum are experienced in middle school. Elementary schools are adopting curricula that mimic middle school curricula.

The American kindergarten curriculum has taken on a vast change to incorporate primary school expectations. Preschoolers are expected to memorize a series of facts and figures and to behave as primary school children. Even the American toddler curriculum promotes preschool and even kindergarten expectations and content.

Are these changes worth it? *Are these changes producing more competent, intelligent children who are productively working to change our society for the better? No, but we have ten and eleven year old adolescents who are pregnant, suffer from alcohol and drug* *addictions, and who are murdering fellow classmates and teachers. When children are forced to grow up too fast, the changes do more damage than good.*

The content, expectations, and interactions of the American curriculum might have changed, but the child's natural momentum for working through developmental stages has not. All children go through specific developmental stages. Children generally experience these stages in the same order, and roughly around the same ages.

Educators must pay attention to these stages and mandate an appropriate curriculum that gives the child what she needs to develop, not any more, not any less. This is what developmentally appropriate practice means. It is imperative to understand what is appropriate at each stage of development so we can produce the best crop possible.

(Reprinted with Permission from the National Association for the Education of Young Children, Hirsh, 2000, p. 81.)

Each plant in the garden has specific needs. The right type of soil, water, and sun are crucial. Without soil, water, and sun, the plant would die. Too much fertilizer burns the plant. Not enough stunts the plant's growth. Natural fertilizers are healthier for plants and for the environment around the plant. The right conditions produce a healthy plant that can withstand the elements.

Each child deserves the care a good gardener gives her plants. Careful consideration and thoughtful planning must be bestowed upon each child in the classroom. *Too much too soon,* and *too little too late,* can negatively influence the development of a child. A purposeful balance is crucial and requires a developmentally appropriate environment.

The *Impatient Gardener* emphasizes a common, inappropriate approach to early childhood education. Bredekamp and Rosegrant (1999, p. 3) define this approach as "elementary child error." The elementary child error approach takes an elementary model of education and pushes it down to the early childhood curriculum. Expectations, content, and methodologies appropriate for older children are forced upon younger children in the hopes of achieving higher academic standards (Bredekamp & Rosegrant, 1999).

Bredekamp and Rosegrant (1999, p. 3) define a second inappropriate approach to early childhood curriculum that involves the opposite extreme, "the early childhood error." The early childhood error approach does not give the appropriate consideration or attention to curricular content. This results in an inadequate environment, materials, and inattention to curricular content. In addition to these errors in implementing an appropriate curriculum for young children, many myths exist regarding the definition and implementation of developmentally appropriate practice.

CLARIFYING MYTHS ASSOCIATED WITH DEVELOPMENTALLY APPROPRIATE PRACTICE It is important to note that many myths exist regarding the definition and implementation of developmentally appropriate practices (Kostelnik, 1992). Many

BOX 1.6	*Common Developmentally Appropriate Practice (DAP) Misunderstandings*

Common developmentally appropriate practice misunderstandings include:

■ the structure of the developmentally appropriate classroom,

■ the methodology involved, the role of the teacher and academics in the classroom,

■ and the expectations for young children enrolled in these classrooms (Kostelnik, 1992).

practices have been implemented under the guise of developmentally appropriate practice and many more have been criticized for misunderstanding what developmentally appropriate practice means. The myths involve the structure, methodology, teacher's role, role of academics, and expectations of the early childhood curriculum.

Structure   The developmentally appropriate classroom is often criticized for its lack of structure (Kostelnik, 1992). There is a myth that in such a classroom, children do *what* they please *when* they please. This is simply not true. A developmentally appropriate classroom is highly structured and organized. The structure develops from the pedagogy utilized, the interests and development of the children in the program, the materials offered, the organization of the environment, and the carefully planned schedule. Kostelnik (1992, p. 17) describes the developmentally appropriate classroom as "... active, but not chaotic; children are on-task, but not rigidly following a single line of inquiry. Overall instructional goals are merged with more immediate ones to create a flexible, stimulating classroom structure." General goals for the curriculum are developed and based on knowledge of child development. Individual goals are developed daily to meet individual children's needs, interests, and learning styles (Kostelnik, 1992).

Methodology   Developmentally appropriate practice (DAP) is not a set, prescribed curriculum, nor is it a methodology. DAP is not a curriculum at all. Rather, it is a *process* or a *practice* of determining what is appropriate in the early childhood curriculum (Bredekamp & Rosegrant, 1999). Many methodologies have been developed utilizing developmentally appropriate principles. There is no singular approach or standard methodology to creating a developmentally appropriate program (Kostelnik, 1992).

An accepted approach to early childhood curriculum that supports developmentally appropriate practice is known as constructivism (Katz, 1999; Gardner, 1991; Piaget, 1963; Vygotsky, 1978; Montessori, 1965; Dewey, 1916). Katz describes the constructive approach as one that views young children "as active constructors of knowledge" (Katz, 1999, p. 1). The contrasting approach is an *instructivist* approach (Katz, 1999), which takes a different view of the child's role in education: "The young child is seen as dependent on adults' instruction in the academic knowledge and skills necessary for a good start for later academic achievement" (Katz, 1999, p. 1). This type of approach can lead to "... schools full of uninterested tourists who view the school experience as though looking from a tour bus window. Occasionally the tour guide, their teacher, sparks their interest through a particularly entertaining story, but for the most part, the content is so thin that it slips right by" (Bredekamp and Rosegrant, 1999, p. 29). Instructivism does not usually provide meaningful experiences, and it promotes a passive approach to education. Constructivism requires the active participation of the child in the curriculum and it is through these active, meaningful experiences that children acquire knowledge.

Role of the Teacher   The teacher does not take a passive role in a developmentally appropriate program. The teacher is very active as an observer, facilitator, diagnostician, instructor, and planner. The teacher balances directed, child-initiated, and collaborative experiences. This approach is often referred to as "collaboration" rather than a teacher-centered or child-centered approach (Bredekamp and Rosegrant, 1999).

Role of Academics   Developmentally appropriate practice has often been criticized for its inattentiveness to, or ignorance of, academics (Kostelnik, 1992). Academics play an important part in any early childhood program. However, academics are best learned in context. Teachers offer meaningful direct instruction, choice of independent experiences, and collaborative projects. All of these experiences are given equal attention and emphasis. Meaningful academic concepts are addressed through contextual experiences.

Expectations   Proper expectations are a key factor in creating developmentally appropriate programs. A teacher must understand what is appropriate for each child's development, experience, interest, and culture (Bredekamp and Copple, 1996). This takes a highly skilled and dedicated individual, and often proves to be a difficult, yet rewarding undertaking.

Summary   Developmentally appropriate practice is not a standard, prescribed curriculum. Rather, it is a critical process of determining what is appropriate in the early childhood curriculum. Understanding developmentally appropriate practice can be overwhelming; therefore, it will be addressed in each chapter, rather than undermining its importance by having only a single chapter dedicated to it. This entire text has been written in a developmentally appropriate context.

Healthy Relationships

The emotional intelligence theory (Goleman, 1995), and the multiple intelligence theory (Gardner, 1993) have given much needed attention to the emotional development of the young child. Emotions play an important role in personal intelligence; however, emotions play an integral role in the development of each intelligence (Gardner, 1999).

Stanley Greenspan (1997) suggests that the emotional aspect of learning is the foundation for learning, intelligence, and brain growth. His theory of the growth of the mind delves deeper into the emotions' responsibility in brain growth and intelligence. The primary architect of emotions is relationships. Therefore, the relationship between the child and her teacher is extremely significant.

The relationship must foster trust, autonomy, initiative, and industry (Erikson, 1950). Children (especially in childcare and after-school care) can spend more waking hours with a teacher/caregiver than with their own parents. It is crucial to recognize the responsibility of being a significant person in a child's life.

Play

Play provides an opportunity for the child to explore, develop, and construct. Hughes's (1989) definition of play addresses the characteristics identified by many play theorists. A true play experience is defined as an experience that is intrinsically motivating, freely chosen, actively engaged in, pleasurable, and nonliteral (Hughes, 1989).

INTRINSIC MOTIVATION American society has become obsessed with punishments and rewards (Goleman, 1995). Children often perform for praise, a sticker, or a piece of candy. A true play experience is motivated from within, and not from an extrinsic reward (Hughes, 1989).

FREE CHOICE Children must be given the materials, time, and opportunity to choose their own play experiences and materials. Instructing a child to play in the block area does not allow the child to choose her own play experience. One cannot choose the experience for the child (Hughes, 1989).

ACTIVE ENGAGEMENT Playing also involves the use of the physical body. Children need to be actively involved in the play experience. Television and video games do not actively involve the child (Hughes, 1989).

PLEASURE A play experience involves pleasure, or at the very least contentment. Organized sports, which can bring children to tears for lack of skill, endurance, or competitiveness, do not provide meaningful play experience (Hughes, 1989).

NONLITERAL (SYMBOLISM)   The final critical component of a play experience is the symbol the experience creates or represents. There needs to be some sort of pretend or symbolic experience involved in the play. Naming a block structure, pretending to answer a play telephone, drawing a representation of an experience, inventing a word, and retelling a story are all symbolic representations of witnessed experiences. Symbol development is crucial in developing an intelligence (Gardner, 1993, 1999). It allows for expression and utilization of cultural disciplines.

Each characteristic of play is meaningful and significant. Through incorporating the five characteristic definition of play, the child is given access to materials that enable him to construct knowledge.

Planning

Planning is usually thought of as the creation of lesson plans. However, every part of the early childhood curriculum demands careful planning. Activities, materials, room arrangement, and scheduling evolve from understanding child development and recognizing needs, and through careful assessment of young children.

ACTIVITIES   Activities are generally thought of as teacher-initiated experiences. The length and content of the activity is planned by a teacher who understands child development, recognizes needs and strengths, and knows her students' interests and stages of development. An entire chapter of the text will be dedicated to planning developmentally appropriate activities that help foster the potentials that exist in all of the intelligences.

ROOM ARRANGEMENT   The organization of the child's environment communicates a value, aids with instruction and choice, and facilitates a sense of community and beauty (Gandini, Edwards, and Foreman, 1993). Many programs pay particular attention to the organization of the child's space. Maria Montessori, Loris Malaguzzi, and Rudolf Steiner have developed methodologies that place a great emphasis on space and room arrangement. Their philosophies, along with strategies for creating developmentally appropriate classrooms that foster the development of the intelligences, will be examined in this text.

MATERIALS   An unprecedented number of materials exist for use in early childhood programs. It is critical to understand the value and use of the many available materials, and to be able to choose appropriate materials for young children. Appropriate materials will be discussed in many chapters throughout the text.

SCHEDULE   Scheduling is one of the most challenging tasks of the early childhood educator. Fostering a natural flow to the day, placing equal emphasis on each part of the day, and balancing quiet and active experiences are the main objectives to master. Each part of the child's day is important and requires careful planning in a developmentally appropriate context. Many goals can be addressed through the purposeful planning of the schedule. The text will offer practical suggestions for creating a schedule and suggest helpful transition techniques.

 Assessment

Assessment has a particular purpose and value in the early childhood curriculum (Chen, Krechevsky, and Viens, 1998). Assessment is used to determine where children are functioning and what they need. It is a critical tool used in the planning process. Planning involves assessing where children are and what they need. Understanding and facilitating appropriate assessment techniques are invaluable assets to the teacher's box. Bredekamp and Rosegrant (1999, p. 10) define assessment as "the process of observing, recording, and otherwise documenting the work children do and how they do it, as a basis for a variety of educational decisions that affect the child, including planning for groups and individual children and communicating with parents." Assessment is an involved process that looks at the individual development and growth of each child and helps to determine the direction of the early childhood curriculum. Assessment includes gathering data and acting on what has been gathered.

A variety of assessment techniques exist. A heavy reliance on one type of assessment technique does not give an accurate picture of a child's growth and development. Standardized tests are one method of assessment that, when used in conjunction with many other assessment techniques, help to determine a child's growth and development (Gardner, 1993). However, a standardized test does not give a complete or accurate measurement of the child's growth.

1.7
Journal Questions

Think about the contents of the box and how those contents influence your personal philosophy of early childhood education. What methodologies do you have experience with? What are your beliefs about content? What and how do you think young children should be learning?

Write a one-page philosophy of early childhood education. Include why you feel the way you do, how you think early childhood education should look, and which theorists are meaningful and relevant to you.

 Using the Box

Curriculum evolves from an understanding of intelligence, play, developmentally appropriate practice, scheduling, activities, relationships, and assessment. Each teacher brings her own understanding of these concepts to the early childhood classroom. This text attempts to take what the teacher brings to the classroom (the contents of the box), offer new explanations, theories, and information, and provide a reflective dialogue with a journal in order to develop an informed personal philosophy for creating curriculum for young children. From that philosophy, the early childhood curriculum can begin.

 References

Bredekamp, S., & Copple, C., eds. (1996) *Developmentally appropriate practice in early childhood programs* (Revised Edition). Washington, DC: National Association for the Education of Young Children.

Bredekamp, S., & Rosengrant, T., eds. (1999) *Reaching potentials: Transforming early childhood curriculum and assessment.* Washington, DC: National Association for the Education of Young Children.

Bronfenbrenner, U. (1979) *The ecology of human development.* Boston: Harvard University Press.

Chen, J., Krechevsky, & Viens, eds. (1998) *Project Spectrum: Early learning activities. Vol 2.* New York: Teachers College Press.

Dewey, J. (1916) *Democracy and education.* New York: Macmillan.

Erikson, E. (1950) *Childhood and society.* New York: W. W. Norton & Co.

Gandini, L., Edwards, C., & Foreman, eds. (1993) *The hundred languages of children.* Norwood, NJ: Alblex Publishing Corporation.

Gardner, H. (1999) *The disciplined mind.* New York: Simon & Schuster.

Gardner, H. (1993) *Frames of mind.* New York: Basic Books.

Gardner, H. (1991) *The unschooled mind.* New York: Basic Books.

Goleman, D. (1995) *Emotional intelligence.* New York: Bantam Books.

Greenspan, S. (1997) *The growth of the mind and the endangered origins of intelligence.* Cambridge, MA: Perseus Books.

Hirsh, R. (2000) "The Impatient Gardener." *Young Children* (May, 2000, Vol. 55, No. 3, p. 81).

Hughes, F. (1989) *Children, play, and development.* Boston: Allyn & Bacon.

Katz, L. (1999) "Curriculum disputes in early childhood." ED436298

Kostelnik, M. J. (1992) "Myths associated with developmentally appropriate programs." *Young Children* (May, 1992, pp. 17–23).

Montessori, M. (1965) *Dr. Montessori's own handbook.* New York: Schocken Books.

National Association for the Education of Young Children and National Association of Early Childhood Specialists in State Departments of Education Position Statement. (1991). "Guidelines for appropriate curriculum content and assessment in programs serving children ages 3 through 8." *Young Children,* 46(3), 21–38.

Piaget, J. (1952) *The origins of intelligence in children.* New York: Free Press.

Shomburg, R., Smith, M., and Tittnich, E. (1986) *Developing your own curriculum.* Pittsburgh: Louise Child Care Center.

Vygotsky, L. (1978) *Mind in society: The development of higher psychological processes.* Cambridge, MA: Harvard University Press.

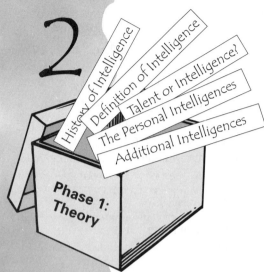

History of Intelligence
Definition of Intelligence
Talent or Intelligence?
The Personal Intelligences
Additional Intelligences

Phase 1:
Theory

Intelligence, a History and Definition

Chapter 1 introduced the four phases of curriculum development. The first phase is theoretical. It is necessary to understand the theoretical foundations for curriculum in order to
plan an appropriate curriculum for young children. We will begin the
discussion of the theoretical phase with this chapter on the history of
intelligence and will continue with each individual intelligence presented in Gardner's theory of multiple intelligences.

The discussion of the theoretical phase of curriculum development in this
text will provide:

1. A historical look at intelligence compared with contemporary views.
2. A complete understanding of each intelligence (or potential).
3. Guiding principles in curriculum content development.
4. A developmental framework for each intelligence.
5. A thorough explanation of the symbol system of each intelligence.

---

*Not everything that can be counted counts and not everything that counts
can be counted.*

— Albert Einstein

2.1

Journal Questions

Before you begin reading, how would you define intelligence?

Do you consider yourself an intelligent person? Why or why not?

How do you think your view of intelligence influences the way you teach children?

Why do you think intelligence tests were developed?

Do you think intelligence tests benefit or compromise a child? Why?

How do you think American schools view intelligence?

Create a list of people you consider to be intelligent.

Create a list of people you consider to not be intelligent.

How does understanding intelligence influence curriculum?

Interview several teachers of preschool, kindergarten, and first grade. Ask them if they administer intelligence tests and if they do, what they do with the results. How do the results change their instruction?

The first chapter emphasized the main goal of early childhood education: reaching potentials. Potential refers to one's capacity in a certain discipline, one's intelligence. Before we continue our discussion, we need to understand the definition of the word *intelligence* and in order to do so, we need to examine historical and contemporary views of the word. Intelligence has meant different things to different people at different times. The research on human intelligence is exhaustive. It would be impossible to present centuries of theories of intelligence in one chapter. This chapter will highlight some of the most influential Western intelligence theorists of the past two centuries. An understanding of the historical view of intelligence will help us appreciate how intelligence shapes contemporary curriculum ideology.

Intelligence is a motivating factor in curriculum development. Defining intelligence is crucial to understanding the motivation and methodology of any given curriculum. A definition of intelligence is influenced by the field of study it originates from and the motivation for providing a definition. The definition of intelligence in this text has been influenced by centuries of research in the fields of cognition, brain development, psychology, anthropology, genetics, and cultural study and is motivated by a curricular perspective.

The definition in the box below is influenced by other Western historical definitions of intelligence and heavily influenced by contemporary theorists such as Howard Gardner. The historical roots of

---

BOX 2.2 | *This Text's Definition of Intelligence*

Intelligence is defined as human potential created from biological and environmental influences. Human potential can exist in many different forms; therefore suggesting there are multiple ways to be intelligent or to possess intelligence. Each culture has specific ideas regarding intelligent behavior.

this definition must be examined to understand how the definition fits into the field of intelligence study and to understand this contemporary view of multiple intelligences.

Historically, intelligence has been studied from a purely biological or environmental perspective, and variations of each perspective. This text's definition embraces both perspectives.

 # Approaches to Intelligence Research

Approaches to the historical study of intelligence can be categorized into biological, psychometric, developmental, and multiple. Each approach brings a unique motivation, perspective, and definition to the field of intelligence research. Not all historical intelligence theories fit into these categories; however, these categories offer a framework for understanding research motivations and for understanding how each definition influenced society.

Approaching Intelligence from a Biological Perspective

Charles Darwin's account of the evolution of man had a great impact in the field of intelligence. Giving attention to genetics, heredity, and innate abilities became an important focus in intelligence research. Darwin influenced such historical theorists as Francis Galton (who was as impressed with Darwin as Darwin was with Galton).

Hereditary factors play an important role in intelligence, although not an exclusive one. Most hereditary theories of intelligence do suggest that environmental stimulation is necessary to develop intelligence.

EUGENICS In 1869, Francis Galton published the *Hereditary Genius,* which supported hereditary factors in determining intelligence. Galton surmised that the manipulation of human genes could improve intelligence and the human species itself (Sattler, 1982). This manipulation of human genes began the foundation of the field of eugenics. In 1883, Galton's further research suggested that intelligence could be gained through understanding the environment, although he still held firm to the belief that intelligence potential itself was hereditary (Sattler, 1982). Galton's theory suggested that individuals of superior races and social status should procreate and individuals of inferior races and social status should not procreate.

Galton believed that individuals learned about the environment through the use of the senses. He concluded that those with the highest sensory discrimination skills would have the highest intelligence (Sattler, 1982). His assumption led to the development of sensory-intelligence tests to measure intelligence. Although this approach

FIGURE 2.1 | Significant Events and Contributors to Intelligence Theory in the Nineteenth Century

1830 (to 1840)	1838	1859	1869	1882	1883	1889	1890	1893	1897
Industrial Revolution begins	Jean Esqural	Charles Darwin	Francis Galton	William Preyer	Francis Galton	Emil Kraeplin	Robert Cattell	William Preyer	Hugo Musterberg
Emphasis on genetic influences on intelligence	First scientific discrimination between "idiots" and mentally deranged	Publishes *The Origin of Species*	Publishes *Hereditary Genius*	From observations of son, reintroduces environmental influences of intelligence and publishes *Mind of the Child*	Introduces sensory discrimination skills into view of intelligence	Develops theory that intelligence is related to real-life experiences	First intelligence testing lab established at University of Pennsylvania	Publishes *Mental Development of Child*	Group intelligence testing on perception, memory, reading, and recall, focused on everyday life experiences
Child's ability to perform long hours of factory work related to intelligence of child		Genetic influences on intelligence investigated	Continued emphasis and support for heredity influences		Develops test to measure sensory discrimination skills	Intelligence test measured perception, attention, memory, and motor skills	influences of tested sensory - integration skills	Emphasis on environmental intelligence	H. Ebbighaur
			"Eugenics" theory: improve human race and intelligence through genetics						Developed intelligence tests in response to German city school teachers

FIGURE 2.2 | Significant Events and Contributors to Intelligence Theory in the Twentieth Century

1900	1903	1900 (–1930)	1916	1917	1920	1927	1929–1939	1940
France develops the first intelligence scales (Binet-Simon scales)	Johann Friedrich Herbart "Ontogeny recapitulates phylogeny" theory of intelligence and physical development	Sigmund Freud Psychosexual stages of development Sexual influences of intelligence Interpretation of dreams Psychoanalysis	John Dewey Breaks away from Herbart's theory Reinvestigates environmental influences on intelligence In order to have an intelligent child, there needs to be an intelligent environment	Robert Yerkes Finds fault with Binet-Simon scales Revises age/scale format	Binet/Simon Revised scales used widely in U.S.	Charles Spearman Two-factor theory of intelligence Edward Thorndike Proposed intelligence has three components: social, concrete, and abstract	Great Depression	David Weschler New intelligence scale Intelligence tests used in schools, clinics, industry, and military

1940	1947	1950	1957	1968	1975	1983	1985	1989
WW II Technological push and influence in intelligence	Jean Piaget Sensorimotor, preoperational, concrete operational, formal operational Environmental and biological intelligence	U.S. Congress passes act to provide funds for gifted and talented education Philip Vernon Hierarchical group factor theory	Sputnik Science and mathematical programs flourish U.S. launches numerous space and science programs	Adrian Dove Develops the Chitling IQ test Cultural bias in IQ testing recognized	PL 94–142 Special education gained funding, support, and attention Further intelligence testing to identify special needs children becomes controversial	Howard Gardner Multiple Intelligence theory	Robert Sternberg Three-factor theory: context, experience, and intellectual components	John Horn Crystallized and fluid intelligence theory

proved to be inaccurate, it opened the door to psychometric measures of intelligence (Sattler, 1982).

Galton's theory led to moral questions and controversies. His theory introduced questions concerning the reproduction of those who do have "good genes" and raised questions such as: Should mentally challenged individuals procreate? Should parents with a history of genetic disease/illness procreate? Should procreation be left only to those who have good families? Moral issues centering on the implementation of the theory emerged. Galton believed that advancement of the human race was to be controlled by those he identified as having "good genes," generally upper-class Europeans.

American theorist Arthur Jensen was a strong supporter of the idea of genetic determinants of intelligence. Jensen supported the measurement of intelligence because it cannot readily be defined. He believed it was easier to identify intelligence using numbers as opposed to using words. Jensen believed that most of the factors that influence the development of intelligence were genetic or biological (Jensen, 1969). Environmental factors had limited influence on intelligence. According to Jensen, environmental factors consisted of the physical environment of the child (as opposed to parental interaction/childcare, etc.). The prenatal environment accounted for the largest environmental influence on intelligence. Jensen (1969) listed many less significant environmental influences such as: birth order, race, social class, prematurity, and nutrition. Parental, familial, or educational interactions were not considered to play an important part in the development of intelligence (Jensen, 1969). He supported this notion by pointing out the failed attempts of school systems to help disadvantaged students (Jensen, 1969).

The manipulation of human genes to create healthier, stronger, gender-specific, and more intelligent human beings is a flourishing field of study in the twenty-first century. In contemporary society, genes are manipulated directly as opposed to the manipulation of genes through selective breeding. Eugenics and genetics remain controversial and moral issues.

2.3

Journal Questions

Do you think eugenics is a moral or scientific issue?

If you could change your hereditary intelligence factors through gene manipulation, would you consider it?

Do you think intelligence is purely biological?

What implications do genetic hypotheses have on intelligence and early childhood education?

Why do you think hereditary factors of intelligence are so heavily criticized?

THE BRAIN AND INTELLIGENCE Genetics is not the sole *biological* theory of intelligence. Discovering and interpreting the mechanics of the brain contributes greatly to the field of intelligence research. Brain research led to the development of an information-processing model of intelligence. In this model, intelligence relates to the brain's ability to process information.

More has been learned about the brain in the past two decades than in any time throughout history. Extensive brain research began in the 1990s when President Bush and the 101st Congress declared the 1990s to be the "decade of the brain."

Decade of the Brain During the decade of the brain, extensive brain research projects took place, due to increased funding for brain research. The findings from the decade are interesting and startling. The early childhood period of development proved to be more crucial than ever believed. Most brain growth is attributed to the early years of life. This has warranted unprecedented attention being paid to those first five years of life and a new interest in providing appropriate experiences early, rather than remedial experiences later.

In *Time* magazine, Madeline Nash (1997) reports that an infant is born with approximately as many nerve cells as there are "stars in the Milky Way galaxy." Billions of nerve cells are present at birth; however, they lack communication and coordination. The infant possesses all of the brain cells he will ever need. Tiny connections referred to as synapses will form in the infant's brain at astonishing speed. By the age of two, the toddler's brain will have formed trillions of synapses, twice as many as a fully functioning adult's brain. Every experience and interaction creates a new connection and furthers the development of the child's brain. Access routes to language, communication, emotional responses, and environmental responses are formed. The toddler's brain (and probably her body as well) consumes twice as much energy as an adult brain.

The first year of life has been shown to be the most critical. The next nine or so years have significant importance as well. During this period of early childhood development, the brain is forming connections, coordinating responses, and laying a framework for the adult brain.

Brain Research Supports Environmental Influence Early interactions, such as play and touch, have a profound impact on the developing brain. Nash (1997) reports that young children who rarely have opportunities to play or to be touched, develop 20 to 30 percent smaller brains as an adult.

In addition to play and touch, other interactions prove important as well. Experiences involving physical movement (Hannaford, 1995), handwork (Wilson, 1998), and music and art (Jensen, 2001) provide necessary "brain food." These experiences are necessary in coordinating brain function, improving health, increasing memory, and improving the ability to learn and apply new information (Jensen, 2001).

As necessary as early interactions are, it is not the interaction itself that causes appropriate brain growth. The experience must be appropriate and meaningful to the child. Inappropriate experiences may hinder brain development. For example, Jane

2.4

Journal Questions

Before reading . . .

Take a moment to create your own IQ test. Write ten questions that you think would determine whether a person was intelligent or not. Share your test with other students. How do their beliefs about intelligence differ from yours? How are they the same?

Ask several early childhood teachers (preschool, kindergarten, first, second) if they use intelligence tests. If they use them, ask how the results affect their classroom practices.

Do you think measuring intelligence is important?

Could the measurement of intelligence have a positive impact on education?

Could the measurement of intelligence have a negative impact on education?

Healy, a neurobiologist, suggests that isolated bits of academic content forced too early on a child may cause a learning disability. Healy (1990) explains that the brain develops in layers. The abstract layer has not yet been developed in young children. Connections to the information contained in the abstract layer may be difficult to form and very difficult to access. When the child's brain matures and is ready for abstract thinking, pathways to abstract information would have already begun to develop. This causes difficulty in calling on the information stored in the abstract layer and encourages the brain to make difficult pathways for additional abstract information.

By around ten years of age, the brain begins to eliminate connections that are rarely or seldom used (Nash, 1997). Cognitive skills or emotional issues that were not dealt with before ten years of age are much more difficult to remediate after that. This finding emphasizes the importance of early interactions.

Approaching Intelligence from a Psychometric Perspective

Most of the intelligence research in the mid- to late-nineteenth century focused on testing and classification of adults and children. The psychometric approach to intelligence originated from genetic and hereditary definitions of intelligence. The nineteenth century intelligence-research community consisted of anthropologists, psychologists, psychiatrists, and geneticists. Germany, England, America, and France were among the leaders of intelligence investigation in the Western world. Each country was motivated in a different direction (Sattler, 1982).

Even though Galton's theory of intelligence relied heavily on genetics, he believed that environment also played an important role in the development of intelligence. Galton believed intelligence was developed through sensory stimulation and discrimination. His assumption led to the development of sensory-intelligence tests to measure intelligence. Although this approach proved to be inaccurate, it opened the door to psychometric measures of intelligence (Sattler, 1982).

James Cattell was very interested in and inspired by Francis Galton (Sokal, 2002). Cattell brought Galton's intelligence tests to America. He revised Galton's work and created his own intelligence tests. Cattell began an intelligence lab at the University of

Pennsylvania in 1890. The lab conducted various "mental tests." Cattell's tests consisted of physiological and psychological tasks. These tasks consisted of such activities as measuring the strength of a squeeze, reaction time for naming colors and sounds, time judgments, sensations, and memory.

Cattell's tests were experimental, designed to find out what tests were useful and what purpose such tests could serve. Cattell realized how interested Americans were in the tests and many other theorists borrowed Cattell's and Galton's tests and/or created their own.

In Germany in 1889, Emil Kraepelin developed an intelligence test that assessed perception, memory, motor functions, and attention (Sattler, 1982). Kraepelin's motivation for this type of assessment was developed through his emphasis on what skills were needed in everyday life experiences. In 1897, H. Ebbinghaus developed one of the first group intelligence tests for a group of German teachers who taught in a city school environment. The teachers requested the development of intelligence tests to aid in instruction and identification of those who had problems. Ebbinghaus developed the first word-completion test component of the intelligence test. A form of this word-completion test is included on contemporary intelligence tests.

By the end of the nineteenth century, intelligence tests were gaining popularity in the United States. Hugo Munsterberg and Joseph Jastrow introduced "mental anthropometry" tests at the World's Fair in 1893 (Sattler, 1982). Participants could have their intelligence tested for a small fee. Interest and competition encouraged many fair participants to take the mental tests.

Intelligence testing in France in the late-nineteenth century was gaining attention and popularity as well. Intelligence began to be thought of as something more than the mastery of physical, reflexive, and sensory tasks. Alfred Binet, Victor Henri, and Theodore Simon came to a groundbreaking realization: the measurement of intelligence had to involve higher-level skills (Sattler, 1982). Previous intelligence tests measured lower-level sensory-motor skills. This motivation opened a new door to intelligence tests in the twentieth century (Sattler, 1982). The first modern intelligence test can be traced to the intelligence scale devised by Binet, Henri, and Simon in 1905 (Sattler, 1982). By the 1920s, the Binet-Simon intelligence scales had been revised and widely accepted and used in the United States.

2.5 Journal Question

How do you think Binet would have felt about the way intelligence tests are used today?

The original intelligence tests were designed with curricular implications. The purpose of the tests was to determine which children would not benefit from the standard curriculum (due to mental deficiency). These children were to be offered an alternative curriculum. Binet cautioned that these tests were not developed to classify children or to be administered to groups with the purpose of using scores for comparison only (without curricular reasons). Revised versions of the Binet-Simon intelligence tests are used in schools today.

In the 1930s, David Wechsler examined the intelligence tests that had already been published and designed eleven sub-tests. The sub-tests were modifications of many other tests. Wechsler became interested in the intelligence field during his time working with the Army's intelligence tests and his sub-tests borrowed from their tests, Binet's tests, and others. Forms of Wechsler's tests are used in schools today as well.

By 1932, 27 percent of U.S. cities were administering intelligence tests to children (Mondale, Patton, Cuban, Andersen, Ravitch, and Kaestle, 2001). The intelligence tests were used for tracking and determining a course of education.

During the 1940s, World War II significantly affected the view of intelligence (McClellan, 1985). The U.S. government realized the advantages of technology in order to preserve the nation's military and political excellence. By 1950, Congress passed an act that would provide funds for gifted and talented education (McClellan, 1985). Intelligence was finally given a federal interest. Giftedness referred to those with superior intellectual ability, creativity, task perseverance, academic aptitude, leadership ability, visual and performing artistic ability, and psychomotor ability (McClellan, 1985).

In 1957, the Russian launch of Sputnik created havoc in the American educational system. Congress immediately passed additional bills to further enhance the scientific and mathematical intelligence of the country (McClellan, 1985). By the 1970s, many programs to promote the advancement of science and mathematics had been put in place. The emphasis on intelligence was refocused on the logical and mathematical aspects of it.

By 1970, intelligence tests were used for placing children in remedial education and in special education (Mondale, Patton, Cuban, Andersen, Ravitch, and Kaestle, 2001). In 1975, Public Law 94-142 was passed. This law protected the education and rights of special needs children and gifted children (McLoughlin and Lewis, 1990). An individualized education plan was now taken seriously by school districts because it was the law. A team had to meet to assess the student's needs and plan an appropriate learning program that would take place in the least restrictive environment. With this law came the investigation into special education programs, particularly those programs that consisted of a large number of minority groups. Programs and criteria were reassessed and previous criticisms of intelligence testing reemerged (Sattler, 1986).

2.6 Journal Questions

Which population did U.S. education law address first, children in need of special education or children in need of gifted education?

Why do you think it was addressed first?

What kind of message might that communicate?

TEST BIAS   Intelligence tests have been determined to be biased from a cultural and gender perspective. Test items were found to be culturally biased in favor of Caucasian, middle-class environments (Ehrlich and Feldman, 1977). In response, alternative tests were developed to address the cultural needs of children. The Chitling Test, created by Adrian Dove, was developed to demonstrate how cultural dialect and experience greatly influenced the child's ability to answer questions correctly (a sample is printed in Erlich, 1977). It showed that experience and language greatly influence the outcome of intelligence tests. Much research was conducted to determine which test items were culturally biased. African-American children were scoring an average of fifteen points lower on intelligence tests (Ehrlich and Feldman, 1977). Further investigation revealed that when Caucasian children from the same socioeconomic background as African-American children were compared, the intelligence scores only differed by four to six points. This was a critical finding. The intelligence tests proved to be culturally biased and not racially biased (Ehrlich and Feldman, 1977). This also shed light on the fact that intelligence itself could not be racially defined, but could be culturally defined. This is quite a contrast to Jensen's perspective on race and intelligence.

Other tests such as the Goodenough Draw-a-Picture test were developed as a way to rule out the cultural bias of language. However, the picture test proved to be culturally biased against Pueblo American Indians. The test was redesigned as a Draw-a-Horse test. The Pueblo American Indian children's intelligence scores increased by twenty points (Ehrlich and Feldman, 1977).

Ehrlich and Feldman's (1977) work questions the role of heredity on intelligence. Children from low socioeconomic families and malnutritive families who were adopted by middle-class families made significant improvements in intelligence scores. This evidence clearly shows that intelligence is culturally based and can only be determined from culture to culture. This evidence also makes the point that intelligence is extremely responsive to the environment. Cross-cultural testing proves to have a consistent bias because the definition of intelligence is not constant among cultures. The effect of the environment, the adaptation of the person tested, and the motivation for the testing situation also influence the intelligence test score. Test scores can also be affected by the development and maturation of the child.

Approaching Intelligence as Developmental

Intelligence has been studied from developmental perspectives, meaning that intelligence is seen as developing in stages. The progression is considered biological; however, appropriate environmental influences are absolutely necessary in the development of intelligence.

Wilhelm Preyer was one of the first individuals to look at intelligence as developmental. Many consider Preyer the father of developmental psychology (Cleverly and Phillips, 1986). In 1881, he published *The Mind of the Child*. Preyer's account of child development was made through observations of his own son. Preyer looked specifically for "when and in what order the child would display various adult abilities" (Cleverly and Phillips, 1986, p. 81). He did not view the child's mind as an "entity worthy of study for its own sake" (Cleverly and Phillips, 1986, p. 81), but as a progression to adulthood. Several decades later, the child was finally studied from an empathetic point of view, a view that respected the child as a child, and one that approached each developmental stage with importance and reverence through the work of Jean Piaget.

While childhood was a necessary step to reaching adulthood to Preyer, childhood was important in itself to Piaget. Jean Piaget (1952) outlined a developmental theory of intelligence through observations of his children as well. He identified four stages of cognitive development: sensorimotor, preoperational, concrete operational, and formal operational (Piaget, 1952). These stages suggested that there were optimal times for successful mastery of specific tasks. Each stage had characteristic expectations within a certain age group. These expectations could not be mastered until the child reached a specific stage of development.

Piaget's theory is influenced by four major factors: maturation, active experience, social interaction, and equilibration (Piaget, 1952). Maturation refers to the biological aspect of intelligence. Certain tasks are more difficult, and sometimes impossible, unless the child has matured to a specific developmental stage. Active experience refers to thorough exploration of an object. The exploration can come through physical movement of the object, or through deep critical thought. Social interaction refers to exchanges between

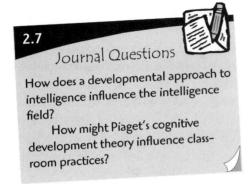

people in the environment. Social interactions are a necessary part of developing intelligence. Equilibration refers to how the child relates information gained through maturation, exploration, and interactions with knowledge he or she already possesses. The child may develop a new category for the information she has learned (assimilation) or fit the new information into an existing theory, thought, or understanding (accommodation).

Piaget's theory suggested tasks that could demonstrate the cognitive developmental level the child is working in. The tasks differed greatly from the psychometric tests of the time. Piaget's tasks were hands-on activities and questions to engage the child. The child's performance was indicative of what stage of cognitive development she was in.

The Multiplicity of Intelligence

In 1927, Charles Spearman developed a theory of intelligence that accounted for multiple factors. His theory suggested a general mental energy factor, known as the g factor, and a task-specific factor (Sattler, 1982). These two factors together accounted for intellectual performance. The g factor refers to a "general mental energy." All tasks require a general mental energy. The more difficult the task, the higher the amount of g, regardless of the discipline (Sattler, 1982). For example, a difficult mathematics problem, musical composition, or linguistic exercise might have the same degree of difficulty. All of these tasks would have the same g factor or require the same general mental energy. The specific factor required to solve each problem is specifically related to the discipline. None of these tasks would share the same specific factor, however all share the same g factor (Sattler, 1982). Spearman's view of intelligence is referred to as unitary. Spearman's view was significant because it led to controversy and a new way of looking at intelligence in multiple forms.

Edward Thorndike challenged Spearman's view and realized that intelligence involves a large number of interconnected abilities. In order to understand this vast number of abilities, he categorized them in three groups: social, concrete, and abstract. This view of intelligence opened the door for multifactor views of intelligence. There are multiple factors to take into consideration when examining the intelligence of an individual. The rise of the multifactor view of intelligence began an investigation into the many aspects of intelligence, such as emotional, cultural, social, intellectual, musical, and so on. Many contemporary theorists have supported the notion of the multiple factors of intelligence, as well as embracing biological and environmental influences on intelligence.

Contemporary Approaches

In 1983, Howard Gardner began to investigate the idea of multiple intelligences. His definition of intelligence is considered "biopsychological." Gardner proposed that there were environmental and biological factors that contributed to the development of intelligence, and that culture defined intelligent behavior. He also proposed that several intelligences existed: musical, interpersonal, intrapersonal, bodily/kinesthetic, spatial, linguistic, and logical/mathematical.

Robert Sternberg's (1985) theory of intelligence utilizes the environmental and genetic influence. His theory emphasizes three components: context, experience, and the intellectual components of information processing. These components are based entirely upon the culture the individual exists in. Culturally, intelligent behavior implies adapting, reshaping, or selecting a new environment. Sternberg (1985) explains that the best demonstration of intelligence is through the completion of an unfamiliar task.

In 1989, John Horn (cited in Yekovich, 1994) developed a theory of intelligence based upon Raymond Cattell's theory of fluid and crystallized abilities. Fluid intelligence consists of intelligence that is demonstrated in new and unfamiliar environments and situations. Crystallized intelligence represents the knowledge an individual has of its culture. Horn firmly states that fluid and crystallized intelligence exist independently from one another.

Contemporary intelligence theorists have begun to move away from the idea that intelligence involves solely cognitive skills. Daniel Goleman (1995) introduced a theory of emotional intelligence that suggested that the traditional means of intelligence did not necessarily make one successful in life. Classifying individuals by traditional intelligence scores reveals that the highest concentration of individuals who commit suicide, would be classified as those possessing the highest intelligence (Goleman, 1995). Goleman explains that emotional health is more important than intellectual superiority. Emotional intelligence consists of: knowing one's emotions, managing one's emotions, motivating oneself, recognizing emotions in others, and handling relationships (Goleman, 1995).

Stanley Greenspan (1997) firmly believes that emotions are the "architect of the mind." It is through emotional connections that intelligence is developed. Greenspan (1997, p. 16) describes intelligence as "the connection between a feeling or desire and an action or symbol." Greenspan proposes stages of emotional development that directly impact intellectual development. These stages will be examined in Chapter 5.

Contemporary research has also shown that there is no magical age where healthy supportive environments must end. William Dickens and James Flynn's (2001) research leads to an interesting conclusion. They say that enriched environments influence intelligence throughout life. Adults demand an attentive environment, just as children do. There is no magical year when the environment can be forgotten.

Curricular Implications of Intelligence

Intelligence has been studied by many different disciplines with a variety of motivations. Theories exist ranging from biological to environmental and every combination in between. Each theory and field of study has curricular implications.

The biological approaches to intelligence suggest that biology and genetics play an important part in determining and developing intelligence. It is important to recognize that some biological influences do exist. Current brain research opens a window into how the brain functions and how these functions affect the classroom environment. The first few years of life are the most significant in brain development. This fact has a tremendous impact on the importance of early childhood education. Even with the extensive technology and sophisticated equipment that is available in the twenty-first century, it has proved impossible to find a singular technique or approach that works definitively (Wolfe, 2001). The research does give insight into the working mechanics of the brain and those mechanics can help illuminate strategies that complement the active part of the brain during specific classroom tasks.

The psychometric approach suggests that intelligence is defined by what can be measured. This view limits intelligence only to skills that can be measured. This view was widely accepted in the nineteenth century and modifications to tests developed then are still in use today. It is critical to realize that psychometric measures may give a glimpse of a child's intelligence on a particular day at a particular time. However, many different types of assessments are necessary in order to get the complete picture of the child.

The developmental approach suggests intelligence is related to maturation, interaction, and active exploration (Piaget, 1963). Early childhood educators need to realize that some children are not ready for specific kinds of materials, interactions, and instruction. Ages and stages play an important role in determining curricular content.

Contemporary research views intelligence as a plural entity, communicates the importance of emotions, and accepts the brain's biological role. Contemporary approaches prevent teachers from limiting experiences for children. This text examines intelligence from an educational perspective with curricular motivations. With this purpose in mind, intelligence is defined as a potential created from biological and environmental influences. The biological influences include genetics, health, and brain function. The environmental influences include cultural, familial, societal, material, and educational interactions. The role of teachers is to understand and accept the genetic, health, brain function, culture, family, and society of children and purposefully plan and implement an educational curriculum that challenges children to reach their potential. Howard Gardner's theory of multiple intelligence most closely matches the philosophy of this early childhood text. His theory will be utilized to investigate the multiple potentials that exist for each child and how the possibility of these potentials shape the early childhood curriculum.

Multiple Intelligences

Howard Gardner's theory embraces the recognized patterns that existed in intelligence history. His definition bridges the gap between environmental and heredity theories. Gardner's theory was created through the critical analysis of past views of intelligence and contemporary views, cultural influences, psychological influences, and biological traits and patterns. His definition of intelligence recognizes how hereditary and environmental interactions both account for intelligence. Rather than presenting his theory as a hereditary or environmental one, he refers to it as "a third perspective, the symbol systems approach" (Gardner, Hatch, and Toriff, 1997, p. 243). This approach readily accepts the hereditary factors of intelligence, but explains that interactions with the symbol system of a specific discipline are responsible for the development of intelligence. The symbol systems are an environmental creation. They do not develop in isolation. Symbol systems are specific to cultural manifestations of the intelligences.

Gardner's theory of multiple intelligences stemmed from intense research on the brain, along with the theoretical viewpoint that multiple intelligences allowed an

BOX 2.8 | *Gardner's Criteria for Identifying an Intelligence*

In order to be identified as an intelligence category, particular criteria had to be met.

1. A potential isolation by brain damage had to be identified.
2. Idiot savants or prodigies had to exist in that area.
3. An identifiable core set of operations had to be established.
4. The intelligence area had to have a developmental history with end–state performances.
5. An evolutionary history to the development of the intelligence had to exist.
6. Support from experimental psychometric tests and tasks had to exist.
7. The intelligence must have its own identifiable encoding or symbol system.

(Gardner, 1993a)

individual to solve a cultural problem or create a product in relationship to the culture the individual exists in. Gardner's research of the brain led to pivotal findings regarding damage to the brain. Individuals who lost the function of particular areas of their brain also lost particular skills. There was a strong relationship and pattern between the part of the brain that was damaged and the skills that were lost. Through brain and educational research, Gardner (1993) identified seven areas of intelligence as a way to categorize the many culturally intelligent behaviors he identified.

The seven intelligence areas Gardner originally defined were logical/mathematical, linguistic, spatial, musical, bodily/kinesthetic, interpersonal, intrapersonal. Naturalistic was not included in the original seven although it is currently accepted as an intelligence. Existential and moral intelligence have been discussed, but not accepted by Gardner (1999). Gardner stresses that more intelligences may be identified. The final number is not as important as recognizing the multiplicity of intelligence itself (Gardner, 1999).

Each intelligence is briefly introduced in Box 2.9. A definition of the intelligence, related cultural roles, and any educational movements that support the intelligence will be provided. More detailed intelligence information will be provided in upcoming chapters.

The first area of intelligence Gardner describes is logical/mathematical. Gardner (1993a) credits Piaget with developing our understanding of logical and mathematical development. Logical and mathematical intelligence has been traditionally valued by Western society. Gardner refers to this as the *westist, bestist, testist* philosophy. The

---

BOX 2.9 | *The Original Seven Intelligences*

- Logical/mathematical—the capacity to problem solve quickly and accurately

- Linguistic—the ability to use, understand, manipulate, and show sensitivity to words

- Spatial—the capacity to perceive an object through the senses with great accuracy

- Musical—the ability to manipulate sound through the human voice, a tool, or through the manipulation of the musical notation system

- Bodily/kinesthetic—the creative and skilled use of the body to perform a culturally acceptable role

- Interpersonal—the capacity to notice distinctions, display empathy, and understand moods, temperament, motivation, and intentions

- Intrapersonal—the ability to understand and express one's own emotional life

cultural values of the West are limited to one view that can be tested (indicative of a nineteenth-century view of intelligence). Logical/mathematical intelligence consists of the capacity to problem solve quickly and accurately. Even before the problem can be articulated, the solution is being constructed. Mathematicians, scientists, and microbiologists possess this kind of intelligence. The "critical thinking" educational movement focuses on logical/mathematical intelligence (Armstrong, 2000).

Linguistic intelligence involves the use of language and verbal symbol systems. Linguistic intelligence is the capacity to use, understand, manipulate, and show sensitivity to words. Journalists, authors, and public speakers have this kind of intelligence. The development of language has remained remarkably consistent across cultures, even deaf cultures. Linguistic intelligence is localized in an area of the brain but other parts of the brain serve the different aspects and functions of language as well. Individuals who lose the ability to form sentences grammatically as a result of brain damage are still capable of performing other linguistic tasks (Gardner, 1993a). The "whole language" movement supports linguistic intelligence (Armstrong, 2000).

Musical intelligence is marked by the individual's powerful reaction to sound. Musical intelligence involves the capacity to manipulate sound through the human voice, a tool, or through the manipulation of the musical notation system. There has not been a definite localization of music in the brain, but individuals who sustained damage to parts of the right hemisphere of their brain suffered from amusia, the loss of musical abilities, which suggests localization. Singers and instrumentalists possess this kind of intelligence.

Bodily/kinesthetic intelligence is localized in the motor cortex. Bodily/kinesthetic abilities involve the creative and skilled use of the body to perform a culturally acceptable role. Surgeons, athletes, sculptors, and dancers exhibit this type of intelligence. The "hands-on learning" movement supports bodily/kinesthetic intelligence (Armstrong, 2000).

Spatial intelligence involves the individual's capacity to perceive an object through the senses with great accuracy. Navigators, chess players, and visual artists possess this type of intelligence (Gardner, 1993). Spatial intelligence is not limited to visual perception. Blind individuals may possess spatial intelligence through the use of other senses. When the area of the brain that controls spatial intelligence is damaged, linguistic intelligence attempts to compensate. The "integrated arts instruction" movement supports spatial intelligence (Armstrong, 2000).

Gardner (1993b) describes the interpersonal area of intelligence as having biological roots. Humans have a prolonged childhood and a need for solidarity that is indicative of interpersonal intelligence. Interpersonal intelligence allows an individual to notice distinctions, display empathy, and understand moods, temperament, motivation, and intentions. The frontal lobes of the brain control interpersonal intelligence. When this area of the brain is damaged, significant personality changes occur that involve the loss of social understanding. Success of the human species relies on interpersonal intelligence (Gardner, 1993b). Teachers, therapists, psychologists, and political leaders exhibit this type of intelligence. The "cooperative learning" movement supports interpersonal intelligence (Armstrong, 2000).

The seventh area of intelligence that Gardner identifies is intrapersonal. Intrapersonal intelligence allows an understanding of one's own feelings. Intrapersonal intelligence can be expressed through the domains of other intelligences, such as linguistic or music. Gardner suggests that individuals with autism may in fact be intrapersonally impaired. The "individualized instruction" movement supports intrapersonal intelligence (Armstrong, 2000).

Summary

The past 200 years have left the intelligence community with decades of research and many pathways to understanding. Theories have been introduced which range from biological, psychometric, and developmental. Intelligence has been viewed as a unitary factor and as an entity with multiple possibilities.

Contemporary views of intelligence respect the emotional health and environment of the child and the adult. Current research on the brain confirms that biology and environment both play important roles in the development of the brain and the formation of intelligence (Nash, 1997).

2.10
Journal Questions

Think back to your box. What beliefs and expectations do you hold about the concept of intelligence? How does the information presented in this chapter influence your beliefs about intelligence?

This text will examine methods of maximizing the early childhood environment while respecting the biological aspects of the developing child. The theory that most closely supports this view of intelligence is Howard Gardner's theory of multiple intelligences. The next four chapters will look at the many potentials that exist for young children and explain how to optimize the environment to help children reach their potentials.

A Story from the Author

As an author, I have been asked many times why I am captivated by the multiple intelligence theory. Why do I use this theory as a basis for an early childhood curriculum text? The answer can be traced back to a kindergarten student I had. Jacob was five. He liked school and was particularly interested in music activities.

Jacob had a very difficult time identifying letters. Even letters in his own name were difficult for him to recall. He became frustrated; he wanted to be able to identify them and noticed how other children in the class could.

As a teacher, I shared my love of music with my students on a daily basis. I would play the flute for them at the beginning of our morning circle time. This was Jacob's favorite part of the day. He would sit and listen in awe. One day, he brought in empty paper towel rolls, aluminum foil, and brass fasteners. He said, with a smile, that he was going to create his own flute. I helped him cut a hole for the mouthpiece and he covered the roll with aluminum foil and poked the brass fasteners in for keys. He sat on the floor and wanted to play along with me. I played the flute while he hummed into his pretend one. The next day, most of the other students brought in paper towel rolls and eagerly wanted to make a flute as well.

Our morning circle time began to turn into a miniconcert. I would play for the children, and they would hum into their homemade flutes. Jacob became increasingly curious about how I knew what to play. "How do you know to play certain notes? How can I know what notes I am supposed to play?" he said. I answered by telling him the notes on the staff paper told me what to play. I read the notes to know what to play next. He asked all kinds of questions about the notes. I began to teach him names of notes (quarter, half, and whole note). I began to tell him about scales, high and low notes, rests, fast and slow tempos. He began to identify several different notes and clap out tempos. He asked for staff paper in the writing corner and began to write out musical scores (in the same way one would use invented spelling). Real notes and invented notes filled the page. Jacob would look at the notes and hum them into his flute. Jacob wanted to know if the notes only worked for the flute. I explained that all music used the same kind of notes. I began to write out colored notes for him to play along on a plastic toy piano (with colored keys). He became fascinated with the musical notational system.

It was then I discovered something. He began to identify letters, and picked them up quickly. Music was a way for Jacob to make the sound/symbol relationship. It was through music that Jacob discovered the meaning, importance, and function of symbols. Remediation did not work for Jacob. However, approaching symbols through music allowed Jacob to make the necessary connections between sounds and symbols. Music allowed his brain to think in symbolic terms.

References

Armstrong, T. (2000) *Multiple intelligences in the classroom*. Alexandria, VA: Association for the Supervision of Curriculum Development.

Cleverly J., & Phillips, D. (1986) *Visions of childhood: Influential models from Locke to Spock*. New York: Teachers College Press.

Dickens, W., & Flynn, J. (2001) "Heritability estimates versus large environmental effects: The IQ paradox resolved." *Psychological Review* (Vol. 108, No. 2, pp. 346–369).

Ehrlich, P., & Feldman, S. (1977) *The race bomb.* New York: Quadrangle.

Eysenck, H. (1971) *The IQ argument: Race, intelligence, and education.* New York: Library Press.

Gardner, H. (1999) *Intelligences reframed: Multiple intelligences for the 21st century.* New York: Basic Books.

Gardner, H. (1993) *Frames of mind.* New York: Basic Books.

Gardner, H. (1993) *Multiple intelligences: The theory in practice.* New York: Basic Books.

Gardner, H. (1991) *The unschooled mind.* New York: Basic Books.

Gardner, H., Hutch, T., & Toriff, B. (1997) A third perspective: The symbol systems approach. In R. J. Steinberg and E. Grigovenko (eds.) *Intelligence, heredity, and environment* (pp. 243–248). New York: Cambridge University Press.

Goleman, D. (1995) *Emotional intelligence.* New York: Bantam Books.

Greenspan, S. (1997) *The growth of the mind and the endangered origins of intelligence.* Cambridge, MA: Perseus Books.

Hannaford, C. (1995) *Smart moves: Why learning is not all in your head.* Arlington, VA: Great Ocean Publishers.

Healy, J. (1990) *Endangered mind: Why children don't think and what we can do about it.* New York: Touchstone.

Jensen, A. (1969) "How much can we boost IQ and scholastic achievement." *Harvard Educational Review* (Vol. 39, pp. 1–123).

Jensen, E. (2001) *Arts with the brain in mind.* Alexandria, VA: Association for the Supervision of Curriculum Development.

McClellan, E. (1985) *Defining giftedness.* ED262519.

McLoughlin, J., & Lewis, R. (1990) *Assessing special students.* New York: Macmillan.

Mondale, S., Patton, S., Cuban, L., Andersen, J., Ravitch, D., & Kaestle, C., eds. (2001) *School: The story of American public education.* Boston: Beacon Press.

Nash, M. (1997) "Fertile minds." *Time Magazine* (February 3, 1997, pp. 55–56).

Piaget, J. (1952) *The origins of intelligence in children.* New York: Free Press.

Sattler, J. (1982) *The development of intelligence.* New York: McGraw-Hill Book Co.

Sokal, M., ed. (2002) *Psychological testing and American society.* New Brunswick, NJ: Rutgers University Press.

Sternberg, R. J. (1985) *Beyond IQ.* New York: Cambridge University Press.

Wilson, F. (1998) *The hand.* New York: Vintage Books.

Wolfe, P. (2001) *Brain matters: Translating research into classroom practice.* Alexandria, VA: Association for Supervision of Curriculum Development.

3

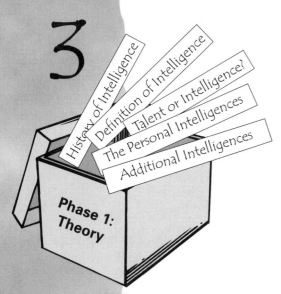

History of Intelligence

Definition of Intelligence

Talent or Intelligence?

The Personal Intelligences

Additional Intelligences

Phase 1: Theory

Traditional Intelligences

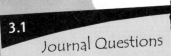

3.1
Journal Questions

Think back to the box mentioned at the beginning of the book. What kinds of tools, experiences, preconceptions, and feelings do you bring with you to the classroom regarding reading, writing, and math? How do you think these feelings, experiences, tools, and ideas will influence your work with children in these content areas?

At what age do you think reading and writing should begin?

How do you think standards and testing affect reading, writing, and math achievement?

Were reading, writing, and math difficult subjects for you in school?

If yes, how did school experiences contribute to the difficulty?

If not, how did school experiences contribute to your success?

Linguistic and logical/mathematical intelligence have historically been the focus in school. Contemporary American culture has also begun to emphasize development of linguistic and mathematical intelligence in preschool. Recognizing that other intelligences exist does not devalue the importance of linguistics and mathematics. The recognition is only meant to emphasize the importance of all intelligences.

Much research and attention has been given to linguistic and mathematical intelligences. Too often children are categorized as "successful" or "failures" based on their achievement in linguistics and mathematics. The multiple intelligence theory suggests that all children (except those with severe disability) can develop a competency in all of the intelligences (Gardener, 1993). Other intelligence strengths can be utilized to help children develop a competency in linguistic and logical/mathematical intelligences.

The early childhood period of development is crucial in creating a foundation for linguistic and logical/mathematical intelligence. A foundation cannot be built simply by providing phonics, shapes, or number instruction. (Providing only those kinds of instruction can even be detrimental.) A thorough understanding of brain development, symbol development, and linguistic and mathematical intelligence is needed in order to address these intelligences intentionally and appropriately in the early childhood curriculum.

# Linguistic Intelligence

Gardner (1993, p. 77) describes linguistic intelligence as a "sensitivity to the meaning of words," "sensitivity to the order of words," "sensitivity to the sounds, rhythms, inflections, and meters of words," and "a sensitivity to the different functions of language." This encompasses many different aspects of language. Phonology, semantics, and syntax are important mechanical domains of language (Gardner, 1993). Phonology involves the sounds, intonations, inflections, and dialects of language. The sound of words can communicate meaning, tonality, purpose, and emotion in language. Semantics, or the meaning of words, is also an important domain of language. Many words have multiple meanings or can be used for specific imagery techniques. Syntax refers to the order of words. Each language has rules for ordering words to make sense. Sensitivity and respect for these rules is crucial. Syntax allows us to understand one another and the manipulation of syntax (knowing when to use and/or break rules) can create startling literary affect.

Language encompasses many functions. Gardner (1993) classifies the functions of language as: rhetorical, mnemonic, explanatory, and reflective. The rhetorical aspect of language refers to "the ability to use language to convince other individuals of a course of action" (Gardner, 1993, p. 78). Politicians, therapists, mothers, fathers, lawyers, and even toddlers take advantage of this aspect of language. The mnemonic aspect refers

TABLE 3.1 | *Careers and Hobbies Associated with Linguistic Intelligence*

Careers with a Primary Linguistic Intelligence	Hobbies/Interests That Reflect Linguistic Intelligence
Author	Reading
Poet	Writing
Politician	Talking
Librarian	Storytelling
Speechwriter	Keeping a journal
Editor	Word games/Jumbles
Trainer/Consultant	

to "the capacity to use this tool to help one remember information" (Gardner, 1993, p. 78). Remembering grocery lists, shopping lists, vocabulary words, directions, and names are made possible by the use of the mnemonic aspect of language. Education has traditionally taken advantage of the explanatory aspect of language. This aspect of language is consistent throughout the intelligences. Most information is explained through explanatory means. Reflective language refers to the ability to use metalinguistic analysis, to "use language to reflect on language."

The International Reading Association (IRA) and the National Association for the Education of Young Children (NAEYC) have formulated a position statement to address the best practices to help children achieve linguistic literacy. The position statement stresses, "the early childhood years—from birth through age eight—are the most important for literacy development" (IRA and NAEYC position statement presented in Neuman, Copple, and Bredekamp, 2000, p. 3). Their position statement does not simply state that all children should read and write, but also should "read and write for their own enjoyment, information, and communication." Reading and writing for these purposes is far more sophisticated than recognizing and recalling print. These skills involve a deep understanding of language and require linguistic intelligence.

The field of brain research has contributed greatly to an understanding of linguistic development. Brain research has shown that reading, comprehending, and speaking words involve different aspects of the brain. Dr. Richard Restak (2001) deems reading to be "one of the most complex cognitive acts our brain performs." There is no single area of the brain that encodes, makes sense of the encoding, and then reads and/or responds to what has been encoded; rather, there are many areas of the brain that are active during reading. The visual cortex, Wernicke's area, Broca's area, the angular gyrus, and the motor area are all hard at work. Print is received by the primary visual cortex, travels to Wernicke's area (the receptive language area), which processes visual and auditory stimuli necessary to encode print. The angular gyrus links the letter symbols to sounds. The arcuate fasciculus consists of a bundle of nerves that allow Wernicke's area and Broca's area to communicate. Broca's area forms the words from the sounds the angular gyrus has processed. The words that are formed travel to the motor area to signal the necessary motor movement involved in speech. The brain's activity during reading suggests that reading is a highly complex, integrated skill.

The presentation of this process is not meant to be memorized, only to illustrate the complexity of language, reading, and print. This revelation has curricular implications. Because language is a complex process, not a single action, a curriculum that fosters language must approach language as a process. The process that has its genesis before birth must find its support throughout the early childhood years.

Linguistic Intelligence in the Classroom

An early childhood curriculum that respects the complexity of linguistic development and the findings of contemporary brain research internalizes four principles:

1. Children construct knowledge of reading and writing through meaningful experiences (Bluestein, 2001). These meaningful experiences are often created during play (Owocki, 1999).
2. Emotions are crucial to the development of formal symbol systems (Greenspan, 1997). Symbol development, and therefore reading, is not possible until the child reaches the appropriate stage of emotional development.
3. Reading and writing are developmental and require a carefully planned environment (Neuman, Copple, and Bredekamp, 2001).
4. Children must understand the function and basic concepts of language before they can read and produce language using the formal (adult) system (Neuman, Copple, and Bredekamp, 2001)

Meaning

Education must be rooted in meaningful experiences (Gardner, 1993). All content areas deserve to be presented in meaningful, relevant ways, but this idea is particularly significant for linguistic development. Reading, writing, speaking, and listening are important tools to learning and communicating in a literate culture. Therefore, these activities must connect the child with her culture. Education involving these activities should be carefully structured around the life of the child and her community. It proves difficult to find meaning and relevance through literature and literature experiences that are planned in another community by a group of adults who may have different goals. This is often the case with basal texts and workbooks whose creators have no idea what is meaningful and relevant to children they have never met (Farris and Kaczmarski, 1988). Often, the stories presented in basal texts are only meant to highlight specific letter combinations or specific skills. A real story is often replaced with a watered-down version due to space, skill, and reading-level considerations. When quality literature is presented in the basal texts, it is most often not presented at an opportune time. It is presented because it is "next," not necessarily because the children need the story or experience presented at that moment.

The teacher is responsible for knowing her students. This means the teacher has a better idea of what material is relevant and necessary to present to her students. Therefore, she becomes a powerful choice maker. She recognizes when appropriate stories are to be introduced and how, and what language experiences may be necessary. Table 3.2 demonstrates how to appropriately choose linguistic materials based on children's

TABLE 3.2	*Using Clues to Plan Developmentally Appropriate Linguistic Experiences*
Clue (Observed Experience)	Developmentally Appropriate Linguistic Experience Planned as a Result of the Observation
A kindergarten teacher notices that a group of five-year-olds are pretending to deliver mail to friends. He notices that the children are role-playing and beginning to gather props.	1. The teacher schedules a field trip to the neighborhood post office. 2. The teacher provides books in the class library related to mail carriers and the post office. 3. The teacher presents some vocabulary relevant to the post office (mail carrier, mail bag, stamp, letter, postcard). 4. The teacher creates student mailboxes in the classroom and adds letter writing materials to the writing center. 5. The teacher adds a list of the children's names next to their pictures in the writing center. 6. The teacher demonstrates the proper way to put a stamp on the letter and explains why the stamp must go in that spot. 7. The teacher has the children write letters to their grandparents or parents. He provides letter-writing materials (the children may draw pictures, use invented spelling, etc.). The teacher walks the children to the post office to mail their letters. 8. The teacher invites the school's mail carrier in to speak to the children.
A preschool teacher notices that a group of preschoolers are making fun of a four-year-old who has recently gotten glasses.	1. The teacher presents a puppet show about an animal who could not see and was in need of glasses. (The puppet show demonstrates how important glasses are for safety and how bad the animal felt when he was made fun of.) 2. The teacher adds glasses to the dramatic play area. 3. The teacher reads stories about glasses and explains some of the vocabulary that is associated with wearing glasses. 4. The teacher invites an ophthalmologist in to check the children's vision. The ophthalmologist brings a special pair of glasses in to show how the child who has to wear glasses sees the world without her glasses.
A group of first graders have been investigating fall weather.	In the writing center, the teacher adds fall-related vocabulary words. She writes the word "leaf" on a cutout leaf, "tree" on a cutout tree, and the words "cold," "season," and "fall" on corresponding cutouts. She fills the writing center with books about fall, colored charcoals, leaves, and pictures/paintings of fall. The teacher invites the students to write and illustrate fall stories in the writing center.
A kindergarten child loves to write stories. She often uses invented spelling; however, she consistently asks how to spell the word "the."	The teacher puts the word "the" on a shape card. (This is a card that shows the visual shape of the word.) The teacher teaches the child the word "the" as a sight word. The teacher may develop a folder game to encourage the child to recognize and remember the word "the."

interests and developmental needs. The "clue" represents the behaviors that spark the linguistic activity prepared by the teacher.

The suggested experiences involve reading, writing, speaking, and listening activities. Each of these experiences provides developmentally appropriate methods of facilitating linguistic intelligence. Meaning not only connects the child to the content, but is also necessary for remembering, recalling, and applying that information. Memory and brain development are directly connected to emotions and meaningful experiences (Bluestein, 2001).

Many of the clues described in Table 3.2 came about in play experiences. Play is extremely significant in determining curricular content. Often, linguistic needs and interests will be determined by observations and questions children pose during play (Owocki, 1999).

The children also create meaning. Children create their own meaning from reading and writing (Manning and Manning, 1995). Many times young children will be able to read back the invented spelling and symbols they have used in a story. In invented spelling, children generally choose symbols that are of interest, importance, and relevance to themselves and their experience with the world. These symbols begin to reflect phonetic and word knowledge, which makes invented spelling a meaningful experience for young children. Instead of having the pressure of memorizing spelling words at a young age, children have the freedom to express the phonetic sounds they do know through invented spelling. They are not limited to a few words they have learned, but open to the possibility of using any word that is connected to their story or experience. Providing and encouraging meaning makes language real to students; it allows them to feel language and take advantage of the emotional impact of language.

Emotions

Stanley Greenspan (1997) suggests that language cannot develop appropriately or accurately without the meaningful emotional nurturance. Greenspan views emotions as the "architect of the mind." A specific emotional level must be reached in order to develop age-appropriate language and to be able to create, understand, and identify written symbols. (Greenspan will be covered further in the discussion of the personal intelligences.)

Putting stress on, rushing, or holding inappropriate expectations of children can create an unhealthy emotional environment. Drilling young children with flash cards, forcing children to write letters correctly, and demanding they spell vocabulary and spelling words correctly creates an emotionally unhealthy environment. An environment that is emotionally unhealthy will not create confident, better readers. Instead, it often creates stressed, unconfident readers who begin to use only words they are sure of. It can create a dislike for reading, writing, and speaking. An inappropriate environment might even lead to a possible learning disability (Healy, 1999).

Reading and Writing Are Developmental

Reading and writing are developmental (Neuman, Copple, and Bredekamp, 2000), meaning that they develop in stages. Neuman, Copple, and Bredekamp (2000) suggest that the developmental steps involved in reading and writing occur in five phases.

Phase One is a foundational stage, *awareness and exploration*. Children begin to explore letters, sounds, genres, and storytelling. They begin to become aware of different types of print in the environment. Children in this phase will make attempts at creating symbols and letters; often these symbols will only be recognizable to the child (Neuman, Copple, and Bredekamp, 2000). See Figure 3.1 for an example of Phase One.

The awareness, exposure, and exploration of the preschool child will lead into the next stage, Phase Two. Phase Two typically involves the kindergarten child. The exploration turns into *experimentation with reading and writing*. Children will write more recognizable letters of the alphabet. They will begin to write words they see often, such as their name, labels, and street signs. They will begin to recognize words such as their name, "mom," or "love" (Neuman, Copple, and Bredekamp, 2000). Children in this phase will invent spellings for words and elaborate themes for their stories. Figure 3.2 is an example of experimentation with reading and writing.

The experimentation of the kindergarten child leads to more formal reading and writing representations. The child transitions to Phase Three, *early reading and writing*. This phase typically involves the first-grade child. The child can sound out words, recognize many sight words, and read short stories independently (Neuman, Copple, and Bredekamp, 2000). The child can write short stories, often using a mix of invented and formal alphabetic symbols. (See Figure 3.3 for an example.)

BOX 3.2 | *Developmental Phases of Reading and Writing*

Developmental phases of reading and writing:

- Phase One—Awareness and Exploration (Preschool)
- Phase Two—Experimental Reading and Writing (Kindergarten)
- Phase Three—Early Reading and Writing (First Grade)
- Phase Four—Transitional Reading and Writing (Second Grade)
- Phase Five—Independent and Productive Reading and Writing (Third Grade)

(From Neuman, Copple, and Bredekamp, 2000)

FIGURE 3.1

FIGURE 3.2

FIGURE 3.3

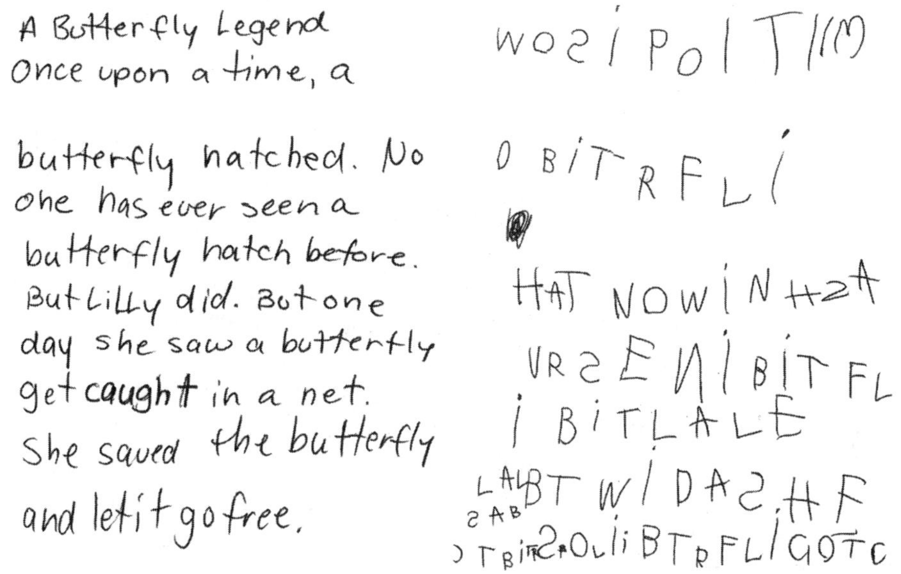

A Butterfly Legend
Once upon a time, a

butterfly hatched. No
one has ever seen a
butterfly hatch before.
But Lilly did. But one
day she saw a butterfly
get caught in a net.
She saved the butterfly
and let it go free.

WO2 I PO I T I(M

0 BIT R F L I

HAT NOW I N H2T

VR2 E M I BIT FL

i BITLALE

LAYBT W I DA2 H F
2 AB
) T BiR2ROLli BTRFLI GOTC

Phase Four is referred to as *transitional reading and writing*. This stage typically involves second graders. During this phase, the child understands and incorporates more formal rules of reading and writing. The child can read and write with increasing fluency and begins to call upon strategies in figuring out unknown words (Neuman, Copple, and Bredekamp, 2000).

The final phase, Phase Five, is referred to as *independent and productive reading and writing*. This stage typically involves third graders. A child in this phase is a much more fluent reader and writer. The child observes formal reading and writing rules, employs many reading strategies, and can write for a variety of audiences and purposes.

The phases described above provide a foundation for linguistic intelligence and a foundation for accessing information related to other intelligences.

Understanding the Basic Concepts and Functions of Language

The previously mentioned phases of reading and writing communicate the developmental aspect of language. Children must understand the basic concepts and functions of language in order to be able to understand and use formal symbols (Neuman, Copple, and Bredekamp, 2000). Reading and writing begin with language and stories. This point cannot be stressed enough. Before any type of formal symbol presentation is expected or directed, the child must have an understanding of the basic concepts and functions of language. This occurs through interaction with language and print during the first five years of life.

Language, Storytelling, and Speaking

At the core of linguistic development is language (Gardner, 1993), the primary tool of communication. Every culture on earth communicates using some form of language.

Before facilitating the development of language in children, it is necessary to instill an appreciation and love of the language the child speaks. Expose children to the beauty of language before they even open a book in the classroom. Talk with children about how changing the way we speak can communicate a variety of meanings. Encourage children to listen to the intonation, inflection, and pronunciation of their language as they speak and as they hear others speak.

An exciting but often forgotten language experience is storytelling. The art of storytelling communicates history, cultural importance, and the beauty of language, and reinforces the wonder of listening. Not all cultures value literacy, although all cultures have stories. Storytelling has a multitude of functions and responsibilities. Storytelling shares news, offers the history and relevance of culture, and introduces and/or enforces cultural morals. Storytelling involves speaking and gestures, no pictures or written words.

Many books for young children use telegraphic speech and picture identification. The use of these texts is acceptable periodically, but children need to be immersed in rich language experiences through storytelling. Fairy tales, myths, and legends offer rich language, a sense of history and place in the world, develop imagination, instill a sense of pride, and reinforce universal moral codes in school-age children. Nature stories, carefully chosen fairy tales, stories about the children themselves, and poems offer appropriate storytelling experiences for the early-childhood period of development.

In contemporary society, many times children are talked *at*. There are limited opportunities for the child to be talked *with* (Whaley, 2002). Storytelling can present an opportunity for a shared language experience. Stories can be developed *with* children as their ideas, thoughts, and suggestions are incorporated into the story.

Storytelling Techniques

Young children begin their story writing with storytelling. There are many ways to encourage children to tell stories. Whaley (2002) suggests such techniques as: sentence stories, theme stories, descriptive stories, picture stories, grab stories, and "finish the story." These techniques can be used with preschool and school-age children. *Sentence stories* involve children's ideas as each child contributes one sentence to the story. In *theme stories,* children suggest and agree upon the theme of the story that will be told. *Descriptive stories* are often a humorous approach to storytelling. The teacher can suggest a sentence such as "The cat ran up the tree." The children can be encouraged to come up with as many descriptive words as possible in the sentence. For example, "The fat, muddy cat ran slowly up the scratchy large tree trunk." *Picture stories* can sometimes add a personal touch to storytelling. Children can bring in pictures from home or use pictures taken of them at the center. Each child can make up a story using the pictures. The child can tell a story after arranging the pictures in a sequence that makes sense to her. The picture stories can also be created using pictures from a magazine or old books, flash cards, or other sources. *Grab stories* offer an exciting approach to storytelling. A number of objects are placed in a box, bag, or a special storytelling bag. Each child takes a turn pulling out one of the objects. After picking one of the objects, the child adds a part to the story that relates to the object she pulled out. *Finish the story* can be implemented in a number of ways. The teacher can begin a story and have the children come up with the ending. The teacher can also supply the ending of the story and encourage children to come up with what might have happened in the beginning. The middle of the story can also be left out, then filled in with children's suggestions (Whaley, 2002).

Puzzle-piece stories are another interesting storytelling strategy. The teacher can draw a picture on a piece of large poster board and then cut it into puzzle pieces. Each piece should contain an object or character. The children put the puzzle together by telling a story. Each child contributes a piece of the story that is relevant to his puzzle piece. (The children can choose their own puzzle piece or be given one randomly.) Teachers can also choose to tell stories with flannel boards, props, and/or puppets.

Another storytelling technique is the use of storyboards. Storyboards have been used extensively to promote and assess linguistic development at Project Spectrum (Chen, Krechevsky, and Viens, 1998, p. xiii). Project Spectrum is "a 10 year research project dedicated to developing an alternative approach to curriculum and assessment. . . ." This project was based on Gardner's multiple intelligence framework. Storyboards have related props, scenery, and figures available for children to use to create their own story. Spectrum uses the storyboard to assess linguistic development. Storyboards can also be used to promote linguistic development. Storyboards can contain new props and scenery to create imaginative stories or they can contain props from a familiar story. Children can retell the story, make up new endings, and add new characters. Many variations on the storyboard theme can be incorporated into the classroom.

Many storytelling techniques exist. Storytelling is an irreplaceable language tool in the early childhood classroom. It offers a meaningful foundation for the child's language and can be used to facilitate the development of other languages.

Second Languages

Current brain research has led to the belief that there are "windows of opportunity" for language development (Restak, 2001). The "windows" are time periods critical for development in a specific area. For example, the opportunity for full language development to occur is from birth to five years of age. Children who are not exposed to language during this time period will not be able to fully develop their potential for language.

This window also holds true for second languages. Children exposed to other languages before the age of five will become more fluent in the language and speak it without an accent (Restak, 2001). This occurs because the child's primary language's constraints have not been permanently set up in the brain (i.e., the brain has not set up a specialization for the primary language). After a child is five years old, language specialization begins to take place and it is more difficult to learn a second language fluently and speak it without an accent (Restak, 2001).

Expose children to the syntax, phonology, and semantics of other languages regularly. This will introduce them to the beauty of other languages and inspire them to learn another language. During the preschool years, children can begin to be exposed to other languages and encouraged to speak them. It is important for the child's second language to be spoken by someone fluent in that language. Children will respond and learn the sounds more effectively from a native speaker or someone fluent in the language (speaks without an accent).

Invite children to learn and witness the beauty of sign language. Sign language proves to children that the body can be used to communicate to others and that words are not always necessary for communication.

Discuss with children the importance of accepting and recognizing other languages. Language and stories provide the experience and interaction necessary for linguistic symbols to emerge.

 # Linguistic Symbol Systems/Writing

The symbol system of each intelligence is extremely significant. Gardner (1993) designated the existence of a symbol system as one of the criteria for determining an intelligence in his multiple intelligence theory. Symbols are of great concern to early childhood educators. Children begin to create, recognize, use, and understand symbols during the early childhood years. Understanding and using the symbol system of an intelligence is far more complicated than encoding print or reading numbers. Before a formal symbol system is even presented to children, certain questions regarding symbol systems must be answered in the early years of life (Gardner, 1991).

1. What is a symbol system?
2. Why use a symbol system?
3. Why is a symbol system important to me?
4. When should I use a symbol system?
5. What are the functions of the symbol system?
6. Can I invent my own symbol system?

These questions, of course, are not answered directly. Rather, the early childhood environment communicates and invites the child to discover the importance, use, function, invention, and creation of symbol systems. This is where writing really begins, with the exposure to writing. Before any marks can ever be made on a piece of paper, the child needs experience and exposure to print. One of the most effective methods of addressing these issues in a linguistic context is through creating a print-rich environment. An environment that is print rich is one that displays, and encourages children to interact with, print of different forms on a daily basis.

The Print-Rich Environment

A print-rich environment is more than one that contains a display of letters. A print-rich environment exposes children to a variety of print mediums. Owocki (1999) categorizes these different mediums as environmental, occupational, informational, and recreational. Each form of print has a place and purpose in the classroom.

ENVIRONMENTAL PRINT   Environmental print consists of the words and symbols witnessed every day on street signs, storefronts, calendars, schedules, name tags, price tags, and menus (Owocki, 1999). Environmental print can be created by children or provided to them. "Street signs" can be added to the classroom that signal play areas or special events. Children can be provided with materials to create store signs to go along with their play theme. Materials can also be provided for children to create their own street signs for a gross-motor or bike area, or building signs for the block area. Picture and word schedules can be displayed for children to see. Environmental print in the community can be pointed out during walks and field trips.

OCCUPATIONAL PRINT   Occupational print consists of the words and symbols used by specific occupations (Owocki, 1999). For example, menus contain occupational print for a restaurant. Patient files contain occupational print for a doctor's office. Table 3.3 provides a sample of occupational print materials that are appropriate in the early childhood classroom. These materials can be teacher-created and/or child-created.

INFORMATIONAL PRINT   Informational print consists of factual print used for storing and accessing information (Owocki, 1999). Informational print is found in technical

TABLE 3.3	*Samples of Occupational Print Materials to Include in the Classroom*	
Area in the Classroom	**Career**	**Samples of Occupational Print**
Dramatic Play	Doctor	File folders, pretend patient files, pretend hospital ID cards, receipts, labeled body charts
	Store Clerk	Price tags, food labels, store signs, grocery lists
	Waiter/waitress	Menus, order pads, receipts, restaurant signs
	Mechanic	Tool labels, car manuals, invoices
	Teacher	Books, attendance sheets, grade sheets, notepads
Block Play	Architect	Building plans, building signs, street signs
Publishing Center	Author/illustrator	Children can create their own stationery, books, poetry, manuals

manuals, newspapers, biographies, calendars, and telephone books (Owocki, 1999). A class telephone book can be made with children's names and telephone numbers. Class newspaper and newsletters can be created to share what's happening in the classroom. Contributions to the newsletters can come from children, teachers, parents, and class visitors. A classroom calendar can mark special days and events. A classroom schedule with pictures and words can be posted at eye level. Biographies can be made of each student. The biographies can include photographs, likes, dislikes, family information, and age. The biographies can be completed through interviews, or children can create them (autobiography). Informational books can be created by children on topics they are investigating or interested in.

RECREATIONAL PRINT   Recreational print consists of words or symbols used for leisure purposes (Owocki, 1999). Books of different interests, genres, and forms are important to include in the classroom library, along with magazines, newspapers, cartoons, poetry, and songbooks. Books authored by the child should also be included in the recreational print selection. Choosing appropriate books for young children is critical and should be done with thought and purpose and should respect developmental knowledge of the children in the classroom.

CHOOSING APPROPRIATE LITERATURE   Choosing recreational print for young children can prove to be difficult. The quantity and variety of books targeted at young children today is unprecedented.

Hurst (1994) suggests that emerging readers should be exposed to literature that has a natural flow. These books are predictable and the pictures play an important role in deciphering meaning. These books are, however, not boring or choppy. Unimaginative stories have been created for children, especially in basal readers, in an attempt to make them easy for beginning readers. These stories are often unpredictable, make little sense, are full of short sentences, and are unmotivating. Children who are exposed to this kind of literature tend to write using the same, short, sentences that convey appropriate grammar, but little meaning (Hurst, 1994). One-word books can be extremely exciting for emerging readers and offer a more successful alternative than the unimaginative short-sentence stories. These stories often have exciting plots and by reading the one word that is repeated throughout the story, the child feels successful and confident about reading (Hurst, 1994). Literal stories with clear pictures can also instill this kind of confidence. Folktales that use a repetitive phrase that is built upon throughout the story and stories with this similar theme are also important to facilitating language. These stories offer a way for the child to discover new words and themes, promote imagination, and offer a framework for writing stories. The stories encourage the child's self-confidence and motivation for reading *and* writing (Mooney, 1994).

Development of the Written Symbol

The symbol system of language stirs controversy. Debates over when a formal symbol system should be presented and expected of children are numerous. It is not really a matter of when the alphabet should be presented to children, but a question of how to facilitate the development of symbol systems throughout the child's early school experiences. It is critical to understand how symbol systems develop in order to create an environment that facilitates their growth and to adopt a methodology that supports literacy throughout life.

Exposing children to the linguistic symbol system creates excitement, interest, and genuine enthusiasm for learning formal symbol systems (Gardner, 1991). The purposeful exposure of print and rich storytelling are necessary components of the early childhood curriculum.

Through the exposure of print, children begin to recognize its features. They begin to recognize features in a progression. The features are outlined by Gretchen Owocki (2001) in *Make Way for Literacy*.

Early Feature Discoveries:

■   Letters can be named.
■   Print carries meaning.
■   There is a difference between drawing and writing.

Print Can Label Objects:

■   Print is used for labeling objects.
■   Most early writing on drawings consists of labels.

Print Is a Physical Representation of Objects:

- Early print is a spatial representation of the object.
- Characteristics of the object play an important part in the child's early print representation.

Print Is Recognized as Separate from the Object:

- Children recognize that print is not related to the physical characteristics of the object.
- Children begin to recognize that words must look different from one another.
- Words on a child's page may not be right next to the object they are labeling or writing a story about.

Relationship between Speech and Print:

- Children begin to match their printing to their speaking.
- Children move their finger across words as they speak (not reading the actual words on the page).

Relationship between Letters and Speech Sounds:

- Children begin this relationship by using one letter or symbol for each syllable they hear. The letter they symbolize with will not usually relate to the sounds they hear.
- Children then use one letter to mark the sound of each syllable they hear. (For example, MN for mountain.)
- Children begin to use more phonetic letters to represent words.

Word Spacing:

- Children begin to use spaces in words for punctuation.
- Children begin to experiment with dots, dashes, and other markings to signify punctuation.

Other Forms of Punctuation:

- Children begin to experiment with other types of punctuation and symbols to add meaning to their print.
- These forms are not always conventional.

Adapted from *Make Way for Literacy* by Owocki, 2001

It is important to recognize that these features of print are not taught. The child develops an understanding of these features through interaction with the people and materials in her environment. Ample time must be given to explore language, reading, and writing through play and child-initiated experiences (Owocki, 2001).

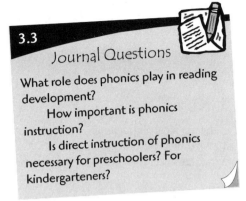

Journal Questions

What role does phonics play in reading development?

How important is phonics instruction?

Is direct instruction of phonics necessary for preschoolers? For kindergarteners?

PHONICS One of the features of reading and writing that Owocki mentions is the relationship between symbols and sounds, referred to as phonics. Phonics are the sounds associated with letters, syllables, and letter combinations.

In examining appropriate methodologies and practices in creating optimal linguistic environments, it's important to look at phonics. There is a lot of misinformation concerning the importance and use of phonics in the early childhood classroom. They are an important part of speech, reading, and writing. An early childhood classroom should not ignore them, nor should it make them the focus of the early childhood reading environment.

Invented spelling is an activity that is rooted in understanding and making sense of phonemes. Children listen to the sounds that are present in the words. The emphasis should be on the sound (the phoneme), not on exact spelling. Children develop a sound/symbol relationship based on the phonemes they hear and the letter symbols they know. Invented spelling is also mixed with creative symbols that resemble hieroglyphics. Children use phonetic awareness and imagery in their first attempts at writing. Instead of providing whole-group instruction on specific letter names and phonemes (instruction that occurs out of context), the child should develop an understanding of the symbol/sound relationship in the context of writing. The skills are taught in context, where they matter. As a result, children do not lose information in the process as they transfer what they have learned to the "real world." They are already learning reading and writing skills in a "real-world" context. It has been argued that the alphabet needs to be formally presented to children in order for them to move ahead with reading instruction. This often occurs at the preschool or kindergarten level. Teachers spend an entire year or two on letters and sounds in the guise of academic preparation. While learning letters and sounds is important to reading, devoting months to it is unnecessary.

Recalling letter names is the least complex of the processes in reading. Kids can learn the names of twenty-six children or twenty-six objects quite quickly. They do not need an entire school year or several months. A curriculum that centers on letter names is not necessary either. It is questionable, then, why schools and preschools spend so much time on letter names. Children *seem* to require many months to learn these letter names when they are presented at the preschool or early-kindergarten level. Children are required to be accountable for this information too early in their education. If letters were formally introduced in the second half of the kindergarten year, or even in first grade, the emphasis and repetition generally needed with younger children would not be necessary. Formal presentation may not even be necessary for children who were able to acquire letters in a literacy-supported environment. Many children might only need a few formally presented.

Brain research suggests that presenting children with formal symbol systems too early can have a negative impact on brain development. Jane Healy (1990) suggests that there is research to support the discouragement of isolated skill development in young children. Isolated skill development in the preschool years can lead to brain connections that may be more difficult to access when the child is older. Healy (1990) also suggests that inappropriate linguistic education and too-early expectations may even create a learning disability.

Hannaford (1995) outlines a model of brain development that highlights specific experiences that feed the cerebral cortex at different times of development. Hannaford stresses that brain development is continuous; however, there are ages at which specific areas of the brain seem to flourish. The limbic system, gestalt hemisphere, and the logic hemisphere areas of the brain are the areas most relevant to the ages of the targeted children of this text. Between the ages 1½ to 4½, the limbic system—or relationship part of the brain—is developing and growing. This part of the brain is responsible for an understanding of the self, emotions, language, memory development, gross motor proficiency, memory development, and social development (Hannaford, 1995). From 4½ to 7 years is generally the time for gestalt hemisphere (or right-brain) elaboration. Whole-picture processing, cognition, imaging, movement, rhythm, intuition, and integrative thought characterize the gestalt hemisphere. From the ages of 7 to 9, the logic hemisphere (or left brain) is growing and developing. Detail and linear processing, refinement of elements of language, reading/writing skills, and linear math processing, are characteristic of this area of the brain.

Recognizing when specific areas of the brain go through growth spurts has curricular implications. Image, emotion, and spontaneous movement (engaged in through play) encourage the gestalt hemisphere to develop (Hannaford, 1995). If specific skills are introduced during this period of brain growth, the skills must be introduced through imagination, movement, and emotion. In the next stage, the brain of the seven-year-old begins to expand and the logic hemisphere of the brain begins to develop (Hannaford, 1995). The brain during this period of growth is ready for direct instruction, skill development, and formal symbol system presentation.

3.4

Journal Questions

Look back at your answers to the previous journal questions: Have any of your answers changed from reading this section? If so, how?

Linguistics and Special Education

Thomas Armstrong (2000, p. 103) explains that historically, special education has worked "from a deficit paradigm—focusing on what students *can't* do—in an attempt to help students succeed in school." The multiple-intelligence theory, in contrast, looks at children as having varying strengths and challenges. The children's strengths serve as a bridge for helping them address their challenges. This approach focuses on what children *can do* to succeed in school. Content can be approached from the child's intelligence strengths instead of consistently remediating a deficit. The example at the end of Chapter 2 clearly demonstrated how a child's strength was able to address the child's challenge. Jacob was able to understand the relationship between symbols and sounds through music.

Armstrong (2000) explains that utilizing the multiple-intelligence theory in special education can lead to fewer referrals, a greater emphasis on strengths, increased self-esteem, and a deeper appreciation for students. The multiple-intelligence theory promotes collaboration between teachers and specialists and encourages more appropriate instruction (Armstrong, 2000).

3.5

Journal Question

You have a child in your first-grade class that is showing difficulty with story comprehension. This child has shown a strong musical and bodily kinesthetic strength in your classroom. What activities could you develop to help the child deal with his challenge?

Utilizing the multiple intelligence theory in special education requires careful assessment and documentation of the child's strengths and challenges. The challenges serve as the child's goals. The strengths offer a pathway for the child to reach her goals. See Table 3.4 for an example of using the intelligences to address linguistic challenges. The strategies presented in the table can help Chris deal with his challenges by allowing him to access linguistic content through his strengths and by adapting the linguistic environment.

Linguistics and Culturally Appropriate Education

The multiple-intelligence theory gives each particular culture the responsibility of defining intelligent behaviors. This has significant implications for the classroom. It is important to understand the cultures represented in the classroom and make sure culturally relevant materials are a part of the daily classroom routine (as opposed to something that's added for a week in the name of multicultural education.)

TABLE 3.4 | *Special Education Strategies*

Child's Name: Chris
Age: 5
Current Placement: Kindergarten

Description:
Chris is a five-year-old male. He is currently enrolled in a regular kindergarten program in a suburban school district. His teacher and parents have expressed a concern over his linguistic delays.

Challenges:

Linguistic

- Chris's receptive language is age appropriate.
- Chris's expressive language indicates a two-year delay.
- Chris has difficulty articulating several sounds—indicating a delay in articulation.
- Chris is currently receiving speech therapy for articulation and expressive speech delays.
- Chris does not demonstrate any knowledge of sound/symbol relationships. He cannot distinguish between letters and numbers.
- Chris has difficulty sitting for lengthy stories and often loses interest. Group stories are particularly difficult for him to sit through. He does not eagerly participate in circle time and his responses are often confusing and not related to the circle-time content.
- Chris has difficulty following the plot in a story. He has great difficulty retelling a familiar story.

Strengths:

Bodily/Kinesthetic

He moves his body with purpose and skill in the environment.
Chris's gross and fine motor skills are more coordinated than his peers.

Spatial

Chris demonstrates preschematic art representation with most art mediums (clay, crayons, paints).
He moves his body with purpose and skill in the environment.

Musical

Chris participates in music-related activities with eagerness and excitement.
Chris is able to mimic, create, and follow a rhythm.
Chris can manipulate several classroom instruments to produce a melody.

Interests:
Chris loves movement, drawing, music, and exploring outdoors. He loves his puppy and takes care of two goldfish at home.

Learning Support Strategies (These are strategies developed to tackle linguistic development directly and through observed intelligence strengths.)

Linguistic Strategies:
- Shorter stories of Chris's choosing should be read to him or available for Chris to look at several times during the school day.

TABLE 3.4 | *Continued*

- Circle time may be difficult for Chris because he does not have the necessary expressive language to communicate to his peers. Avoid putting Chris on the spot. When asking him questions, phrase them as "I wonder" or "Maybe . . . " to allow Chris to be comfortable and offer a response.
- Play match and go-fish games one-on-one with Chris. Use cards that have pictures of words he is working on in speech class. Invite him to play, rather than instruct him to practice.
- When Chris is talking, sit on the floor with him at eye level. Offer him full attention. Pause after he finishes talking to let him know he has time to finish his thoughts.
- When Chris misarticulates a word, repeat the phrase he has said, using the correct articulation. (Do not point out that he has said the word "wrong.") This practice is used to let him hear the correct articulation of the word and to let him know you understand what he says.

Spatial Strategies:
- In the block area, provide story props as well. Facilitate theme development with Chris to build a sense of story.
- Chris can begin letter representation by making the letters in his name out of clay, drawing them in shaving cream, or using a stick to draw them in rice.
- During lengthy stories, offer Chris crayons and paper to draw pictures of the story. Encourage Chris to tell about his drawings to build his expressive language and to create a comfortable atmosphere for conversation.

Bodily/Kinesthetic Strategies:
- Provide props or storyboards related to stories that are read in class. Invite Chris to play with the props. Chris might demonstrate *better comprehension skills or develop comprehension skills* by role playing and manipulating props.
- Chris can be asked to "act out" the end of a story or to "act out" a new ending to a story read to him.
- The sign language alphabet might be performed for Chris to assess an interest in sign language. Chris can begin to symbolize letters with his hands. This might spark an acknowledgment and interest in the alphabetic symbol system.
- Letters of the alphabet might also be acted out with the body.
- Chris can use his fingers to trace over sandpaper letters.

Musical Strategies:
- Encourage Chris to tell a happy story with musical instruments, a sad story, and an angry story.
- Provide songbooks for Chris to look at in the classroom. Point out the musical notation system simply by talking about it (to see if there is an interest in knowing more about it.)
- Encourage Chris to make sound effects during stories with musical instruments.
- Encourage Chris to communicate moods through music.

Integrating culture into the curriculum is difficult. Many approaches have been attempted. The National Association for the Education of Young Children (Bredekamp and Rosegrant, 1999) describes three common, but inappropriate, approaches to diversity in early childhood education: European-American culture-centered, difference denial, and multicultural.

The European-American approach typically looks at education from the perspective of the mainstream culture. Every aspect of the classroom, including holidays, traditions, celebrations, and curriculum content are influenced by the European-American culture. This communicates to children an inappropriate emphasis on a single culture (Bredekamp and Rosegrant, 1999).

The difference-denial method approaches diversity from the standpoint that humans are basically the same. This approach emphasizes similarities between people. Bredekamp and Rosegrant (1999) warn that this approach quickly turns into the European-American approach. Because differences are not emphasized, similar customs and culture are presented to the children.

The third approach is referred to as the multicultural approach. Bredekamp and Rosegrant (1999) explain this approach as something that occurs "in addition to the regular curriculum." Differences are addressed, and other cultures are brought into the classroom. However, other cultures are not truly *integrated* into the curriculum. This approach typically reinforces stereotypes and quite frequently misrepresents a particular culture. Activities are often added on as a cute art or movement experience, instead of occurring in context.

An antibias, multicultural program provides cultural experiences in context. Context is the difference in providing appropriate cultural experiences. This means that an antibias multicultural curriculum will look different in each classroom. The curriculum must respond to the interests and cultural practices of the children in the program. This text will not attempt to offer generic tips and strategies for implementing an antibias, multicultural curriculum. Instead, this text will offer a description of a real child, Joy. She will be used in each intelligence section of the text. Her description will be used as a focal point for deciding what cultural experiences in each of the intelligences would be appropriate. Joy is a four-year-old Chinese American. She is certainly not stereotypical of all Chinese Americans. This is one child from one family who brings quite a different culture to the early childhood classroom.

After the description of Joy is presented, linguistic strategies will be offered that pertain to Joy and her family. The strategies are not prescriptive for all Chinese-American children. This is offered as a tool to see firsthand how an early childhood teacher can integrate culture into the curriculum based on a real child's cultural history.

NAME: *Joy*   **AGE:** *4 years old*   **PLACEMENT:** *Preschool*

Joy is a four-year-old Chinese American female. Joy is tall and slender, has short black hair, a fair complexion, and dark brown eyes.

Joy comes from an affluent family and is the only child. Joy and her parents live in a small affluent Chinese-American community. Both of Joy's parents speak English, but neither speaks English in the home. Chinese is the only language spoken in the home. For the first two years of Joy's life, she was taken care of by her grandmother. Her grandmother lived in China and came to the United States to take care of Joy. When Joy was two, her grandmother had to return to China. Joy's parents took Joy to an English-speaking childcare center. Joy's caregivers spoke only English. Key phrases were taught to Joy's primary caregivers.

Currently, Joy speaks English and Chinese fluently. Chinese characters are used and taught in Joy's home. Joy's family primarily prepares traditional Chinese food. Joy's family regularly participates in most Chinese holidays. Chinese New Year is an especially significant holiday for Joy's family. Joy's family participates in American celebrations of Christmas, Easter, and Thanksgiving. Her parents are most interested in the academics of the preschool curriculum.

Joy has strong bodily/kinesthetic strength. Her gross- and fine-motor skills are advanced for her age. She is able to manipulate very small objects with ease and efficiency. Joy exhibits advanced problem-solving skills.

Integrating Culture and Linguistic Intelligence

This section will focus primarily on how to integrate Joy's culture into the linguistic experiences of the classroom. Joy has an interest in Chinese characters and has been learning them at home. In the writing center of the classroom, calligraphy pens and high-quality paper are offered, along with familiar (to Joy) displays of Chinese characters. Joy's family supports a more traditional way of encouraging Chinese character development. They prefer for Joy to learn characters with calligraphy tools and felt-tip pens. This is something that will always be offered in the writing center. Joy, and the other children in the classroom, will have a choice as to using the materials to practice and create Chinese characters. These are not materials added to the writing center periodically to address the Chinese culture. Rather, these are materials that become an inte-

FIGUR 3.4

gral part of the writing curriculum, because they are of cultural interest to Joy and her family.

Fairy tales often offer a history of people from different cultures. Fairy tales offer a view into how different cultures see the world and how different cultures explain varying phenomenon (such as the creation of the sun, why grass is green, or why an elephant has a trunk). It would be important to incorporate Chinese fairy tales into the literature selection of the classroom. Joy's family can offer suggestions for familiar fairy tales. Chinese versions of familiar fairy tales can be read and added to the literature selection as well.

Books, sandpaper letters, alphabet boards, and other materials offer exposure to the English alphabet in the classroom. It would be important to offer these materials in Chinese as well. A Bo Po Mo board (Chinese character board) could be available for all children to use. Chinese character books and Chinese characters children could feel and touch would be important tools in the classroom to help Joy achieve English and Chinese literacy.

Books with Chinese characters would be important to offer in the literature collection of the classroom. Again, these books would become part of the literature collection, not something added periodically, but something that would be offered daily.

Each child in the classroom should have an opportunity to have family members come in and read favorite stories. Joy's family would be no exception. Because Joy's family reads and speaks Chinese at home, they would be welcome to read favorite stories in Chinese to the children.

Books about daily routines, holidays, and traditions are part of the classroom. Books that specifically represent routines, holidays, and traditions from Joy's family should also be incorporated into the daily literature selection. The books should be checked by Joy's family for accuracy to avoid stereotyping or misrepresentation of Joy's culture.

It would be important for Joy's teachers to learn any Chinese names Joy has for special people, toys, events, or objects.

These antibias multicultural linguistic strategies offer a way to integrate Joy's culture into the curriculum on a daily basis. The daily attention and purposeful inclusion of Joy's culture validates it and communicates to the other children that these things are an important part of their environment.

Joy's description will be presented in each intelligence section throughout the text. Intelligence-specific strategies will address antibias multicultural concerns.

Summary of Linguistic Intelligence

Linguistic intelligence is one of two intelligences that have been traditionally attended to in the classroom. This section of the text offered a definition of linguistic intelligence, examined the development of the linguistic symbol system, offered special educational strategies, and included antibias multicultural curricular implications. The next section will focus on the other traditional intelligence, logical/mathematical.

3.6

Journal Questions

Name two ways you could facilitate linguistic intelligence in the classroom.

Name one way you could facilitate your own linguistic intelligence.

In your own words, describe linguistic intelligence.

Observe a kindergarten classroom. How is reading viewed in the classroom? What changes, if any, would you make if you were the kindergarten teacher in that classroom?

How was your linguistic intelligence supported or not supported in the school you attended?

How does the text's approach to antibias multicultural curriculum respect Joy and her family?

3.7

Journal Questions

How do you think children develop mathematical thought?

Is it something they are taught, discover, or construct?

Did you like math in school?

Look at your tool box. What ideas, emotions, feelings, and strategies do you bring with you to the mathematical classroom?

Logical/Mathematical Intelligence

Gardner (1993, p. 143) describes logical/mathematical intelligence as "the ability to recognize significant problems and then to solve them." A mathematician seems to "sense a solution, or a direction, long before they have worked out each step in detail" (Gardner, 1993, p. 143). This definition suggests powerful reasoning ability. It also indicates that mathematical knowledge reaches far beyond a memorization of facts and algorithms.

Mathematical intelligence involves a process. A problem must be identified, recognized as something worth solving, an algorithm is then identified and/or created, and a solution is attempted. Intelligence in this area requires a true understanding of how mathematics and logic work in the real world, in everyday life. Understanding the *why* in mathematics truly indicates an understanding of mathematic processes.

The National Council for the Teaching of Mathematics (NCTM) defines mathematics as the attainment of mathematical power. "Mathematical power includes the ability to explore, conjecture, and reason logically; to solve nonroutine problems; to communicate about and through mathematics; and to connect ideas within mathematics and between mathematics and other intellectual activity. Mathematical power also involves the development of personal self-confidence and a disposition to seek, evaluate, and use quantitative and spatial information in solving problems and in making decisions" (NCTM, 1989, p. 1). Mathematical power instills confidence and certainty. Mathematical power allows the child to develop, create, and control numerical thought processes. The NCTM (1989) has identified thirteen curricular standards that help children gain mathematical power. The standards are applicable to children from kindergarten to fourth grade. Learning these key mathematical concepts

TABLE 3.5 | *Careers and Hobbies Associated with Logical/Mathematical Intelligence*

Careers with a Primary Logical/Mathematical Intelligence	Hobbies/Interests That Reflect Logical/Mathematical Intelligence
Scientist	Number games
Mathematician	Mysteries
Engineer	Computer games
Biologist	Science
Geneticist	Math
Paleontologist	
Pharmacist	
Doctor	
Emergency medical professional	
Computer programmer	
Software engineer	
Inventor	

helps the child develop mathematical power, which creates the necessary foundation for mathematical intelligence.

The standards include the following mathematical concepts:

Problem Solving
Communication
Reasoning
Connections
Estimation
Number Sense and Numeration
Whole Number Operations
Whole Number Computation
Geometry and Spatial Sense
Measurement
Statistics and Probability
Fractions and Decimals
Patterns and Relationships

Concepts taken from the curriculum standards in
Curriculum and Evaluation Standards for School, NCTM, 1989

Logical/Mathematical Intelligence in the Early Childhood Classroom

An early childhood curriculum that acknowledges the implications of mathematical power and respects the comprehensiveness of logical/mathematical intelligence is guided by four principles:

1. Mathematics involves confrontation with the physical world (Gardner, 1993).
2. An autonomous approach to mathematics is crucial, especially in the early childhood years (Kamii, 1985).
3. Logics and mathematics are developmental (Piaget, 1952; Richardson and Salkeld, 1999).
4. Opportunities for mathematical development occur daily (Richardson and Salkeld, 1999).

Confrontation

The young child is constantly confronted with objects. The infant is confronted with a mobile, a mirror, a familiar face. The toddler begins to realize that once confronted with an object, she has the ability to act upon the object with intentionality. The preschooler carefully assesses and chooses confrontation with specific objects in the environment. Her deliberate manipulation causes specific expected and unexpected results. Gardner (1993, p. 129) explains, "For it is in confronting objects, in ordering and reordering them, and in assessing their quantity, that the young child gains his or her initial and most fundamental knowledge about the logical-mathematical realm." The confrontation encourages the child to act purposefully on the environment, to see what will happen. Confrontation occurs through interaction with interesting materials, objects, and people in the child's environment. Intelligence can develop through the confrontation when the environment is safe, supportive, and encourages autonomy.

Autonomy

In order for the child to develop logical and mathematical thinking, the learning environment must promote autonomy. The traditional mathematics classroom promotes heteronomy, which values and prefers the group to an individual (Kamii, 1985). The heteronomous classroom teaches to the group as a whole, ignoring individual differences and preferences. Traditionally, mathematics has been regarded as facts, with an accepted set of practices that are conducive to solving logical and mathematical queries. Many adults may be able to solve mathematical problems using learned algorithms; however, few can explain why or give the reasoning behind the algorithms. In an autonomous classroom, children take their responsibility for learning quite seriously and discover the processes behind the algorithms (Kamii, 1985).

Constance Kamii (1985) explains that children are quite capable of inventing their own algorithms to solve a problem. Figure 3.5 illustrates an example of a child figuring out a method for solving her mathematics problem. A six-year-old was playing in the doll corner. She had four dolls and twelve doll cookies. She wanted to give each of her dolls the same number of cookies.

FIGURE 3.5

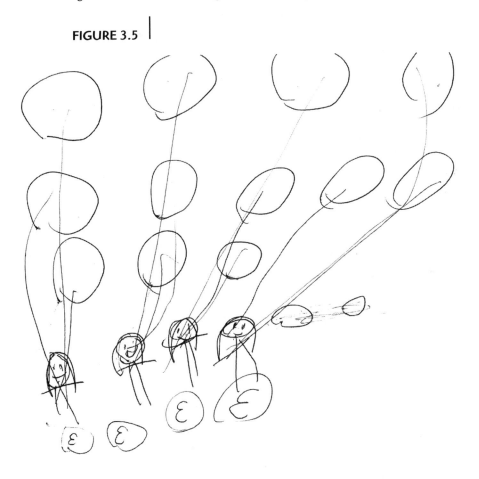

The algorithms children create are inspired by confrontation and reflect an understanding of their mathematical view of the world. Kamii (1985) and Piaget explain that children construct their own knowledge of mathematical concepts. It is an internal process, which develops with interaction, as opposed to direct instruction (Kamii, 1985). According to Kamii and Piaget, it is impossible to teach concepts of number. Direct instruction of mathematics concepts can confuse and interfere with the child's mathematical development. An environment that supports social interaction with people and materials is vital to the development of number. In this type of environment, there are no right or wrong answers; only answers that are questioned and asked to be proven by the teacher and other children. The child must validate his/her responses through the use of language and symbols. Accountability lies within the process, not within the answer. The child is encouraged to verbalize and demonstrate their disagreements with other children in a socially appropriate manner. This can be accomplished through setting up an environment that allows the children to choose materials that are interesting to them. Encouragement should be given to children who choose to create their own rules and processes for using the materials. The children should also be encouraged to work in small groups and share, accept, and reject ideas from classmates. Conflict over processes, solutions, or ideas encourages children to think for themselves and provides the confrontation necessary to develop mathematical thought. When something is confusing or challenging, children are encouraged to question, explore, and find the validity in the theory proposed. The teacher provides a safe environment for children to question and feel free to *disagree*. The teacher listens and observes the disagreement. When children have difficulty resolving the disagreement, the teacher can step in to offer solutions to help the children solve their conflict without telling them the "right" answer to their query (Kamii, 1985).

The child should be viewed as an active constructor of knowledge, rather than a passive receptor of information. Approaching mathematics in this way encourages the development of an autonomous relationship with peers, the environment, and the child's logical/mathematical thinking ability. This approach not only benefits the child in the school setting, but will also enable the child to solve conflicts, present a logical argument, and feel confident in her validation of her beliefs.

Logic and Mathematics Are Developmental

Confrontation initiates logical/mathematical thought. An autonomous environment encourages logical/mathematical thought to develop. Logic and mathematics develop in stages and the stages offer a framework for providing appropriate materials, experiences, and expectations of young children.

Genetic epistemologist Jean Piaget developed a theory of intelligence that Gardner (1993) credits as a theory of logical/mathematical intelligence. Piaget identified four stages of cognitive development: sensorimotor, preoperational, concrete operational, and formal operational.

Following is a description of Piaget's stages of cognitive development. The preoperational stage will be emphasized due to its relevance to the targeted ages of children discussed in this text.

The *sensorimotor* period of development is a time for sensory and motor exploration. The child develops an awareness and appreciation of objects in the environment. He learns about objects through sensory exploration and accidental and/or purposeful manipulation. He also develops an understanding of object permanence during this stage.

The *preoperational* period of development spans the early childhood years of growth. This stage of cognitive growth is marked with egocentric thought, hierarchal classification, precausal reasoning, inability to understand reversibility and conservation, and the ability to use and manipulate symbols. The child's experience is egocen-

TABLE 3.6	*Piaget's Stages of Cognitive Development*	
Stage	**Age Range**	**Characteristics**
Sensorimotor	Birth to 2 years	Cause/Effect Object permanence
Preoperational	2 to 6 (7) years	Symbolic play Egocentric Difficulty with reversibility and conservation Classifies by one or two attributes
Concrete Operational	6 to 12 years	Child can conserve quantity, size, length, and volume Understands reversibility Can classify by many attributes Realizes others' point of view
Formal Operational	12 years to adulthood	Abstract thinking

tric: she only acknowledges and utilizes one point of view during this stage of development—her own. Her interactions and experiences with people and objects in the environment are influenced by her point of view. She does not have the ability to empathize and may have difficulty sharing, taking turns, and waiting.

The child is able to recognize and classify an object through attributes, called hierarchical classification. Although the child in the preoperational period of development is able to classify objects by hierarchal arrangement, he may have difficulty with subclasses.

This stage is also marked with an inconsistent understanding of reality and fantasy. The child's conclusions reflect a kind of logic that is influenced by imagination and fantasy. Her conclusions are often illogical and confusing.

The preoperational child has not yet developed the cognitive skill known as reversibility. Reversibility allows one to reverse a situation in one's head; to think of the situation in reverse or in the negative.

The preoperational child does not yet understand conservation, the idea that something remains the same in quantity even if the shape or arrangement of the object changes. When an object changes spatial form and arrangement, the child believes the object changes in quantity as well.

The preoperational child makes an important discovery, the discovery of symbols. The preoperational child can pretend, identify/use/create symbols, and recognize the function of symbols. This is a crucial discovery in cognitive thought. Children might not recognize the formal symbols that represent mathematics, but they are able to symbolize their mathematical thinking.

FIGURE 3.6

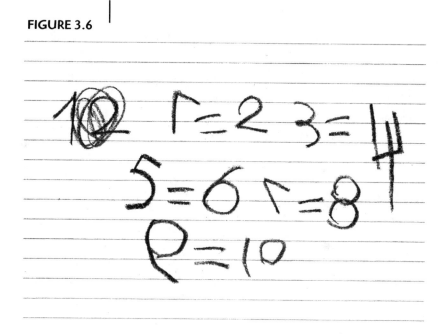

The child in the *concrete operational* period of development exhibits reversibility, decentration, the ability to classify several attributes, and conservation. The child is able to think in reverse and concepts that revolve around the negative (subtraction, division).

The concrete operational child can decenter her viewpoint: Instead of experiencing and interacting with life from their sole point of view, they are able to see multiple points of view. They demonstrate empathy, can share, take turns, wait, and understand why something may be important to another.

The concrete operational child can recognize that an object has many attributes and can be classified in many different ways. The concrete operational child is able to conserve space, volume, solids, and liquids. The child recognizes that when an object changes shape or arrangement, the quantity of the object remains the same. The concrete operational child needs experiences that allow him to learn through hands-on experiences in which he can see and manipulate objects.

At around age twelve, the adolescent moves into the *formal operational* period of development. The adolescent can think and understand abstract concepts and no longer needs concrete experiences to acquire information and solve problems. He can reason and think out problems and solutions.

CURRICULAR IMPLICATIONS OF PIAGET'S THEORY   The preoperational period of development has significant curricular implications for the early childhood years. A curriculum that emphasizes relevant situations, manipulatives, problem solving, choice, discussion, cooperation, experimentation, and individual attention would be the most appropriate type for a child in the preoperational stage. The child needs to be given the opportunity to make choices, manipulate materials, identify problems, and discover solutions.

The preoperational period is marked with an inability to understand reversibility and conservation. The inability to think in reverse makes it difficult for the preoperational child to understand subtraction and division. The preoperational child can think of what can be added to a situation, but not what can be taken away from the situation (Kamii, 1985). Therefore, while addition is appropriate for first grade, subtraction is not appropriate until the child understands reversibility and can recognize the negative of the situation. Piaget explains that young children think in the positive. They think about what they can add to a situation, to a block structure, to their picture, but not what can be taken away from it (Kamii, 1985). Negative, reverse, or reciprocal actions are constructed later in development, as the child moves into the concrete operational stage. Subtraction develops *out of* addition, not along with addition (Kamii, 1985). Kamii (1985) advocates teaching subtraction in the second grade.

The early childhood teacher must recognize that the preoperational child is egocentric and create an environment where children become slowly aware that other children see the world in different ways. Kamii (1985) emphasizes an environment where children are free to disagree and express their point of view. This begins to acquaint the preoperational child with the idea that other points of view exist, so the concrete operational child can understand these points of view and react appropriately to them.

Opportunity for Logical/Mathematical Development

Math is everywhere. Piaget explains that mathematics terminology is social and relative to the language of a culture. However, mathematical processes and operations are universal. Normal life experiences offer children confrontation with their environment; the opportunity to recognize, identify, create, and utilize symbols; and the opportunity to develop an autonomous relationship with the mathematical world. This opportunity is stifled by judgment, evaluation, and by providing the right answers.

Children's discovery of mathematical concepts leads to logical/mathematical intelligence. Being able to regurgitate a list of facts and algorithms may demonstrate a good memory, but not strong logical/mathematical intelligence. Piaget believed that mathematical concepts had to be constructed; they were not something simply taught to the child. Math is something that must be internally constructed through manipulation and interaction with the environment (Kamii, 1985). The realization that mathematical concepts are constructed poses a challenge to the traditional way mathematical concepts have been presented to children in school.

The controversy stems from debates between a skill-based, teacher-centered approach and a child-centered or child-constructed approach. The skill-based curriculum has traditionally focused on facts, drills, memorization, worksheets, competition, and has focused on whole-group instruction. Skills are developed in isolation through drills and worksheets.

On the other side of the debate is the constructivist approach, which emphasizes relevant situations, manipulatives, problem solving, discussion, and cooperation. Skills and concepts are discovered by the child and developed in context. Contextual learning promotes an easier transfer of skills to similar experiences and problems.

It is often asked, What's the harm? What's the harm in presenting skills to children before they are ready? Contemporary research is beginning to suggest that it may be harmful to expose children to specific isolated skills before they are ready for them (Elkind, 1988; Healy, 1999; and Kamii, 1985). At the very least, it is useless. However, it can prove to be harmful. Research also suggests that presenting isolated skills too early may wire the brain in such a manner that when these skills are accessed later, it may actually take longer and may result in a learning disability (Healy, 1999). Elkind (1988) documents research which shows less (if any) remediation is needed if children are introduced to concepts when they are developmentally ready for them. Kamii (1985) explains that teacher-directed instruction that occurs too early interferes with the child's ability to construct mathematical concepts and fully understand and appreciate them. When children do have difficulty constructing or understanding mathematics, other intelligences can be used to build upon the child's difficulty.

Special Education and Logical/ Mathematical Intelligence

3.8

Journal Question

You are teaching in a first-grade classroom. One of your students is having difficulty identifying numbers and counting objects. This student has musical and bodily/kinesthetic strengths. How could you use the student's strengths to help him deal with his mathematical challenge?

As stated in the linguistics section of this chapter, special education has traditionally been guided by identifying and remediating deficits (Armstrong, 1999). The multiple intelligence theory approaches challenges by identification and utilization of strengths. The following describes a seven-year-old girl who is considered gifted by her teachers and parents. Jaleesa's mathematical ability is well above her peers. She can quickly come up with creative algorithms and other children turn to her for help in solving problems.

TABLE 3.7 | *Special Education Strategies*

Name: Jaleesa
Age: 7
Placement: First grade

Description:
Jaleesa's logical/mathematical ability is well above her peers. She becomes bored and frustrated with the ease of the mathematical experiences appropriate for her peers. Jaleesa often puts her head down and sighs when other children express difficulty with mathematical concepts.

Challenges:

Logical/Mathematical

■ Jaleesa's mathematical ability is far above her peers. She is not appropriately challenged, exhibits boredom and frustration.

Interpersonal

■ Jaleesa becomes frustrated with peers who cannot master mathematical concepts as quickly as she can.
■ She often refers to other students as "stupid" and "slow."

Spatial

■ Jaleesa demonstrates preschematic art representation, which is slightly below age expectation. Other spatial representations (such as through blocks, and other art medium) also indicate a slight challenge with representing materials spatially.

Strengths:

Logical/Mathematical

■ Jaleesa has a strong logical/mathematical capacity.
■ Jaleesa demonstrates a strong understanding of reversibility, conservation, and can classify objects by several attributes.

Musical

■ Jaleesa plays the violin and can read and write simple compositions.
■ Jaleesa expresses a deep love and interest in music.

Naturalist

■ Jaleesa can easily identify patterns in nature.
■ Jaleesa can classify natural objects by many attributes.
■ Jaleesa exhibits a deep appreciation and love of the natural world.

Strategies:

Logical/Mathematical

■ More challenging math experiences will be incorporated into the classroom during free choice-time (such activities would include geometric solids, geoboards, abacus, golden beads, hundred board, Montessori checkerboard, seguin board, multiplication boards, fraction manipulatives, and bankers game—most of these are Montessori materials). The teacher can show Jaleesa the process of the activity and then have the activities available for her during free choice/play time and during math activity time.

TABLE 3.7 | *Continued*

- If the teacher knows a concept will be too easy, or that she has already mastered it, the teacher will introduce one of the materials above or plan a more challenging math experience for Jaleesa.
- Jaleesa will have the opportunity to use more challenging math activities during group activities that are too easy for her.
- Jaleesa will be involved in peer tutoring; the tutoring will be facilitated to encourage and model appropriate peer feedback.
- Jaleesa will be introduced to geometric problems and spatial math concepts. These types of activities will challenge Jaleesa's problem-solving ability and build spatial concepts.

Spatial

- Spatial concepts will be addressed through a problem-solving approach. For example, in the block area, the teacher may have a building made, but with a structure problem, such as the roof is falling down. Jaleesa will be asked to brainstorm solutions to the problem and try them to see if they work.
- Jaleesa will be encouraged to express mathematical processes visually, through pictures or manipulatives to encourage spatial development.
- Jaleesa will have drawing or building materials available to her to use when she has finished a math activity early. The materials will be presented with a problem for Jaleesa to solve through the manipulation of them.

Logical/Mathematical Intelligence and Culturally Appropriate Education

3.9 Journal Questions

You are teaching in a preschool and implementing several logical/mathematical strategies suggested in this chapter. A group of parents is afraid their children will not be ready for kindergarten. They request worksheets and direct math instruction. How would you explain to parents how your methods are facilitating mathematical development?

Are there any new feelings and/or strategies you would add to your box regarding logical/mathematical and linguistic intelligence?

What role does isolated skill development play in the early childhood curriculum?

The linguistics portion of the chapter presented a description of a four-year-old Chinese American girl, Joy. Joy's description will be utilized throughout the text. Reread her description in the previous section. The following strategies are provided to demonstrate an antibias multicultural approach to logics and mathematics.

Joy's family has a strong interest in her mathematical abilities. Joy has demonstrated an interest and strength in mathematics. Joy's mother explained to the staff that many manipulatives are used in China to develop mathematics. Joy's mother brings in some of the manipulatives to share with the teacher. The teacher incorporates some of the manipulatives into the math center of the classroom. Chinese numbers are presented through books, pictures, and math materials. Math equipment and materials will be marked with both English numbers and Chinese numbers.

Summary of Logical/ Mathematical Intelligence

It is amazing to witness young children discuss a particular mathematical or logical concept on their own, create their own rules to a game, set up and conduct their own experiment, creatively problem solve, or debate a conclusion. It is more gratifying to realize that these children did these things without being taught or told to. In this kind of environment, children can develop a motivation for mathematics that replaces the fears of children who did not have access to this environment. These children will develop into autonomous learners who have a desire to explore, make sense of, and challenge their environment.

3.10

Journal Questions

Think back to your own schooling. What feelings were communicated to you regarding reading and mathematics? What feelings and values concerning mathematics might you communicate to the children you teach?

References

Armstrong, T. (2000) *Multiple intelligences in the classroom.* Alexandria, VA: Association for the Supervision of Curriculum Development.

Bloom, B. S., Ed. (1956) *Taxonomy of educational objectives: The classification of educational goals: Handbook I, cognitive domain.* New York: Longmans, Green.

Bluestein, J. (2001) *Creating emotionally healthy schools: A guide for educators and parents.* Deerfield Beach, FL: Health Communications Inc.

Bredekamp, S., & Rosengrant, T., eds. (1999) *Reaching potentials: Transforming early childhood curriculum and assessment.* Washington, DC: NAEYC.

Chen, J., Krechevsky, M., & Viens, J. eds. (1998) *Project spectrum: Early learning activities. Vol 2.* New York: Teachers College Press.

Elkind, D. (1988) *The hurried child.* Cambridge, MA: Perseus Publishing.

Farris, P., & Kaczmarksi, D. (1988). "Whole language, a closer look." *Contemporary Education 59,* 77–81.

Gardner, H. (1999) *The disciplined mind.* New York: Simon & Schuster.

Gardner, H. (1993) *Frames of mind.* New York: Basic Books.

Gardner, H. (1991) *The unschooled mind.* New York: Basic Books.

Greenspan, S. (1997) *The growth of the mind and the endangered origins of intelligence.* Cambridge, MA: Perseus Books.

Hannaford, C. (1995) *Smart moves: Why learning is not all in your head.* Arlington, VA: Great Ocean Publishers.

Healy, J. (1999) *Endangered mind: Why children don't think and what we can do about it.* New York: Touchstone.

Hurst, C. (1994) "First books for emergent readers." *Teaching K–8*, 50–53.

Kamii, C. (1985) *Young children reinvent mathematics: Implications of Piaget's theory.* New York: Teachers College Press.

Manning, M., & Manning, G. (1995). "Whole language: They say, you say." *Teaching K–8*, 50–54.

Mooney, M. (1994) "Developing the whole child." *Teaching Pre K–8*, 24(8) 46–48.

National Council of Teachers of Mathematics. (1989) *Curriculum and evaluation standards for school mathematics.* Reston, VA: NCTM.

Neuman, S., Copple, C., & Bredekamp, S. (2000). *Learning to read and write: Developmentally appropriate practices for young children.* Washington, DC: NAEYC.

Owocki, G. (2001) *Make way for literacy!* Washington, D.C.: NAEYC.

Owocki, G. (1999) *Literacy through play.* Portsmouth, NH: Heinemann.

Piaget, J. (1952) *The origins of intelligence in children.* New York: Free Press.

Restak, R. (2001) *The secret life of the brain.* Washington, DC: Joseph Henry Press.

Richardson, K., & Salkeld, L. (1999) "Chapter 12: Transforming curriculum organization" (pp. 167–176). In *Reaching potentials: Transforming early childhood curriculum and assessment,* vol. 2 (ed. Bredekamp, S., & Rosegrant, T.) Washington, D.C.: NAEYC.

Richardson, K., & Salkeld, L. (2001) "Transforming mathematics curriculum." *Reaching potentials: Transforming early childhood curriculum and assessment.* Washington DC: NAEYC (Vol. 2, pp. 23–41).

Whaley, C. (2002) "Meeting the diverse needs of children through storytelling." *Young Children* (Vol. 57, No. 2, pp. 31–34).

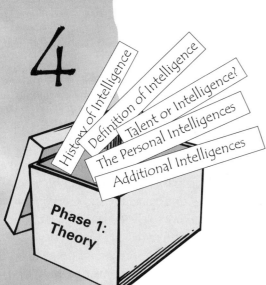

4

Phase 1: Theory

Talent or Intelligence?

Traditionally, the American school system has facilitated the development of two basic intelligences, linguistic and logical/mathematical (Gardner, 1993). The nineteenth century's intelligence-research community was driven by a need to test and categorize intelligence (Sattler, 1982). This motivation led researchers to define intelligence in measurable terms. Language and mathematics can be more readily measured than other intelligences. Language and mathematics also have an easily identifiable symbol system and these symbol systems greatly influence American cultural life. Other intelligences have been viewed as talents. Music, dance, art, and so on traditionally have not been given the place that language and mathematics hold in curriculum. Usually these talents are not given formal attention until linguistic and mathematical literacy have been achieved. Gardner's (1993) definition of intelligence causes us to look at the traditional view of talent versus intelligence differently.

4.1
Journal Questions

Do you believe that skill in music, art, and movement is due to talent or intelligence? Why? Do you believe music, art, and movement have an important place in the curriculum? As important a place as math and reading?

BOX 4.2 | *Gardner's Definition of Intelligence*

Gardner (1993, p. x) views intelligence as "The ability to solve problems, or create products, that are valued within one or more cultural settings . . ." (Source: *Frames of Mind, 1993*)

Culture plays an important role in defining and facilitating intelligence. Contemporary American culture values dance, art, music, sports, and emotional and social life so it is not a fair assumption to state that the American culture solely values linguistic and mathematical strengths. American culture values many strengths and this needs to be reflected in the way intelligence is defined and facilitated in the classroom. Contemporary brain research also supports the validity of addressing these talents with more importance and purpose. Brain research confirms that these *talents* are necessary for healthy brain growth, and contribute to a robust emotional, physical, and intellectual life (Jensen, 2001).

How does this understanding of intelligence affect the early childhood field of development? At the beginning of this text we stated that intelligence is a significant determinant in curriculum. An unprecedented number of children are enrolled in early care, childcare, and preschool programs. The most significant brain development and interactions take place in the early childhood years. The foundation for all intelligences is begun in these early years as well. Careful curricular attention and consideration must be given to these special early years. It is important to understand each intelligence and its curricular implications in order to provide a healthy foundation for the intelligence to flourish. By providing an early childhood environment supportive of multiple intelligences, unexpected strengths may be discovered, challenges may be revealed, and an early learning profile can be established (Gardner, 1993).

This chapter will look at intelligences that have traditionally been viewed as talents. Sports, dance, and physical movement will be attributed to bodily/kinesthetic intelligence. The arts and manipulation of objects and space will be discussed in terms of spatial intelligence. Music will be attributed to musical intelligence. This chapter will define the intelligences, offer a cultural validation of each, and explain the development of the symbol system(s) associated with each intelligence.

Bodily/Kinesthetic Intelligence

Bodily/kinesthetic intelligence involves the functional and expressive use of the body and the ability to use objects skillfully and purposefully (Gardner, 1993). Bodily intelligence involves mainly gross-motor skills, while kinesthetic intelligence involves mainly fine-motor skills. Isolated skills are necessary in the development of bodily/kinesthetic intelligence; however, there is a creative side to the definition of bodily/kinesthetic development. The body can be used to express emotions, communicate moods, relay information, and express feelings. The body can also be used to create personalities, actions, animals, natural phenomena, and abstract concepts (Gardner, 1993). Body gestures are interpreted constantly and many times may be more indicative of meaning than spoken words. An individual can tell an entire story through body and kinesthetic movements.

Bodily Intelligence

The core of bodily intelligence is the control of the body. Gardner (1993, p. 206) describes bodily intelligence as the capacity to "use one's body in highly differentiated and skilled ways, for expressive as well as goal-directed purposes." The child needs to be able to assume various body positions and relationships, move isolated body parts and coordinate body parts in order to move appropriately in the environment. Bodily intelligence is critical to the development of self-control. A step in gaining self-control is being able to manage impulses. Knowing when to stop and start body movements, and what body movements are appropriate for what moment, are the beginning steps to managing impulses. The child must also be able to move the body intentionally through space and know how to physically respond to the various situations the body will encounter during the day.

CULTURAL VALIDITY OF BODILY INTELLIGENCE   The American culture emphasizes the importance and recognition of bodily/kinesthetic intelligence through various domains. Athletes are highly paid, endorsed, and generally respected for their athletic ability. America spends much leisure time and money participating or watching those who possess bodily strengths. Many Americans watch or take part in such bodily intelligence modalities as: football, baseball, hockey, soccer, wrestling, ballet, opera, dance, acting, miming, exercise, yoga, gardening, and so on.

Kinesthetic Intelligence

Bodily intelligence involves whole-body movements and gross-motor skills. Kinesthetic intelligence involves the manipulation and coordination of fine-motor skills. Gardner (1993, p. 206) describes the core of kinesthetic intelligence as "the capacity to handle objects skillfully." While bodily and kinesthetic tasks can be independent, many physical tasks require both the ability to move the body with function and expression (bodily) and the ability to handle objects with skill (kinesthetic) (Gardner, 1993).

TABLE 4.1	*Bodily/Kinesthetic Intelligence Careers/Hobbies*
Careers That Reflect Bodily/ Kinesthetic Intelligence	**Hobbies/Interests That Reflect Bodily/Kinesthetic Intelligence**
Dancer	Sports
Gymnast	Dance
Athlete	Physical games
Marine	Paintball
Surgeon	Handwork
Artist	Woodworking
Carpenter	Yoga
Actor	Ballet
Mime	Exercising
Circus performer	Weightlifting
Seamstress	Gardening
Wrestler	Creative movement
Mechanic	
Sculptor	
Theater	

CULTURAL VALIDITY OF KINESTHETIC INTELLIGENCE   The American culture values and responds to those who possess kinesthetic strengths. Potters, carpenters, surgeons, artists, gardeners, athletes, drafters, and mechanics all share kinesthetic strengths.

SCHOOL AND KINESTHETIC INTELLIGENCE   Early childhood programs have traditionally encouraged the development of isolated kinesthetic skills. Kinesthetic abilities include skills such as cutting, pasting, drawing, sorting, manipulating small objects (blocks, pegs, beads, puzzles, zippers, buttons, and tools) and manipulating art mediums (clay, play dough, paper, crayons, markers, scissors, hole punchers). Kinesthetic intelligence involves more than the acquisition of skills—it involves creation. Kinesthetic intelligence is expressed when the child is involved in physical tasks that allow her to communicate a thought or feeling, symbolize her experience, create a product, share a cultural tradition, or engage in a functional and necessary task. Many times the purpose of kinesthetic development becomes lost when programs focus on isolated skill development. Skills are important and necessary in the development of kinesthetic intelligence. It is necessary, even at the preschool level, to show children techniques and demonstrate how to use materials and tools. It is equally necessary to realize that children need the freedom and time to create and use the tools in personally expressive ways.

Masters in the individual fields of kinesthetic intelligence should be invited to visit the class to discuss techniques and products and share their trade or skill with the students. Masters in kinesthetic fields would include sculptors, artists, carpenters, mechanics, and surgeons.

Bodily/Kinesthetic Intelligence in the Early Childhood Classroom

An early childhood curriculum that truly understands and respects bodily/kinesthetic intelligence follows four guiding principles for integrating the intelligence into the classroom.

1. Bodily/kinesthetic intelligence deserves the same curricular attention that other intelligences receive (Gardner, 1993).
2. The curriculum must address the various modalities that bodily/kinesthetic intelligence presents.
3. Research about the brain confirms the importance and significance of bodily/ kinesthetic development (Jensen, 2001).
4. Bodily/kinesthetic intelligence develops in stages.

Curricular Attention

Traditionally, schools have addressed bodily intelligence through recess, physical education, and participation in sports programs (Gardner, 1993). The Council on Physical Education for Children (COPEC) strongly supports daily physical education and recess. Unfortunately daily participation in these activities is quite limited in contemporary American school life and many schools are not following the COPEC guidelines. In some programs, recess has been eliminated to provide more instructional time. Physical education might only occur once a week. In addition, organized sports have become very stressful and demanding for children. In many programs there is little time, if any, provided for creative use of the body, for children to create games or projects, or engage in movement without the intervention or direction of an adult. While schools have addressed the purely physical aspects of movement, the bodily realm also includes emotional expression, role-play, games, and bodily expression of thoughts, ideas, and information.

Preschool programs have traditionally shown a little more respect for bodily intelligence. Many preschool teachers realize there is a need for children to move and they provide for this need. However, there are many half-day programs that do not provide for physical experiences. These programs claim to focus on the academic life of the preschooler and claim to prepare him for school life. Many times though, physical movement in early childhood programs is provided for children in order to prevent restlessness, to give teachers a break, and for children to blow off steam (Gallahue, 1999).

There are programs that justify their choice to withdraw recess and limit physical education because of curricular constraints. Some programs choose to focus on academics and provide more time for such experiences as reading and math. That leads to a debatable issue: *Is it even necessary to address recess and physical education in school?* The National Center for Chronic Disease Prevention and Health Promotion states that physical education reduces the chance of dying from heart disease, decreases colon cancer, diabetes, and high blood pressure. It maintains healthy development of muscles, bones, and joints. Physical education reduces anxiety and relieves some symptoms of depression. Physical exercise is helpful in maintaining a healthy weight. Movement also has been shown to be an effective treatment in ADHD (Hannaford, 1995). These reasons support physical movement.

Early childhood and elementary programs that address physical movement and development generally approach bodily intelligence through recess, outdoor play, and physical education.

RECESS/OUTDOOR PLAY Schools have traditionally provided recess after lunch, consisting of approximately twenty to thirty minutes of supervised free play outdoors. Children usually engage in motor tasks, movement games, or pick-up sports. Adults supervise but usually do not interfere in children's play during recess. Preschool programs typically provided outdoor play, which is similar to recess. Preschool children engage in motor tasks and movement games during this time. Adults supervise and facilitate, but generally try not to interfere.

To maximize the benefits of recess/outdoor play, there needs to be ample time available. Recess should be long enough for children to be able to choose an activity, make up the rules for it, and fully participate in it. At least forty-five minutes would be needed in order for children to do this. Preschool children benefit from thirty to forty-five minutes of outdoor play daily. Preschool children need time to choose outdoor play experiences, take care of animals and insects, observe, and engage in games. By providing ample time, bodily/kinesthetic intelligence can develop; recess should not be limited to physical exercise and movement.

Children have less and less time to engage in child-directed play outdoors. Schools have the responsibility of addressing this time of the day and providing for it fully. Schools will benefit by having children who: have improved brain function; are better able to attend to tasks and teacher-directed experiences; are able to negotiate conflicts and socialize; and simply feel better. Recess should take place daily and occur outside except in extreme weather conditions. If recess cannot be taken outside, it must be accommodated for inside.

PHYSICAL EDUCATION Physical education must be offered daily. Physical education can take place in a gym, outside, in the classroom, or other areas of the school. In preschools, preschool teachers generally take responsibility for physical education. In elementary schools, physical education is usually conducted by a physical education teacher in a gym. For children in the early childhood period of development, education and care are best provided by one teacher or a pair of teachers with whom the child forms a relationship. Young children generally do not have the opportunity to form a relationship with a physical education teacher; therefore, physical education is best provided by the child's teacher. This is not intended to downplay the role of a physical education teacher. A physical education teacher can work with the child's teacher, explaining safety and instructing teachers on specific skills and physical experiences. It is important to have a physical education specialist on staff or to consult with one to plan appropriate bodily experiences. The physical education specialist can demonstrate safe ways for children to exercise and move. Physical education teachers can also be brought into the classroom as "masters" to show children physical skills that relate to the content of the classroom. Other masters such as dancers, gymnasts, athletes, and carpenters can be brought in as well to share their talents, skills, and to do demonstrations. Teachers and/or parents may also have bodily strengths they wish to share and help children develop. Children can explore music, poetry, dance, stories, and community roles through physical movement.

In addition to the attention that bodily/kinesthetic intelligence deserves in recess and physical education, bodily/kinesthetic deserves attention and awareness in all other aspects of the curriculum. There are a number of ways to address and recognize bodily/kinesthetic intelligence in the classroom: through a designated gross-motor room or gym, outdoor play, activities, and rest time.

GROSS-MOTOR ROOM/GYM Preschools may have a room dedicated to gross-motor play. Schools often have a gym available for gross-motor play. If a space is not available, it is important to create a space large enough for gross-motor play indoors. Shelves can be put on wheels so they can quickly be pushed aside. Tables and chairs can also be moved to one side of the room. Young children should have access to materials and equipment that allow them to engage in gross-motor play. Slides, climbing equipment, tricycles, streamers, large hollow blocks, balls, basketball hoops, jump ropes, and hopscotch areas allow children to engage in gross-motor play. The number of choices available for gross-motor play will depend upon the space available. When space is limited, the choices should be limited as well. The materials and focus of the gross-motor/gym room can be changed and can vary between child-initiated, adult-initiated, and collaborative experiences. Children can use the gross-motor room for interpretative dance, storytelling, creative movement, whole-group or small-group games, sports play, role-play, or free choice play.

OUTDOOR PLAY During outdoor play, children can develop bodily intelligence. The outdoors provides a larger area for gross-motor movements and an opportunity to interact with nature on a physical level. Children can respond physically to the wind, weather changes, animals, and insects. They can imitate animal and insect movements, run with the wind, and use their body to respond to changing weather cues.

Kinesthetic intelligence can be developed through the manipulation of tools used to investigate the natural world and through the manipulation, physical classification, and investigation of natural objects. The tools may include magnifying glasses, microscopes, tweezers, bug containers, shovels, and telescopes.

ADULT-DIRECTED ACTIVITIES Each day children should participate in adult-directed learning activities. The learning activities can involve any of the intelligences. A teacher can choose to do specific activities that work on bodily/kinesthetic development. He might teach the children a physical game, involve them in a sport, or encourage the children to jump rope. The teacher might have another adult come in to the classroom to teach dance steps, art techniques, or specific physical skills. The children can participate in interpretative or cultural dance. Young children can be encouraged to move and respond physically to music, color, light, and sound. Music can be played and children can move their bodies any way they like (while respecting their body boundaries and the body boundaries of others). The teacher may take the children on a hike or walk around the neighborhood or invite them to interpret the weather physically. Children can float like a snowflake, pretend to shovel, or march around in deep snow. There are a variety of activities that can specifically address bodily/kinesthetic intelligence that would be appropriate during activity time.

REST TIME Rest time does not seem as if it would provide any type of physical benefit. However, managing impulses is a critical skill in bodily/kinesthetic development. Rest time and relaxation allows children to calm their bodies, become aware of their body boundaries, and helps them to develop impulse control.

Bodily/Kinesthetic Modalities

Bodily/kinesthetic intelligence presents itself in many domains in the early childhood classroom. It is important to keep in mind that bodily/kinesthetic intelligence manifests itself in a variety of forms. Children may have a preference, interest, or ability in one form of expression as opposed to another. The modalities of bodily/kinesthetic intelligence can be categorized into three different forms of expression: dramatic, industrial, and recreational (Jensen, 2001).

DRAMATICS Jensen (2001) explains that dramatics encompasses domains such as dance, drama, mime, theater, musicals, choreography, media play, and improvisation. This aspect of bodily/kinesthetic intelligence is often neglected. However, the ability to role-play and use the body in expressive ways is an important part of bodily/kinesthetic intelligence.

Dramatics can be encouraged in the early childhood classroom through dance, dramatic play, and expressive bodily movements. Mirrors can encourage dramatics and allow the child to assess their dramatic interpretations and expressions.

INDUSTRIAL Industrial arts refer to the functional aspect of bodily/kinesthetic intelligence. Industrial arts include woodworking, auto repair, metalworking, construction, sculpting, and design (Jensen, 2001). Industrial arts has had a traditionally negative association and some people associate "slower" children with attendance at a trade school. However, this view is simply not accurate. All children can benefit emotionally, physically, and cognitively from participation in industrial arts. Industrial arts makes a significant contribution to healthy brain growth and promotes self-confidence and mastery (Jensen, 2001).

Participation in industrial arts can be encouraged in the early childhood classroom by providing tools for children's use. A woodworking table encourages motor manipulation, creativity, construction, and design. An art center can provide the child access to a variety of visual art materials to encourage one-, two-, and three-dimensional representations using sculpture, paint, and paper. A discovery center can include radios, telephones, computers, and appliances for children to take apart.

RECREATIONAL Recreational arts include exercise, rough-and-tumble play, games, scavenger hunts, adventures, obstacle courses, and sports (Jensen, 2001). It is important to point out that recreational arts involve enjoyment. They are not something the child is forced to participate in or does not enjoy. These are arts that one chooses in leisure time.

The recreational arts can be incorporated in the early childhood classroom through choice during free play or through organized adventures, competitions, and games, such as scavenger hunts, games, and obstacle courses.

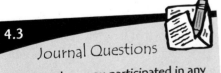

4.3
Journal Questions

Do you or have you participated in any dramatic, industrial, or recreational bodily/kinesthetic experiences? Do you enjoy these activities?

The Brain and Bodily/Kinesthetic Intelligence

Physical movement in itself is crucial to brain development and learning. Hannaford (1995) explains that physical movement is responsible for the creation of new nerve-cell networks. These networks can be considered the "essence of learning."

Eric Jensen summarizes the neuro-scientific validation for bodily and kinesthetic development. Jensen (2001, p. 71) explains that contemporary brain research concludes that kinesthetic arts "contributes to the development and enhancement of critical neurobiological systems, including cognition, emotions, immune, circulatory, and perceptual-motor." Exercise and movement increase blood flow (which has been linked to better cognitive performance), increase levels of brain cell–growth hormone, and have been shown to have a positive effect on neurotransmitters—the mood-altering chemicals of the brain (Jensen, 2001; Hannaford, 1995). The chemicals that are released during exercise help the body focus, increase attention, and help the body feel better (Hannaford, 1995).

Incorporating dramatic, recreational, and industrial arts into the early childhood classroom has significant impact on the developing brain (Jensen, 2001). Dramatic arts have been shown to develop creativity, improve self-concept, aid in ability to follow directions, improve timing and coordination, encourage expression, increase social skills, and encourage emotional attunement (Jensen, 2001). They also aid in the development of cognition and activate the systems that control memory and attention (Jensen, 2001). Industrial arts encourage memory, visualization, cognition, and intrinsic motivation, which improve and coordinate brain function (Jensen, 2001). Recreational arts allow the brain to relax. Relaxation permits the individual to try out cultural roles in a nonthreatening environment (Jensen, 2001). Many research studies have suggested that an integrated arts program increases cognitive performance and helps more children reach appropriate grade-level expectations (see studies cited in Jensen, 2001).

The Development of Bodily/Kinesthetic Intelligence

Bodily/kinesthetic intelligence is developmental, meaning that it develops in stages that are relative to the child's age, maturation, and experience.

The development of the *fundamental movement phase* encompasses the early childhood period of development, roughly between the ages of two and seven. The fundamental movement phase suggests that the child is learning fundamental physical tasks. Mastery is not expected or anticipated. This phase has three distinct stages, the *initial, elementary,* and *mature* (Gallahue and Ozum, 1995). The *initial stage* typically

BOX 4.4 | *Development of Bodily/Kinesthetic Intelligence*

- Reflexive movement phase—Birth to 1 year
- Rudimentary movement phase—1 to 2 years
- Fundamental movement phase—2 to 7 years
- Specialized movement phase—7 to adult

As presented in Gallahue and Ozmun (1995).

involves two- and three-year-old children. During this stage, Gallahue (1999, p. 132) explains that children make "relatively crude, uncoordinated movements. Children at this age make valid attempts at throwing, catching, kicking, jumping, and so forth, but major components of the mature patterns are missing." Children experiment with bodily movements they have seen others make. Time for experimentation and movement are critical in order for children to become more coordinated and purposeful in their attempts to move their bodies.

The next stage is referred to as the *elementary stage*. Coordination and rhythm improve for the four- and five-year-old in this stage; however, mastery is not yet attained and children often lack fluidity (Gallahue, 1999).

With appropriate support and environmental stimulation, the six- or seven-year-old progresses into the *mature stage*. Appropriate support and stimulation are critical, for maturation alone will not bring the child into the mature stage. This stage is characterized by refined physical skill and the ability to use the physical skills in the appropriate environment and cultural activity (Gallahue, 2001).

Bodily/Kinesthetic Symbol System

Bodily/kinesthetic intelligence's developmental stages can be assessed through the representation of its symbol system. Each intelligence expresses itself through one or more symbol systems. A wide variety of bodily/kinesthetic expression and symbol systems exist and each domain of bodily/kinesthetic intelligence has its own specific symbols. For example, dance's symbol system is the movements that are named and recognized as dance steps. Plié, arabesque, and the five positions are symbolic of ballet. The symbol system of painting includes brush strokes, techniques, and materials.

The preschooler is generally working on initiative (Erikson, 1950) and begins to develop her own symbols in response to her experience with the world. A child may put together a series of dance movements and call it ballet. A preschooler needs experience and minimal generalized instruction with tools and techniques, but must be given the time and opportunity to explore and discover with them. The instruction given should be general. For example, a preschool teacher may introduce watercolors by wetting the child's paper, wetting the brush, using a color, and wetting the brush again. In this way the child learns the process of watercolor painting and can then be given time to experiment with color, with modifying the technique (such as putting the paintbrush in all of the colors without using water to clean the brush) and observing the results.

The school-age child is generally working on industry (Erikson, 1950). They have an interest in and need to learn more about the tools of the adult world. School-age children can benefit from instruction on techniques and tools from masters in the field. The child who has learned the process of watercolor painting will be open to more specific watercolor techniques. An artist can show children how to blend colors for a specific effect or demonstrate various brush strokes. Children can begin to understand the watercolor symbol system more clearly and incorporate more adult-like techniques into their work. A sculptor might come in and demonstrate one technique for children to practice in addition to the techniques they have already discovered and applied during the preschool years. A dancer may come in and perform for children. That ballet dancer may then take a few children who are interested and teach them the five positions. The child interested in ballet may then incorporate the five positions into their understanding and interpretation of the ballet symbol system that was begun in the preschool years. Many times the child will modify their understanding of the symbol system during the school-age years as their understanding of the adult symbol system increases. The child's symbolic representation of bodily/kinesthetic intelligence might signify a particular strength and challenge in bodily/kinesthetic domains.

Special Education and Bodily/ Kinesthetic Intelligence

The use of other intelligences in the development of bodily/kinesthetic intelligence has implications for special education. As explained in the linguistics section, the multiple-intelligence theory takes full advantage of the child's strengths. Table 4.2 provides a description of a child with bodily/kinesthetic challenges. Strategies that utilize other intelligences will be addressed along with bodily/kinesthetic adaptations.

TABLE 4.2	*Special Education Strategies Using the Multiple Intelligence Theory*

Child's Name: Mica
Age: 6
Current Placement: Kindergarten

Description: Mica has been diagnosed with spina bifida. She is currently enrolled in a regular kindergarten program. She receives physical therapy and speech at her school. Mica has a shunt implanted to prevent fluid from accumulating around her brain.

Challenges:

Bodily/Kinesthetic

- Mica wears braces on her legs for walking. She is able to walk slowly and tires easily.
- Mica has difficulty with fine-motor tasks.

Linguistic

- Mica's expressive language is somewhat delayed.
- She has difficulty articulating many sounds; she attends speech therapy.

Interpersonal

- Mica does not participate in group meetings or sharing times.
- Mica becomes frustrated when other children cannot understand her.

Spatial

- Mica bumps into objects in the environment. She has difficulty maneuvering in tight spaces.
- Mica demonstrates a random scribbling stage of art representation. Her marks often go off the page.

Strengths:

Naturalist

- Mica goes horseback riding with a group of children who have physical challenges. She has several pets at home. She loves the zoo, can identify many animals. She knows interesting facts about animals that her peers do not.

Musical

- Mica listens and responds to music. She makes special requests at music time and taps her braces together to keep a beat.

Interests:
Mica loves animals and listening to music.

Learning Support Strategies:

Musical Strategies:

- Mica has shown an interest in and love of music. Musical experiences to encourage specific movements and physical skill development may help Mica deal with her physical challenges.
- Songs that work on the sounds she needs help with can be incorporated into daily classroom routines and activities.
- Musical games that encourage cooperation may be initiated to help Mica with interpersonal relationships.
- Group meetings may involve songs to encourage her participation.

<INST>TABLE 4.2</INST> | <SUPTTL>*Continued*</SUPTTL>

<H2>*Naturalist Strategies:*</H2>

- A classroom pet can be brought into the classroom. Mica can have the responsibility for caring for the pet to encourage her fine motor development. The pet, along with her knowledge and love of animals, can be used in the classroom to facilitate expressive language development.
- Mica can be encouraged to take pictures of her pets at home and of her horseback riding. The teacher and Mica can put a book together describing different animals. Mica can dictate information to the teacher about her photographs. The book can be read to the class, emphasizing her knowledge of interesting animal facts.

Linguistic Strategies:

- Mica can dictate a story or poem before circle time that the teacher can share with the class. This will help Mica contribute to meeting times without having the pressure of speaking in front of a group.
- Mica can choose to use a puppet to communicate through during some meeting times. The puppet might make her comfort level a little better for talking in front of a group.
- Avoid putting Mica on the spot for answering questions in front of her peers. Questions can be asked privately or during free choice time.
- The teacher should repeat what Mica says in conversation back to her with the correct articulation. (This is done to let Mica know you understand her and for her to hear the correct articulation of words. This is not done to make Mica feel badly about her speech or to correct her.)

<H2>*Bodily/Kinesthetic:*</H2>

- Make sure Mica has accessibility to the classroom. The classroom must be organized, neat, and permit large pathways for Mica to move freely in.
- Balance active and quiet experiences. Provide Mica ample time to rest after the class has participated in physical experiences.
- Incorporate all strategies offered by her physical therapist.

<H2>*Interpersonal:*</H2>

- Empathize with Mica's frustrations. Encourage her to express her frustrations in appropriate ways. When Mica is talking to another child, and that child is having difficulty understanding her, the teacher can repeat what Mica has said to the child. The teacher will encourage the other children not to walk away if they do not understand her, but to listen to the teacher's cues and repetitions of Mica's dialogue.

Bodily/Kinesthetic Intelligence and Culturally Appropriate Education

Refer once again to the description of Joy in Chapter 3. This section will address how to meet Joy's bodily/kinesthetic cultural needs. Joy's family has shown an interest in, and appreciation for, traditional Chinese culture. This appreciation extends to traditional Chinese dance. Joy attends a dance school where she learns Chinese dances as well as gymnastics. As mentioned before, masters in various fields from each intelligence are encouraged to come into the classroom and share their skill with the children. Joy's dance teacher can be invited in to share cultural dances and gymnastic movements with the class. The class may also attend public dances featuring traditional and contemporary Chinese folk dance such as the Cloud Gate Dance Troupe (Joy's mother's favorite).

Yoga would also be appropriate to incorporate into the curriculum. Joy's mother and Joy participate in a weekly yoga class. Yoga instructors can be brought into the classroom to demonstrate techniques and explain why particular techniques are used.

 Summary of Bodily/ Kinesthetic Intelligence

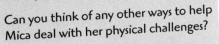

4.5

Journal Questions

Can you think of any other ways to help Mica deal with her physical challenges?

Are there any specific folk dances or physical experiences that are significant to your culture?

Name two strategies for incorporating bodily/kinesthetic intelligence into your classroom (as opposed to simply adding movement and exercise).

Before reading further . . .

Do you consider art experiences important for young children?

Interview a preschool and first-grade teacher. Ask how art is viewed in the classroom. What place does art have in the curriculum?

Physical movement is necessary for health, education, and brain growth. It is undeniably an important part of the child's overall education. Bodily/kinesthetic intelligence is valued and recognized by national children's organizations (NAEYC, COPEC), physical educators, and by the American culture. It is a necessary component to school life and a valuable part of the multiple-intelligence curriculum.

With the increased attention to and publicity about the importance of bodily movement, perhaps physical education will be viewed as something more than a "special" or an extra. Perhaps it will finally get the recognition and attention is deserves.

Spatial Intelligence

Spatial intelligence is defined as the "[capacity] to perceive the visual world accurately, to perform transformations and modifications upon one's initial perceptions, and to be able to re-create aspects of one's visual experience, even in the absence of relevant physical stimuli" (Gardner, 1993, p. 173). Spatial intelligence respects body, material, and environment boundaries. It exists in the visual realm, but is not limited to the visual realm. Spatial intelligence involves sensory perception and all of the senses help to create or recreate an image or experience. For example, a blind person can demonstrate a high level of spatial intelligence. Their tactile and auditory sensory perceptions help them to visualize the environment and move within it appropriately and efficiently.

Spatial intelligence is expressed through the arts, games, movement, architecture, engineering, aeronautics, and navigation. Spatial intelligence requires purposeful design and placement of objects in space.

The Consortium of National Arts Education Associations (1994) has developed art standards that can apply to the different disciplines represented through spatial intelligence. The standards recommend that children understand various techniques, processes, and media; use knowledge of structures and functions; choose and evaluate a range of symbols and ideas; understand how history and culture influence the arts; reflect upon characteristics of the work of others; and make connections between visual arts and other disciplines (Consortium of National Arts Education Associations, 1994).

Cultural Validation of Spatial Intelligence

Spatial intelligence is of great importance to the American culture. Spatial intelligence allows houses, bridges, buildings, cars, and machines to be built properly and safely. Driving, flying, and boating require a great sense of environmental awareness and skill. Individuals need to know where they are in their environment and how to manipulate and move in that environment. Art, physical presentation, and dress are valued in American society as well.

Individuals with spatial intelligence strengths can express their strengths in a variety of ways. Navigators, chess players, artists, draftspeople, interior decorators, designers, architects, and make-up artists all demonstrate spatial intelligence strengths.

TABLE 4.3 | *Spatial Intelligence Careers/Hobbies*

Careers That Reflect Spatial Intelligence	Hobbies and Interests That Reflect Spatial Intelligence
Artist	Art
Navigator	Chess
Architect	Checkers
Engineer	Dance
Pilot	Pottery
Make-up artist	Sculpture

 Spatial Intelligence in the Classroom

An early childhood curriculum that understands and respects spatial intelligence takes three guiding principles into consideration.

1. Spatial intelligence requires an awareness of body and material boundaries.
2. Spatial intelligence develops in stages (Brittain and Lowenfeld, 1964).
3. Spatial intelligence reveals the child's perceptions, interests, and understandings (Brittain and Lowenfeld, 1964).

Boundaries

BODY AWARENESS Three-year-old children will often bump into, step over, and touch one another. This is due to a lack of body boundaries. An awareness of body boundaries is a foundation for self-control. Body boundaries can be explored through mirror play, gross-motor play, and outdoor play. Mirror activities can help the child to see where her body is, and how it moves in space.

Movement is extremely important in the young child's life. Movement indoors and outdoors allows the child to develop an awareness of where her body is and how her body moves through space. This awareness will provide a foundation for being able to move the body skillfully and purposefully in the environment.

MATERIAL AWARENESS After a child has developed an understanding of her body boundaries, she can explore spatial intelligence through material awareness and boundaries.

Many times when a young child of two scribbles, the scribbles go off the paper. As the young child perceives her paper boundaries more clearly, she is able to stay within the boundaries of the paper. As the child's material boundary awareness increases, she is able to keep her materials organized and in close proximity. She respects the boundaries of her materials and of others and can use the materials to express and develop her spatial potential.

ENVIRONMENTAL AWARENESS Awareness of her place in the environment is also significant to the child's spatial development. Preschool children will begin noticing and manipulating shapes in their play environment. They will notice similarities and differences in shapes and structures. They will begin to verbalize an understanding of structural opposites (tall/short, big/little). Opportunities to explore shapes sensorially lead to spatial development. Children will identify, move, create, and manipulate shapes in the environment. Blocks of different shapes and textures, puzzles, gears, nuts and bolts, and other objects of varying shapes and sizes allow children to move, manipulate, and explore shape concepts. Montessori equipment such as geometric solids, metal insets, trinomial and binomial cubes, and knobless cylinders allow children to explore the concept of shape in the environment.

Playing with blocks allows the child to represent their environment through the creation of a model. It also helps the child to develop balance and symmetry, and allows the child to create a scaled-down version of their environment.

Preschool and kindergarten children will be able to locate and recognize familiar landmarks and streets that symbolize the way to grandma's house, preschool, or the park. An unexpected or alternate route to these places will often confuse a child. Young children are also able to recognize the functions of specific buildings in the environment. They recognize the firehouse, police station, school, library, and hospital and have an understanding of the functions of the buildings. The children are interested in landmarks in the environment that are directly related to their everyday life. Preschool and kindergarten children will represent their environment through block structures and art representation. The child might also be interested in simple mapmaking.

As children approach the end of the preoperational period of development, their egocentrism begins to be replaced by an awareness of, and eagerness to know and represent, others. The child acknowledges and recognizes that others may have a different point of view. The child is more interested in gaining a spatial perspective on where he/she is in relationship to others in the classroom, school, community, state, country, world, and universe. Map and globe activities will become important and relevant spatial tools. Maps and globes allow the child to begin to organize the environment and become aware of environmental boundaries that exists outside of the community. The child will create maps of her own.

Perceptions, Interests, and Understandings

In order to maximize the art experience for children and help them develop spatial intelligence, a question must be asked to clarify the purpose of arts education in the early childhood classroom. Lowenfeld and Brittain (1964, p. 52), authors of *Creative and Mental Development,* ask, "Do we study it [art] for our purpose of gaining insight into the child's growth, his experiences, his emotions, his interest? Or do we want to evaluate the child's work for the purpose of showing him his strengths, his weaknesses, his creative abilities, his skillfulness or his lack of skill; in other words, to classify him?" This query is extremely significant. When art is used as a tool of evaluation and classification of children, the creativity and individual expression of the child is lost. The child's potential may not be fully realized in an evaluative art program. Many times adults value, classify, and judge children's artwork without even realizing it. Oftentimes children are told their project "does not look like the model," is messy, or was not made following the directions. Even positive comments can seem evaluative. Calling artwork "beautiful" or "pretty," or telling the child it's "done right" is evaluative. The young child has a need to create art for the sole purpose of creating art. The purpose should never be to please an adult, to copy an adult model, or to meet adult expectations. What an adult might deem as messy may be a physical, artistic outlet of an experience for a young child. When art is used as a tool to gain insight into a child's perceptions, interests, and understandings, the experience itself becomes much more significant and the capacity for spatial development can be realized.

Development of Spatial Intelligence and Symbols

Lowenfeld and Brittain (1964) describe stages of artistic growth, which can be appropriately applied to spatial or perceptual growth. These stages reflect recognizable form development and the spatial representation capacity of the child.

SCRIBBLING Children from the ages of two to four are typically in the scribbling stage of development. There is a progression of scribbling. Children begin with disorganized scribbling. (This disorganization can be applied to other spatial tasks as well.) Children who are engaged in disorganized scribbling make random marks on a page, scatter block materials, have difficulty completing puzzles, have a lack of body awareness, and demonstrate an inability to organize materials.

Disorganized scribbling is indicative of sensory play. Scribbles are made simply for the physical experience. The focus should be on the process of scribbling, not on a final product. The scribbling stage is necessary for the development of spatial intelligence and for creativity to flourish. Slowly, the scribbling becomes more controlled.

Controlled scribbling is indicative of the motor stage of play. The child begins to experiment with and manipulate materials. The child does not often attend to the boundaries. Marks frequently go off the paper and onto the table or the floor. Various unrecognizable forms and shapes begin to appear. Eventually the child will begin to name these forms. The naming process usually consists of the action in the activity. For example, the child will call his picture "running," "hopping," or "daddy driving" (Brittain and Lowenfeld, 1964.) The naming aspect of scribbling signals the beginning of an awareness of symbol functionality. Figure 4.1 is an example of preschematic art representation.

In addition to facilitating body, material, and environmental awareness, sensory perception is significant to spatial intelligence. Experiences which allow the child to use and develop the five senses are critical for the development of spatial intelligence. Lecturing to young children does not encourage full sensory development to take place. Experiences that allow the child to engage in sensory and motor play increase sensory

FIGURE 4.1

this is water while you boil noodles

this is a wizard of oz music

perception. Materials that encourage sensory development include light tables, sand and water, textured materials, and natural materials.

Light tables offer children an opportunity to manipulate objects in space in response to the objects' shape, color, warmth, and texture. Manipulating transparent shapes, colored sand, colored rice, leaves, seeds, flowers, and other objects on the light table can help the child explore his visual and tactile perception and appreciate the aesthetic qualities of the materials.

Sand and water play offer tactile and visual perceptual experiences. Materials with different textures, colors, shapes, smells, and sounds need to be available to children.

Montessori equipment such as kinetic cylinders, color tablets, knobless cylinders, touch boards, touch tablets, thermic bottles, and sandpaper letters encourage spatial growth.

PRESCHEMATIC   From the ages of four to seven, children move into the preschematic stage of development. This stage is characterized by recognizable forms; however, these forms are not detailed and do not have a theme (Brittain and Lowenfeld, 1964). The child experiments with body representations and forms are drawn all over the page. There is a respect for paper boundaries, but no baseline exists in the picture. Block forms become recognizable. The child is able to put together simple puzzles, is able to purposely create original and recognizable shapes, and is able to begin to manage the body appropriately through space and around others. Figure 4.2 is an example of preschematic art representation.

SCHEMATIC   School-age children from ages seven to nine are typically involved in the schematic stage of development. Schematic activities are those that have a common

FIGURE 4.2

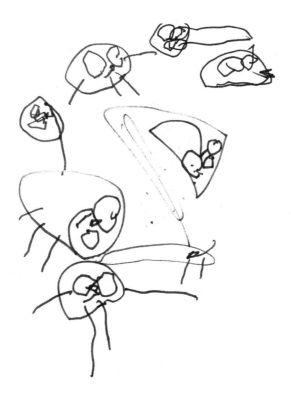

and consistent theme. The ideas behind drawings, movements, projects, and blocks are related to one another. Common themes often are the human body and those that reflect an awareness of spatial relationships. Feelings and actions are incorporated into creative activities that reflect the child's whole self. The development of the schema signifies less egocentric thinking and demonstrates a perception of how others influence the activity (Brittain and Lowenfeld, 1964). Figure 4.3 is an example of schematic art representation.

GANG AGE After a child has become more attuned to others, he/she enters the next stage of development, the gang age. The gang age occurs between the ages of nine and eleven. Children's activities begin to become influenced by social pressures and acceptance. The child begins to express independence and separates from parents. This happens because of the greater understanding the child has of his/her self and the environment. The child develops a deeper understanding of what is real. Generalizations and characterizations are made in creative activities. The child moves away from the schematic representation to a more naturalistic representation (Brittain and Lowenfeld, 1964).

FIGURE 4.3

Responding to Symbol Development

It is necessary to respond to children's symbol making appropriately. An adult can discuss the child's artwork as the process is unfolding if the child is willing. Questions and comments such as, "I see you are using lots of yellow," "Tell me about your picture," and "I can see you are working hard" are appropriate. Questions and comments such as "What is that?" "The sun is yellow, why would you make it green?" and "You're not doing it right," are evaluative and judge the child and would be inappropriate.

The child's presentation of spatial symbols can suggest evidence of a particular developmental stage. The symbols can also be used to assess a strength or challenge that may exist in a spatial domain.

 # Special Education and Spatial Intelligence

Children with spatial challenges may have difficulty with body boundaries, manipulating art materials, and may not be able to visualize. In the bodily/kinesthetic section, readers were introduced to Mica. Her example will be repeated in Table 4.4 to address her spatial challenges.

 # Spatial Intelligence and Culturally Appropriate Education

Each culture has specific methods for expressing spatial intelligence. Paintings, drawings, pottery, handwork, writing, and crafts communicate important cultural messages. Joy's family has an interest in origami, calligraphy, and painting. Her family has an appreciation for historical and contemporary Chinese art, pottery, and crafts.

The art center could have origami paper. Joy's teachers could visit museums to acquaint themselves with Chinese art. A botanical garden near Joy's school displayed a garden influenced by Chinese traditions. Part of the display contained 1000 origami cranes. A field trip could be planned to the botanical gardens to view the cranes to initiate interest and/or an actual origami project. Joy's family and/or a representative of the botanical gardens could come into the classroom and demonstrate origami techniques and share the history behind the thousand-crane display. Materials for creating origami could be provided in the art center of the classroom.

A field trip to local museums could acquaint all of the children with American, Chinese, and other cultural art representations that are significant to them. It would be important to display different forms of art, including Chinese art, in the early childhood classroom.

TABLE 4.4	*Special Education Strategies*

Child's Name: Mica
Age: 6
Current Placement: Kindergarten
Description: Mica has been diagnosed with spina bifida. She is currently enrolled in a regular kindergarten program. She receives physical therapy and speech at her school. Mica has a shunt implanted to prevent fluid from accumulating around her brain.

Challenges:

Bodily/Kinesthetic

- Mica wears braces on her legs for walking. She is able to walk slowly and tires easily.
- Mica has difficulty with fine-motor tasks.

Linguistic

- Mica's expressive language is somewhat delayed.
- She has difficulty articulating many sounds; she attends speech therapy.

Interpersonal

- Mica does not participate in group meetings or sharing times.
- Mica becomes frustrated when other children cannot understand her.

Spatial

- Mica bumps into objects in the environment. She has difficulty maneuvering in tight spaces.
- Mica demonstrates a random scribbling stage of art representation. Her marks often go off the page.

Strengths:

Naturalistic

- Mica goes horseback riding with a group of children who have physical challenges. She has several pets at home. She loves the zoo, can identify many animals. She knows interesting facts about animals that her peers do not.

Musical

- Mica listens and responds to music. She makes special requests at music time and taps her braces together to keep a beat.

Interests:

Mica loves animals and listening to music.

Learning Support Strategies:

Spatial Strategies:

Spina bifida has presented Mica with many spatial challenges. Her difficulty moving her body with purpose in the environment is frustrating for her. Mica is not always aware of where her body is and how her body is moving.

- Mirror play may help Mica become fully aware of where her body is. This may help Mica develop body boundaries and enable her to move past someone without bumping into them.
- It is important to keep her physical environment organized, safe, and allow her space to move freely.

TABLE 4.4 | *Continued*

- Mica engages in random scribbling. A large piece of paper can be taped to her table inside of a small hula hoop. The hula hoop can be taped to her table as well. The hula hoop offers Mica physical boundaries for her spatial representations. The boundaries may help Mica develop more control over her scribbling. This may enable her to move into more controlled scribbling attempts.

Musical Strategies:

- Body movement songs can be played to isolate specific physical movements. Mica can perform the movements in front of a mirrored wall.
- Mica can be encouraged to draw to the tempo of a musical selection. This will help her drawings become more controlled and purposeful as she draws faster to fast music and slower to slow music.

Calligraphy tools were mentioned in the linguistic section of Chapter 3. They are also important tools for spatial development. Chinese characters are representative of writing and art. Placement of each stroke is important and communicates meaning.

4.6
Journal Questions

Plan a visit to preschool, kindergarten, or a first grade classroom. What kind of art do you see displayed? Does all of the art look the same, or is individual expression encouraged?

Gather a drawing from a three-year-old and a seven-year-old. How are the drawings different? Are there any similarities? What stage of development does each picture represent? (Refer to Lowenfeld's stages of art representation.)

Before reading further. . .

How important is music in a classroom? Is it more important in a preschool than a first-grade classroom? Why or why not?

 # Summary of Spatial Intelligence

Spatial intelligence is a necessary and important part of the early childhood classroom. Tapping into spatial strengths fosters brain development, aesthetic development, self-control, competence, and specialized skill.

 # Musical Intelligence

Musical intelligence is marked by an individual's powerful reaction to, and manipulation of, sound. Musical intelligence includes the ability to manipulate and experiment with sound using the voice, an object, or manipulation of the musical symbol system (Gardner, 1993). The importance of music often goes unrecognized. Music is usually an extra activity that is added to fill time or to highlight seasonal holidays. However, musical intelligence is as important as any other intelligence. Amusia, the loss of musical abilities, has been

TABLE 4.5 | *Musical Careers, Hobbies, and Interests*

Careers That Reflect Musical Intelligence	Hobbies and Interests That Reflect Musical Intelligence
Songwriter	Music
Composer	Dance
Musician	Songwriting
Singer	Poetry
Dancer	

documented in individuals with localized brain damage (Gardner, 1993). This provides evidence of a specialized area in the brain that is responsible for music.

Cultural Validity of Musical Intelligence

The American culture seems obsessed with music. Music is played in the car, at work, and during dinner. It accompanies many parts of the day. Successful musicians are highly regarded and highly paid in America. Music is a valued part of the American life. This is evident in the number of individuals who choose music as a part of leisure activities and pay to see someone perform; the number of music CD's that are purchased annually; and the overwhelming amount of music-related products. Music is even marketed at pregnant women and women with young children. There are a large number of music-related products that are available for infants and young children. There are products that are available for play and to develop an interest in music, and there are music-related products that are specifically designed to boost IQ, strengthen skills, and prepare children for academics later in life (or so these products claim). The

BOX 4.7 | *The Music Educators National Conference (MENC) Music Standards*

The MENC (1994) standards address content such as:

- Singing alone, expressively and with others
- Playing a musical instrument
- Creating music
- Responding to music

- Understanding music
- Listening and analyzing music
- Performing
- Reading and writing musical notation

Music Educators National Conference (1994) has developed standards to address important musical concepts in the early childhood classroom. (See Box 4.7.)

Approaching Musical Intelligence in the Early Childhood Classroom

The MENC standards indicate that there is much more to music than listening to it in the background while performing unrelated cognitive tasks. Musical intelligence involves understanding, interpreting, responding to, and creating music. Opportunities to interact with music should be available daily. Fully integrating musical intelligence into the classroom is possible while respecting and understanding the following principles.

1. Music facilitates brain development (Jensen, 2001).
2. Early childhood music experiences should revolve around understanding, interpreting, responding to, and creating music (Andress, 1999).
3. Music is facilitated through musical education (Gardner, 1993).
4. Musical intelligence develops in stages.

Brain Development and Musical Intelligence

Music has an effect on brain growth and bodily systems. Jensen (2001) reports that music reduces stress and enhances the function of the immune system. Music can help children relax or can be used to excite. It affects the heart rate, blood pressure, and improves blood flow (Jensen, 2001) and also has an effect on memory. It develops the memory through melody and beat, and through its connection to the emotions. Music can also improve coordination and the ability to listen and respond.

The tempo and genre of a musical selection influences blood pressure, relaxation, respiration, and body temperature. Music that is loud and fast can slightly raise body temperature, quicken respiration, and elevate blood pressure. Music that has a slower tempo and is softer can lower body temperature and slow respiration. Music has an effect on brain chemicals and physical systems in the body (Jensen, 2001).

Understanding, Interpreting, Responding, and Creating

Music involves interaction (Andress, 1999). It is not a passive experience, but an active one. The interaction occurs through understanding, interpreting, responding to, and creating music. In order to interact with music, music must be listened to, as opposed to being heard. Hearing and listening involve two very different processes. Hearing is a passive physical process that is used to take in stimuli (Jensen, 2001). Listening involves the ability "to filter, analyze, and respond to sounds" (Jensen, 2001, p. 43).

How does one facilitate listening in the early childhood classroom? Through creating experiences to understand, interpret, respond to, and create music (Andress, 1999). Talk to children about the music they hear. Ask what the music sounds like; is it fast or slow; what kind of feeling does it communicate; what instruments might be involved; what instruments could they use to recreate it? Provide opportunities for children to manipulate objects to create sounds, play musical instruments, and clap out musical beats. Children may respond to music by talking about it, dancing, moving, and creating representations of it through drawing, clay, or other medium. Children should have the opportunity to create music through construction of musical instruments, experimentations with the notation system, and through pretending to be a conductor or musician.

Musical Education

As stated many times throughout this section, music involves more than hearing music. Musical intelligence requires interaction within the musical realm (Gardner, 1993).

MOZART EFFECT   During the last decade or so, there has been incredible media hype concerning the effects of Mozart's music on intelligence and performance (Weinberger, 2000). Claims are made that suggest listening to Mozart for only a few minutes can increase attention, spatial ability, intelligence, and performance on intelligence tests. Many of the claims are unsupported by documented research. The studies that do exist do not support these claims. The research study that began the interest in the Mozart effect was conducted in 1993 by Frances Rauscher, Gordon Shaw, and Katherine Ky. The researchers concluded that listening to a few minutes of Mozart before engaging in a spatial task may help the brain to perform the spatial task more easily (Weinberger, 2000), although the effect only lasts a few minutes. The music may simply serve as a tool for warming up the brain. The researchers do not make any claims suggesting that a few minutes of Mozart increases intelligence. Some individuals performed slightly better on spatial tasks after listening to the music. The study has been difficult to replicate.

Norman Weinberger (2000) cautions us about the recent media hype relating Mozart, young children, and intelligence. It is important to note that the research that has been carried out on the Mozart effect has been centered on adults in controlled situations. Teachers and parents have been bombarded with CDs and cassettes that claim to boost a child's potential through classical music. Women are even encouraged to play Mozart to their unborn child. The hype over the Mozart effect could be attributed to America's never-ending quest for the quick fix (Weinberger, 2000). Many parents, teachers, and educators buy into the hype because it promises increased intelligence with only a couple minutes of listening a day. However, musical intelligence involves a great deal more than simply listening to classical music a few minutes each day. This is not meant to downplay the idea of classical music in the early childhood classroom. There is a benefit in just listening to classical music for the sake of listening to it. It is important to note that supplying background music for children is appropriate at times, but not all the time. Children should also have the benefit of working in a quiet environment, devoid of background noise. When music is played in the background, many children only regard the music as background noise, and may filter it out as they would a dog barking or an airplane flying overhead. Music should be played for children purposefully, when they can fully attend to it.

Children can respond to the music in a variety of ways. It's critical for the early childhood teacher to understand that music is important and beneficial in the classroom. Classical music is not a quick fix, though. Educators should use caution when approached with a quick-fix method regarding any area in education. This includes quick-fix approaches to intelligence, behavior, and test performance.

WHAT DOES MOZART OFFER CHILDREN?   Should the criticism of the Mozart effect discourage the use of classical music and other types of music in the classroom? Certainly not; however, it does bring to light the importance of music *education* (as opposed to playing a few minutes of classical background music). Musical intelligence is something that develops in children out of interaction with people and materials in the environment. It is not a frill or something that can be attended to in a few minutes. Music must be fully integrated and attended to in the early childhood classroom. While a few minutes of Mozart may not have an effect on performance, music education has a lifetime effect on an individual.

Mozart offers children beautiful music to listen to, respond to, connect with, interpret, internalize, and symbolize. It may inspire a future musician, composer, or conductor. The music may elevate mood, encourage imagery, and increase musical awareness. The music of Mozart represents a beautiful part of humanity that needs to be shared, enjoyed, and valued with children.

In addition, music fosters many mathematical skills. Interaction with music and music education may develop and stimulate areas of the brain that will be needed for complex mathematical operations. Listening to a few minutes of music may not do this; however, experience and interaction with music on an ongoing basis may have an effect on the musical part of the brain that prepares or creates connections to the logical/mathematical part of the brain.

VALUE OF MUSIC EDUCATION   The criticism of the Mozart effect emphasizes the importance of music *education* and musical intelligence. Research has supported the value of musical education to other intelligences.

Music offers the child experience with patterns, rhyming, sounds, boundaries, rhythms, left to right orientation, and auditory discrimination skills. All of these experiences are vitally important to the development of other intelligences.

Manipulation of the voice is another critical and valuable musical skill. The voice can be manipulated and experimented with through singing, reciting poetry, musical games, and puppetry. The manipulation of the voice helps to facilitate linguistic intelligence as well.

Music provides a developmentally appropriate way to expose children to other cultures. Music and dance can also provide opportunities to use and manipulate language and the body. This manipulation enhances verbal and nonverbal communication skills.

Teacher-directed and child-directed musical experiences need to be incorporated into the rest of the program to fully foster musical intelligence. Teacher-directed musical experiences can create interest in music, ease transition times, and provide a comfortable routine. Child-directed activities allow him or her to engage in musical activities that he/she is intrinsically motivated to investigate. This allows for further development of self-esteem, musical competence, and self-knowledge of musical interests and abilities.

There are a variety of musical materials available for use in the classroom. Instruments can be purchased, made by the children, or obtained through donations from local organizations and parents. Cassette tapes or CDs providing a variety of different types of music are important. Local musical groups may be willing to perform for the children, which will put the children in touch with how different cultures interpret musical intelligence. Many books offer musical games, rhymes, and interpretations. Puppets and dolls can also be used to encourage children to sing and experiment with different sounds. Puppets and dolls are especially helpful when a child is embarrassed about their voice or embarrassed to perform in front of others. Puppets are allowed (and are supposed) to sound different and funny.

The child's environment is full of sounds. Play guessing games with the children and have them identify familiar sounds. Take the child outside to listen to nature's music. Try to identify different animal and environment sounds. The child can try to imitate these sounds and create a melody with them. The natural world was man's first music. Many of the instruments that exist today were inspired by natural sounds in the environment.

Teachers need to be aware of musical skills in order to facilitate them in children. It is recommended that a musical specialist be on staff or one can be consulted to provide in-service training for staff. A music specialist can also introduce specific musical skills to the children. Musicians can be invited into the classroom to demonstrate various types of music and musical instruments.

It is important to keep in mind all the musical interests of the classroom. It is also important to communicate that music is an integral part of daily life. Musical experiences can be incorporated into the housekeeping, block, manipulative, woodworking, science, and reading areas of the classroom. Music is everywhere and is not isolated from the rest of the world. Musical experiences bring people together. Each child and adult may interpret the meaning of a musical experience differently, but still appreciate and share it. Music should be an integral part of the classroom, and not limited to separate experiences that reflect limited awareness of, and appreciation for, the musical arts.

The comfort and language experience of music begins early in life and music is often an early source of comfort for an infant.

Development of Musical Intelligence

Music is developmental and is characterized by the use and understanding of the musical notation system. The development of music can be compared to the developmental framework presented in the spatial section of this chapter.

Initial Stage (Age 1 to 3 or 4)

The initial stage can be referred to as the scribbling stage. Children's attempts to use music, move to music, and represent music are disorganized and random. Often children will equate the tempo of a musical selection with the pressure and intensity with which they draw. Fast music may be represented through hard swirling strokes with crayons. Slow music will be characterized with somewhat more controlled, lighter shapes. Formal presentations of the notation systems are abstract and make little sense during this stage.

Inventive Stage (Age 4 to 6 or 7)

At around age four, the child enters the inventive stage This stage resembles the preschematic stage of spatial development. In music, the child begins to "invent" notes. The child invents notes in much the same way he uses invented spelling. Symbols are used to represent notes, convey messages, and communicate musical meaning. The child of this stage can invent a melody or rhythm with musical instruments, communicate meaning through physical movement, and invent musical instruments. The child of this stage will represent musical genres through invention as well. For example, the child will invent various shapes with his body to represent ballet or jazz. The child may even name the shapes, utilizing familiar terms he may have heard, or will invent names of dance steps. (See Figure 4.4.)

Industrious Stage (Age 7 to 9)

During the industrious stage, the child represents music similarly to the schematic stage of spatial representation. The child will be able to begin playing an instrument such as the pentatonic flute. The child recognizes there are rules and specificities to musical instruments and genres. The child will be able to identify different musical genres. A theme is clearly represented in his musical creations and symbols. The child will be able to identify and utilize formal notation and will begin to incorporate it into his composition. The child also begins to develop the rules for creating music, recognize scales, and interpret music with sophistication and relevance.

FIGURE 4.4

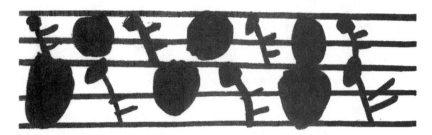

Formal Notation Stage (Age 9 to adult)

The child in the formal notational stage will be able to read and write music fluently. The child will acknowledge and respect music rules for different musical genres. The child will be able to play a complicated instrument and identify tempos, rhythms, and melodies.

 Choosing Music for Young Children

Choosing music for children should be approached as carefully as choosing literature, stories, and/or play materials. In the linguistic intelligence section of this text, a variety of stories and literature were suggested. Stories that exposed children to the beauty of language were as important as stories that young children can read. Short, choppy, non-sensical stories are often found in basal texts and in some children's books. The stories may be easy for children to read, but offer the child little in the way of storytelling, language, or imagery. Music can be looked at in the same way. Children need to be exposed to the beauty of music. All genres are appropriate for young children. Children's music is certainly important and traditional rhymes, songs, and musical games are an important part of musical development. However, children's music is usually limited in genre and scope. Children need to be immersed in quality music. Children enjoy and can respond to classical, jazz, blues, rock, country, and culturally specific music.

Music development is important in the early childhood classroom. It is often overlooked or addressed at later stages of development. Music can offer an entry point for challenging content or create a pathway into the symbolic world. Musical intelligence can be used to address challenges in other intelligence areas.

Special Education and Musical Intelligence

The second chapter of this text concluded with a story about a boy who had difficulty thinking symbolically. A pathway to symbol development was made possible through music. Table 4.6 will look at Jacob and offer further suggestions for tapping into his musical strength.

Musical Intelligence and Culturally Appropriate Education

As with the other intelligences, musical strategies to address Joy's culture must be integrated into the daily function of the classroom. Playing a week of Chinese music is not meeting Joy's cultural music needs. Joy's family enjoys music and has been asked to bring in copies of their favorite songs in Chinese. These songs can be integrated into the musical repertoire of the classroom. Throughout the year, musicians that play traditional Chinese instruments such as the er-hu, xiao, or yang-qin may be asked to come in and play for the children. If instruments are presented in class according to their type (percussion, woodwind, brass, horn)—the Chinese classification (metal, wood, silk, bamboo, gourd, clay, skin, and stone) system of instruments can also be introduced through games, stories, and activities. Materials such as metal, wood, silk, bamboo, gourds, clay, skin, and stones can be introduced in the art center or music center for children to create their own instrument.

Chinese music often utilizes a pentatonic scale. The scale can be introduced to children with music, tones, bells, a pentatonic flute, or through movement exercises.

TABLE 4.6 | *Special Education Strategies*

Child's Name: Jacob
Age: 5
Current Placement: Kindergarten
Description: Jacob demonstrates a musical strength. He has difficulty using linguistic and mathematical symbols.
Challenges:

Musical

- Jacob is not challenged musically in the classroom. He is eager and often asks for music activities and experiences.

Linguistic

- Jacob has no interest in linguistic experiences and materials.
- He has only recently made a connection between linguistic sounds and symbols.
- Jacob has difficulty articulating several sounds and is receiving speech therapy.

Strengths:

Musical

- Jacob has a great musical strength.
- His understanding and response to music is above most of his peers.
- Jacob can identify and create rhythms.
- Jacob can identify several musical genres.
- Jacob has an interest in musical instruments and experiences.
- Jacob can skillfully play several classroom instruments. (He can play the color-coded piano and follow notes written out in colors.)

Intrapersonal

- Jacob responds and interacts appropriately with peers.
- He is well liked in the classroom.

Interpersonal

- Jacob is aware of his challenges and strengths.
- He asks for help when needed and also asks for more challenging tasks when appropriate.
- He manages impulses and channels emotions appropriately.

Interests:
Jacob loves music and telling jokes. He enjoys interacting with peers and expresses a love and passion for music. Jacob is especially fond of flute music.

Learning Support Strategies:

Musical Strategies:

- Jacob is ready for a more challenging instrument. His interest and enthusiasm for flute music encourages the presentation of a pentatonic flute. Jacob can take lessons from his teacher or from the school's music instructor.
- Staff paper and pens would be important to add to the writing or music center of the classroom. Jacob can experiment with his knowledge of the formal musical notation system.

TABLE 4.6 | *Continued*

- Musical materials can be added to the music center to offer Jacob challenge. For example, Montessori equipment such as: tone bars, bells, and note position boards.
- Music may provide an entry point for linguistic experiences. Storytelling can involve songs and movement. Jacob can be asked to create music to signify different characters.
- Songs that incorporate the sounds Jacob has difficulty with can be integrated into the classroom.
- To encourage further linguistic symbol appreciation, Jacob can play musical games with linguistic symbols.

Linguistic Strategies:

- Personal and classroom objects will be labeled to create an awareness of print.
- Books that contain the alphabet and one-word books will be available for Jacob to read or the teacher to read to him.
- Books with musical concepts will be available to facilitate an interest in literature.
- Jacob can create sound effects for group stories.

Summary of Musical Intelligence

Musical, spatial, and bodily/kinesthetic intelligence have traditionally been addressed as talents in the classroom. They are things that have been presented in addition to the regular curriculum. This text presents these intelligences as worthwhile aspects of the curriculum that deserve the same attention and respect as language and mathematics. These intelligences help facilitate the development of other intelligences, encourage brain growth, provide opportunities for growth of self-esteem, offer useful analogies and entry points, and offer the teacher alternative ways of presenting core concepts.

> **4.8**
> **Journal Questions**
>
> What information from this chapter might you add to your box? Do you feel differently now about the importance of music, art, and movement? Do you consider music, art, and movement talents or intelligences?

 References

Andress, B. (1999) "Transforming curriculum in music." *Reaching potentials: Transforming early childhood curriculum and assessment.* Vol. 2. Bredekamp and Rosegrant, eds. pp. 99–108.

Brittain, W,. & Lowenfeld, V. (1964) *Creative and mental growth.* New York: MacMillan Books.

Consortium of National Arts Education Associations. (1994) *National standards for arts education.* Reston, VA: Music Educators National Conference.

Erikson, E. (1950) *Childhood and society.* New York: Norton & Co.

Gardner, H. (1993) *Frames of mind.* New York: Basic Books.

Gallahue, D. (1999) "Transforming physical education curriculum." *Reaching potential: Transforming early childhood curriculum and assessment.* Washington, DC: NAEYC. (Vol. 2, pp. 125–143).

Gallahue, D., & Ozmun, J. (1995) *Understanding motor development: Infants, children, adolescents, adults.* Dubuque, IA: Brown and Benchmark.

Hannaford, C. (1995) *Smart moves: Why learning is not all in your head.* Arlington, VA: Great Ocean Publishers.

Jensen, E. (2001) *Arts with the brain in mind.* Alexandria, VA: Association for the Supervision of Curriculum Development.

Music Educators National Conference (MENC). (1994) *Opportunities-to-learn standards for music instruction: Grades preK–12.* Task Force chair P. Lehman. Reston, VA: Author

Sattler, J. (1982) *The development of intelligence.* New York: McGraw-Hill Book Co.

Weinberger, N. (2000) *"The Mozart effect":* A small part of the big picture. MuSICA Research notes. University of California.

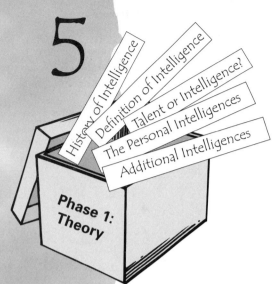

5

The Personal Intelligences

Phase 1: Theory

History of Intelligence
Definition of Intelligence
Talent or Intelligence?
The Personal Intelligences
Additional Intelligences

M anaging, interpreting, and expressing emotions is crucial for success in life (Goleman, 1995). These personal abilities enable us to develop significant relationships with others. The foundation for these abilities is developed through the earliest relationships. The infant's relationships significantly affect the child's ability to form appropriate later relationships with peers, adults, and siblings. Relationships are influenced by the child's interpersonal and intrapersonal development. This chapter will define the personal intelligences and present information on how relationships influence the development of the personal intelligences.

 ## The Personal Intelligences

Emotions and relationships are at the center of the personal intelligences. These intelligences are perhaps the most important—and the most over-looked—in the classroom. With the contemporary emphasis on academic standards, standardized tests, and achievement, little attention is given or allotted for emotional and interpersonal aspects of the curriculum (Goleman, 1995; Teele, 2001). It is crucial to understand and facilitate healthy emotional development in the early childhood classroom. It is equally important to value and create healthy, nurturing relationships with children.

5.1

Journal Question

Look at the list of the following people. Who would you consider intelligent?

Rachel Carson

Mother Theresa

Thomas Edison

Albert Einstein

Mohandas Gandhi

Amadeus Mozart

Ludwig Beethoven

Pablo Picasso

Eleanor Roosevelt

Maria Montessori

Jean Piaget

Mikhail Baryshnikov

Gardner (1993) describes two intelligences that deal with the emotional life of the child: interpersonal and intrapersonal. *Intra*personal intelligence is the individual's capacity for understanding and expressing one's own emotional life: *Intra*personal intelligence deals with the self. *Inter*personal intelligence is the individual's capacity to understand and interpret another's emotional and cognitive intentions: *Inter*personal intelligence deals with relationships with others. Look at the list of people in Box 5.1. Who would you consider intelligent?

All of these people had significant gifts to offer others and the world. It would be impossible to determine which gifts were more significant than others. It is also quite difficult to determine who among this list is *not* intelligent. All of these people exhibited intelligence strength. Their strength may not have been identified as intelligence in the traditional sense; however, including emotional potentials in the definition of intelligence leads us to reexamine the traditional view of intelligence. All of these people manipulated the symbol system of their discipline with expertise and skill. All of them were highly respected in their field and demonstrated a gifted capacity for their discipline. These were intelligent individuals. Some of these people demonstrated mathematical, logical, or linguistic strength; others demonstrated musical, spatial, or bodily/kinesthetic strength. The others demonstrated strength and intelligence related to their emotions.

Mother Theresa and Mohandas Gandhi are beautiful examples of individuals who excelled in interpersonal intelligence. Their empathy, sincerity, compassion, interpretive skills, and relationship skills were far superior to most. To say their behavior was not intelligent behavior would be an insult. Their abilities to understand emotions, form relationships, interpret feelings and mood, and to communicate emotional issues were certainly an indicator of intelligent behavior. The world certainly benefits from those gifted in the personal intelligences. The benefit is even greater when each child receives a healthy foundation for the development of personal intelligences.

Contemporary theorists have been concerned with the emotional health of the young child. Daniel Goleman, author of *Emotional Intelligence,* agrees with Gardner's view that school knowledge is disassociated with real-world knowledge. Traditional preparation of the student has little to do with the student's emotional preparation for life (Goleman, 1995). Goleman refers to interpersonal and intrapersonal development as

TABLE 5.1 | *Personal Intelligences Careers/Hobbies*

Careers That Reflect the Personal Intelligences	Hobbies/Interests That Reflect the Personal Intelligences
Psychologist	Diary/Journal
Journalist	Self-help books/conferences
Teacher	Yoga
Psychiatrist	Meditation
Politician	
Nurse	
Motivational speaker	
Counselor	

emotional intelligence. Goleman's theory of emotional intelligence consists of five domains: knowing one's emotions, managing one's emotions, motivating oneself, recognizing emotions in others, and handling relationships. All of these domains are critical in developing both interpersonal and intrapersonal intelligence.

The Joint Committee on National Health Education Standards (1995) emphasizes the importance of intelligence in their address of intrapersonal and interpersonal content and in their description of the health-literate individual. The Committee's health standards address mental and emotional health, relationships, and family life. The Committee's Standards (1995, p. 5) describe a health-literate person as "a critical thinker and problem solver; a responsible, productive citizen; a self-directed learner; and an effective communicator." This description defines and presents the capacities that are necessary in order to develop intrapersonal intelligence.

5.2
Journal Question

How do you feel about your own intrapersonal intelligence? It is important to think about the way you handle emotions, set goals, and manage your feelings. You are a model for the young children you teach. Your intrapersonal skills will be viewed and interpreted by the children you teach.

Intrapersonal Intelligence

Possessing *intra*personal intelligence allows an understanding of one's own emotions, mood, intentions, feelings, self-control, impulses, reactions, and interpretations. Gardner (1993, p. 239) describes intrapersonal intelligence as "the access to one's own feeling life— one's range of affects or emotions: the capacity instantly to effect discriminations among these feelings and, eventually, to label them, to enmesh them in symbolic codes, to draw upon them as a means of understanding and guiding one's behavior." The sophistication of the emotional encoding and representation increases with age and experience. Intrapersonal intelligence provides for accomplishments, anxieties, goal setting, and goal attainment. Intrapersonal intelligence also allows an individual to make intelligent choices regarding paths in life (Gardner, 1999).

Interpersonal Intelligence

*Inter*personal intelligence emphasizes the intentions, moods, reactions, impulses, feelings, expressions, and interactions of and with others. It allows an individual to notice distinctions, display empathy, and understand moods, temperament, motivation, and intentions of others (Gardner, 1993). These are life skills that can strongly influence the adult's life and determine the emotional success of an individual (Goleman, 1995). Traditionally, interpersonal skills have only been taught remedially to children who are labeled with emotional disabilities (Goleman, 1995). Why wait until it's too late? Interpersonal development can be fostered from birth (Karr-Morse and Wiley, 1997).

Cultural Validity of the Personal Intelligences

The cultural validity of these intelligences emerges from the recent activity of America's youth. In the 1980s, unprecedented acts of violence began occurring in schools. Children began shooting and killing fellow classmates, teachers, and sometimes themselves. American children had found a very high-profile method of dealing with depression, teasing, boredom, frustration, relationship difficulties, bullying, mental illness, intolerance, and pain. Statistically, the chance of being murdered by a fellow classmate is low. However, the emotional manifestations, the fear, and the inter/intrapersonal deficits these actions represent are far more devastating than statistics can show.

In addition to the murder epidemic plaguing America's youth, Goleman (1995) reports disturbing juvenile crime statistics. In 1990, the United States witnessed the highest arrest rate for violent juvenile crimes. Forcible rape doubled, suicide rates and venereal diseases tripled, and teen murder quadrupled (Goleman, 1995). Heroin and cocaine usage increased by 300 percent with teens, and there was a staggering increase in mental illnesses. These statistics led Goleman to conclude that the emotional intelligence of the country was rapidly declining. Goleman (1995) proposes that emotional literacy needs to be made an integral part of the education process. The success of the American culture depends upon it.

In addition to the failing intrapersonal skills of America's youth, adults have difficulty with relationships, exhibiting appropriate conduct at work, controlling impulses, and controlling rage (Gardner, 1995). This is evident in the unprecedented divorce rate, depression diagnoses, sexual and physical harassment of adults at work, and road rage. As a result, many adults and children are in counseling, therapy, and/or on medication. There is an obvious need for attention to intrapersonal and interpersonal intelligence in the classroom.

The Personal Intelligences in the Early Childhood Classroom

The social development of young children has traditionally been marked by observable behaviors such as sharing (Chen, 1998). Jie-Qi Chen, the editor of Project Spectrum's Early Learning Activities (1998, p. 171) explains that a curriculum that utilizes the multiple intelligence theory approaches social development through "children's perceptions and understandings, on how they view the world of social relationships and their role within it." The "observable behavioral" view identifies social abilities. The view expressed by Chen takes responsibility for children's social development and involves the internal processes that are responsible for emotions and relationships.

The social development of elementary-school children has traditionally been addressed in a deficit archetype. Intrapersonal deficits are addressed in the disciplinary or remedial realm of the classroom. The child who does not have self-control is punished. The child who cannot manage or channel emotions appropriately is punished or referred for special education. The child who exhibits severe emotional difficulties is placed in an emotional support class. Waiting until a problem exists is too late (Karr-Morse and Wiley, 1997). The multiple-intelligence theory looks at intra/interpersonal potential as critically as other potentials. Intra/interpersonal development is vital to success in the classroom (Gardner, 1993) and to success in life (Goleman, 1995). Intra/interpersonal intelligence in the early childhood classroom is addressed through the purposeful planning, attention, and inclusion of intra/interpersonal content and materials. Successful implementation of the personal intelligences is facilitated through the following principles:

1. Emotions are not limited to the personal intelligences (Greenspan, 1997; Gardner, 1999).
2. The personal intelligences develop in stages. These stages emphasize a specific crisis. The resolution of the crisis sets the foundation for the resolution of the next crisis (Erikson, 1963).

3. Intra/interpersonal intelligence requires an emotionally safe environment (Bluestein, 2001).
4. It is essential to establish a sense of community in the classroom (Vance and Weaver, 2002) in order to develop the personal intelligences.
5. Relationships are crucial to the child's emotional development and the child's ability to learn (Greenspan, 1997). It is through social interaction that emotions develop (Greenspan, 1997; Hyson, 1994).

Emotions and Intelligence

Before examining the curricular implications of the personal intelligences, it is critical to point out that emotions are not limited to the personal intelligences (Gardner, 1999). While the personal intelligences deal with emotional development, emotions do not exist independently from cognition (Greenspan, 1997). Greenspan (1997) refers to emotions as the "architect of the mind." They are not separate from cognition, but are necessary in creating the structures that govern cognition (Greenspan 1997). Emotions facilitate brain growth. Emotional experience and interaction are crucial in order for the developing brain to be able to symbolize. All experiences are emotionally charged and require emotional response in order to be processed by the brain (Greenspan, 1997).

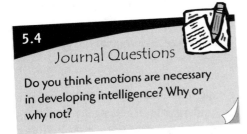

5.4
Journal Questions
Do you think emotions are necessary in developing intelligence? Why or why not?

Upon a reexamination of the intelligences in the 1999 publication of *Intelligences Reframed,* Gardner (1999, p. 43) emphasizes the "emotional facets of each intelligence rather than restrict emotions to one or two personal intelligences."

Development of the Personal Intelligences

Erikson's stages of psychosocial development provide a framework for understanding how the personal intelligences develop. The developmental stages presented reflect the development of both interpersonal and intrapersonal development. While they are separate intelligences, they are both an expression of emotions. One looks at inner life, while the other looks at relationships. Hyson (1994, p. 121) explains that "emotions develop in social context." Emotions cannot develop in isolation; social interaction is necessary (Greenspan, 1997; Hyson, 1994).

Erikson (1950) proposed that a child develops in psychosocial stages. Each stage presents an inner conflict or crisis. Resolution of the crisis in one stage affects the resolution of the crisis in the next stage. The resolution of the crisis is greatly influenced by the parent, teacher, or caregiver's response to it. Erikson suggests that a favorable resolution of the crisis provides a healthy balance for that stage of psychosocial development. His theory also suggests that any crisis can be reworked at a later stage of development. One has a chance to rework the crisis in school, therapy, special education, with skilled parenting, and/or counseling.

The first four stages of Erikson's theory will be focused on in this section of the text because of their direct relevance to the ages of the children that the curriculum is intended for. These stages include trust, autonomy, initiative, and industry. The later stages involve identity, intimacy, generativity, and ego integrity.

TRUST   The first stage is referred to as the *oral-sensory* stage. This stage presents a crisis centered on trust. The first crisis, *trust vs. mistrust,* lays the foundation for the child's culture, relationships, and place in society. This crisis emerges during the first year of life and lays the foundation for resolution of the conflicts that follow and for future relationships with friends, teachers, spouses, and children.

The crisis revolves around the issues of trust and consistency. In order to develop trust, the infant must have her basic needs met consistently. This means the child's needs are responded to and the child feels safe. When the infant's needs are consistently and genuinely met, the infant develops a trustful relationship with her parents, caregivers, and with the world. If the infant's needs are not consistently met or the infant is abused, he will develop a general mistrust of life and relationships. The favorable resolution is a balance of trust and mistrust that instills drive and hope in the child (Erikson, 1963).

Trust in the Classroom   The relationship the child and her teacher create is a crucial one. In many instances, the child's preschool or kindergarten teacher may be the first nonfamilial relationship. Those interactions can be an opportunity for the child to establish a trustful relationship outside of her extended family and the opportunity to begin to foster the development of trust between peers.

The teacher can create a sense of trust in the environment by establishing a predictable routine, responding consistently and appropriately to the children, creating and maintaining a safe environment, intervening when body boundaries are threatened, and by having appropriate expectations of the children.

A predictable routine can be set with flexible scheduling. Schedule blocks of time where certain activities are expected to take place. Provide young children with pictures that signal changes in activities. Post the pictures in the sequence that they will be presented. Exact times are not needed. Free play, center time, activity time, or lunch time may take longer or shorter than expected so flexibility is important. As children begin to tell time and understand the linguistic symbol system, the pictures of the activities can be replaced with clocks and words. The children need to know what to expect from their teacher. By responding to the children consistently, their expectations are met, and they continue to develop a sense of trust.

Safety is of extreme importance. The child must feel safe in her environment. Her environment must be challenging, but manageable; free from clutter; organized and predictable; and have clearly defined limits. The child must also be safe from other children. Expectations for interactions must be clearly communicated.

AUTONOMY   This next stage is referred to as the *muscular-anal* stage. It focuses on the conflict between *autonomy* and *shame/doubt*. This crisis usually occurs during the second and third years of life. During this crisis, the child wrestles with trying to balance being independent with dependency. The child realizes she is a separate being from her mother, with specific wants, needs, and views of the world. The ambivalence of the child leads to frustration, temper tantrums, and vocalization to do things by herself (Erikson, 1963).

Autonomy involves feelings of self-worth, self-confidence, and power. Children who feel powerless will react by trying to impose power on other children and adults. Teachers need to help the child create an appropriate balance of power. Let the children have choices of activities during the day. Let the child also have the option of not participating. As a teacher, examine your feelings on why you want a child to behave in a particular way. Is there a developmental or safety reason why a child should not be engaged in a particular behavior, or is it simply because you do not want the child to engage in a particular behavior? It is important for you to evaluate your own sense of autonomy before helping the children deal with this issue.

If the child is constantly dominated and not allowed to figure things out on his own, he will develop shame and/or doubt. The child will begin to question his efforts in exploring and mastering his environment and relationships in his environment. The child develops autonomy through supporting her efforts to try things on her own, creating an environment that offers challenging but manageable experiences, avoiding power struggles, and by valuing her as a unique human being. The favorable resolution of this crisis is a healthy balance between autonomy and doubt. This balance instills a sense of self-control and willpower in the child (Erikson, 1963).

It is important to note that the child continues to work through trust during this stage as well. Trust is worked on in each stage; however, each stage emphasizes a predominant crisis (Erikson, 1963). The child working through autonomy also works on trust issues that deal with autonomy.

Autonomy in the Classroom   A classroom that promotes autonomy is one that recognizes the need for children to make choices regarding materials, problem-solving techniques, and areas of interest. An autonomous classroom supports and shares each child's point of view. A heteronymous classroom supports one view—the teacher's or basal text's view. The heteronymous classroom accepts only one right answer, one way of doing things, one way to succeed (Kamii, 1985). An autonomous classrooms respects the differences children have, respects the multiple ways a problem can be solved, and expects each child to succeed in his own way. Autonomy can be supported through allowing children to debate or brainstorm ideas and solutions to problems, acknowledging diversity in the classroom, and respecting each child's intelligence strengths and challenges.

INITIATIVE   The preschool child operates in the *locomotor-genital* stage. This stage revolves around the conflict between *initiative* and *guilt*. The three- to four-year-old begins to engage in self-initiated experiments and activities. The child of this age is capable of thinking about an experience, gathering materials together, engaging in the experience, and putting materials away. The child can initiate an activity and provide closure to the activity. The child develops her own way of encoding the world and encoding the intelligences. The child will explain conclusions in fantastical terms. Impulses are channeled into appropriate, child-initiated outlets. Initiative allows the child to think for herself, trust in her convictions, and become comfortable expressing her own ideas.

Of course, every expression of initiative cannot possibly be encouraged in the classroom. The child needs to understand the appropriate use and context of initiative. This can be achieved by a skilled teacher who allows choices, allows children to share ideas, but does not allow the child to hurt, endanger, or dominate the classroom.

If the child's attempts at initiative are constantly thwarted, the child will develop a primary sense of guilt. The favorable resolution to this crisis is a balance of initiative and guilt, which creates a sense of direction and purpose (Erikson, 1963).

Trust and autonomy are also worked on during this stage; however, initiative is the predominant crisis for the preschool child. Trust and autonomy issues related to initiative surface again and will continue to arise throughout the remaining crises.

Initiative in the Classroom   Initiative is developed by providing children with choices, allowing and respecting play in the early childhood program, encouraging independence, encouraging children to problem solve, and allowing children to discuss, debate, and question each other's ideas in an appropriate and respectful manner. Choice is a critical component in the early childhood classroom. Choice encourages initiative and allows the child to access materials that reflect strengths and build upon challenges.

INDUSTRY   The *latency* stage deals with the conflict of *industry* versus *inferiority*. Learning the adult ways of doing things is appealing and motivating for children. The child is interested in adult tools and adult roles. These tools include formal symbol systems, art tools, carpentry tools, literary tools, musical instruments, formal dance techniques, and so on. The child is ready and eager to take part in adult-like experiences.

This is the time when cultures teach the use of weapons, tools, roles, and literacy (in literate cultures). It is important not to concentrate on just one role or tool, such as literacy or mathematics. A good relationship with all the skills and tools of society is necessary in order to be prepared for the next crisis concerning identity. The favorable resolution of the industry crisis is a balance between industry and inferiority. The balance should lead to method and competence (Erikson, 1963).

Trust, autonomy, and initiative are also dealt with in this stage. Industry remains the predominant crisis; however, the child continues to work through trust, autonomy, and initiative. Issues of trust, autonomy, and initiative that relate to industry are emphasized. Trust, autonomy, initiative, and industry will surface in the remaining four crises as well.

Industry in the Classroom   Industry can be encouraged by acquainting the child with techniques and tools of many disciplines. The child can work as an apprentice to develop the techniques of a role that interests her. The child should have the opportunity to see the roles and tools in action and to use the tools in context to the specific discipline.

Erikson (1963, p. 274) explains that without these basic virtues "and their reemergence from generation to generation, all other and more changeable systems of human

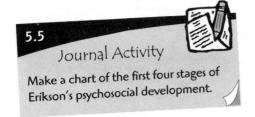

values lose their spirit and their relevance." Hope, will-power, purpose, and competence are important humanistic tools that are necessary not only for success in life, but for success of the human race.

Symbol Systems and the Personal Intelligences

The formal symbol system of intrapersonal intelligence is expressed in specific disciplines such as psychology, counseling, or motivational speaking. The symbol system of intrapersonal intelligences is marked by emotions, control, and impulses. The child reacts emotionally to all stimuli. The child cries, giggles, screams, smiles, looks at, listens to, touches, and smells the world around her.

The child then reacts physically to emotional impulses. For example, the child hits, kicks, throws herself on the floor, hugs, or kisses in response to feelings and emotions.

The older toddler/preschool child represents emotions through motor movements and words. The child begins to say, "I am angry," "I am sad," or "You are angry," "You are sad." The preschool child can begin to draw pictures of faces that symbolize different emotions.

The preschool child can also begin to explain why they feel a particular way. The child is able to create pictures that represent an emotional theme or emotional experience. The child can illustrate journal pages to communicate emotional responses to experiences. Figure 5.1 depicts a preschooler's representation of a feeling.

The kindergarten/first-grade child is able to describe the mood, intention, and action of her emotional expression. The child can initiate discussions regarding emotions. The child can talk about the emotions, intentions, and motivations for characters in stories. Original stories based on emotional themes can be created by children and discussed. Figure 5.2 demonstrates how a kindergarten child can represent feelings and causes for feelings in a journal entry.

The elementary child begins developing the formal symbol systems for intrapersonal intelligence through journal writing, debate, conversation, discussion, and story writing. The elementary child uses formal symbols to communicate and interpret intrapersonal development.

Emotional symbols will develop in an emotionally safe environment. This is an environment that nurtures, challenges, and cares for children in a safe, supportive atmosphere.

The personal intelligences bring the issues of emotions and relationships into the classroom. These issues have been discussed and emphasized in the past couple of decades with the advent of Daniel Goleman's emotional intelligence theory and Howard Gardner's attention to interpersonal and intrapersonal intelligence. Another theorist,

FIGURE 5.1

FIGURE 5.2

Stanley Greenspan (1997), believes the role of emotions and relationships are not taken seriously enough by historical and contemporary theorists. Greenspan does not see the emotions as separate, or as a separate intelligence.

Emotions and Symbols

Greenspan outlines six levels of emotional development in *The Growth of the Mind and the Endangered Origins of Intelligence*. Greenspan's stages of emotional development illustrate the maturation of the emotions and the emergence of the ability to symbolize. Each stage presents a different way for children to construct their own emotional development.

Level one—Making Sense of Sensations
Level two—Intimacy and Relating
Level three—Willed Exchange of Signals and Responses
Level four—Purpose and Interaction
Level five—Images, Ideas, and Symbols
Level six—Emotional Thinking

The foundation for emotional development begins during the child's first months of life. Greenspan explains that Level One "involves learning to organize life's wondrous sensations as well as the body's responses" (1997, p. 4). In this level the infant has two tasks: to decode sensations and to move the body with purpose and intent (Greenspan, 1997). The infant is bombarded with sensations. It is the infant's task to differentiate and accept the vast sensations she experiences. The infant must also begin to move the body purposefully in order to explore and control her environment. The end of this level is marked by the infant's ability to calmly accept sensations and to intently explore her environment (Greenspan, 1997).

Greenspan (1997) refers to the second level as *intimacy and relating*. This level begins the love affair between parent and child. The child reacts to the parent's attempts at closeness and engagement. The parent reacts to the child's emotional expressions with empathy, love, and concern. This exchange of emotions results in a sharing of humanity and enables the child to form relationships with other people (Greenspan, 1997).

The third level is marked with a "willed exchange of signals and responses" (Greenspan, 1997, p. 55). The willful exchange symbolizes intent. The infant communicates purposefully, in order to receive some acknowledgement for his exchange (Greenspan, 1997). There is meaning and purpose to human exchanges; they communicate a message. Body gestures and sensations communicate meaning. Through the exchanges, the infant begins to realize he is separate from his parents.

Now that intent has been realized, the child moves to the fourth level, *purpose and interaction* (Greenspan, 1997). The young toddler's exchanges with her mother become more purposeful and communicate a deeper sense of meaning and understanding. The child can communicate effectively with gestures, body language, and sounds. The child's interpretations of the body language of others begins at this level. It is through this presymbolic interaction that the child first learns about the culture and the values of her primary caregivers (Greenspan, 1997).

The fifth level marks the beginning of symbolic expression. This expression takes the form of *images, ideas, and symbols* (Greenspan, 1997). The toddler can pretend and present the world in symbols. This ability allows the toddler more control over her impulses and feelings. She can symbolize her feelings and impulses with words, rather than with physical actions (Greenspan, 1997).

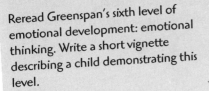

5.6

Journal Activity

Reread Greenspan's sixth level of emotional development: emotional thinking. Write a short vignette describing a child demonstrating this level.

The sophistication of the use of the symbol marks the sixth level, *emotional thinking*. The preschool child can reason. He can give reasons for actions, events, and feelings. His sophisticated symbolic thinking leads to an internal construction of the events, actions, and feelings that affect his life. These events, actions, and feelings manifest themselves through emotional expressions, pretend play, words, and pictures. The ability to connect emotions with experiences continues to grow in sophistication throughout maturity (Greenspan, 1997).

This text targets children from ages three to eight so Greenspan's levels five and six fall within this text's concentration. What can be done as a teacher to encourage the healthy development of these emotional levels? Teachers have an extremely significant role in fostering emotional development. Greenspan (1997) suggests five principles for fostering healthy emotional development:

1. Effective teaching must tune in to the child's own developmental level.
2. Effective teaching presents children not with information to assimilate but with problems to solve through active initiative and participation.
3. Effective teaching takes seriously the child's natural inclinations and perspective and uses them as a means of broadening her understanding and experience.
4. A teacher must present material in steps, at a pace appropriate to the child's cognitive abilities and learning style.
5. Effective teaching involves structure and limits.

These five guiding principles are presented in
The Growth of the Mind by Stanley Greenspan (1997).

Greenspan's principles promote individualized education. Each child is different; therefore education for each child should look different. Their interests, development, perspectives, and experiences are crucial in determining content and materials. Children are active participants in life and therefore, should be active participants in their education. However, the activity must occur within appropriate structure and limits. Enabling a child to explore his interests and involving the child's perceptions and experiences does not give license for the child to do anything he wishes. Structure and limits promote emotional health and well-being. Greenspan's developmental principles create an emotionally safe environment. Emotionally safe schools are essential in producing intelligent, competent, children who have the ability to express themselves meaningfully and appropriately.

 # Emotionally Safe Schools

Creating an emotionally safe school is essential in developing intrapersonal and interpersonal intelligence (Bluestein, 2001). Emotionally safe schools can be established through creating environments where children feel safe, can take risks, are challenged but not overly stressed, and where play, pleasure, and fun are facilitated (Bluestein, 2001).

Safety

In order for trust to be established, children must feel safe (Bluestein, 2001). If a child goes to school with fear of being bullied, beat up, or murdered, personal intelligence (along with most other intelligences) is not going to develop appropriately. A safe environment is created by not allowing one child to invade another child's body, space, and material boundaries. A safe environment is one which has clear expectations regarding the safety of all students. Bullying is not tolerated. Conflict resolution skills are taught and modeled by teachers.

Risk Taking

An emotionally safe school allows the child to fail without feeling he is a failure (Bluestein, 2001). Appropriate challenges are facilitated by teachers. Children are not pressured to receive a particular grade or obtain a particular score. Children are expected to debate, discuss, and problem solve. If they come to an incorrect solution, they are encouraged to try again or to try another method of problem solving. Children are not belittled, punished, or embarrassed when they do not succeed or meet their own goals. The child's worth is not determined by his test score or performance. The child is valued because she is a member of the class. In an emotionally safe classroom, teachers make mistakes. They share these mistakes with children and sometimes elicit the children's help in solving their problem.

Stress

Contemporary schoolchildren bring many forms of stress with them to the classroom. The stress can take the form of academic pressure, familial pressure to perform, being part of a single-parent family, hurried schedules, and pressure to grow up too fast (Elkind, 1988; Bluestein, 2001). The pressure can come from school, home, or the media.

Stress causes wear on bodily systems and when one is overstressed, the immune system can be directly affected. Stress uses up energy reserves, demands a greater amount of energy, and forces the body to respond physically through aggression, outbursts, or illness (Elkind, 1988).

Stress can be reduced by making sure children's basic needs are met, they feel safe, and they are able to take risks without fear of failure; and by having appropriate expectations of children at specific ages.

Play, Pleasure, and Fun

Part of developing intrapersonal intelligence is being able to freely engage in pleasurable experiences and recognizing that pleasure, fun, and play are a normal and healthy part of life. Play can encourage the personal intelligences in a variety of ways. A quiet center can be incorporated into the classroom. This is a space where the child can retreat, rest, be alone, work on journals, or calm down. Soft, soothing sensory materials can be available for children to look at or touch. A cardboard box for a child to crawl into with pillows and blankets can be created for children who need to get away from the normal routine for a few minutes. (This is not used as a punishment, but as a child-initiated or teacher-suggested experience to help a child who needs to be alone for a few minutes.)

Puppetry can offer the child an opportunity to communicate feelings and emotions in a nonthreatening environment. The author has made some interesting observations as a puppeteer. Children often try opposite roles with puppets. For example, a child who responds very physically or aggressively will often choose a shy or timid puppet. An introverted child will often choose an aggressive, loud, or large puppet. Children with emotional disorders often prefer to share emotions through the use of a puppet.

The dramatic play area can have props available to encourage children to explore different familial and community roles. Children can begin to establish empathy through role-playing and risk-taking. The dramatic play and music area can also offer culturally appropriate props and instruments. Props that accurately represent various cultures that are relevant to the children's lives can be available for exploration and play.

The personal intelligences can be integrated throughout the rest of the classroom with appropriate facilitation. If a conflict arises between two children, the teacher can help facilitate a resolution. The conflict can be resolved by helping the children to verbalize the situation and allowing each child to state her/his side of the conflict. Acknowledge the child's feelings with words such as, "I can see that made you angry," or "I can see that you are frustrated by this." This validates the child's feelings without judging them. After both sides have been stated, encourage the children to discuss and brainstorm possible solutions to the problem. The teacher should then accept the solution (as long as it respects the safety of the children involved), even if the teacher disagrees with it. This type of conflict resolution encourages the child to take responsibility for the situation, encourages negotiation, and values each child's ideas and input.

In addition to stress, risk-taking, safety, and fun, teachers also have a responsibility for bringing experiences into the class that are emotionally relevant. Emotional relevance depends upon many factors. Culture, age, developmental level, interest, and experiences influence emotional relevance (Hyson, 1994). Hyson (1994, p. 84) advocates materials that "encourage children to talk about, write about, and play about emotionally important ideas." For example, if a plane crashes nearby and children in the class know about it, planes, ambulances, policemen/women, EMTs, and hospital props would be necessary for children to express the events emotionally and cognitively. If a new baby were expected in the home, new baby dolls and care props (diapers, bottles, pacifiers, etc.) would be added to the housekeeping center. Through providing meaningful emotional experiences, a sense of community develops that greatly influences the child's emotional development.

Community

Erikson's and Greenspan's theories of emotional development necessitate social interaction. Social interaction communicates how specific feelings are dealt with and supported in a family and culture. Facilitating appropriate interactions, attending to emotionally relevant experiences and materials, and building relationships with children creates a sense of community in the classroom. Community is an important and necessary component of the early childhood classroom. Community begins with respect (Vance and Weaver, 2002). Respect is encouraged by teacher models, class meetings, and group problem solving (Vance and Weaver, 2002).

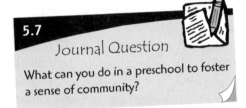

5.7

Journal Question

What can you do in a preschool to foster a sense of community?

Modeling

The teacher has a crucial role to play in promoting emotional development, community, and respect. Her interactions with children, other teachers, and parents create a model of emotional expression. Children pay attention to her body movements, speech patterns, voice level, and words. They pay particular attention to these attributes in times of crisis, anger, or frustration. While it's not possible to approach every situation appropriately, it is essential to approach most situations, especially stressed situations, with the skills one expects children to develop. Every teacher should keep in mind that one of her greatest roles is that of an emotional and social model (Vance and Weaver, 2002).

Class Meetings

Class meetings provide the opportunity for emotional development, personal expression, conflict resolution, and modeling (Vance and Weaver, 2002). Class meetings should occur early in the day to set the tone and to get a feel for the emotional shape the children have arrived in. Class meetings can occur before the beginning of a project, special event, or experience. Class meetings can occur at the end of play, special events, experiences, or at the end of the day. End-of-the-day meetings can serve to acknowledge children's behaviors (Vance and Weaver, 2002), reflect on the day's experiences, talk about challenges and accomplishments, or talk about the direction to take with an activity or project. Class meetings offer a time for problem solving and group discussion of problems that come up in the classroom.

Group Problem Solving

Vance and Weaver (2002) suggest class meetings as a strategy for solving conflicts and problems in the classroom. The meeting may involve the entire class or a few children to whom the problem is relevant to. The process involves, first, stating what the conflict is. Children involved should have the opportunity to describe the problem, uninterrupted, from their point of view. Each child can then state how the problem made him/her feel (Vance and Weaver, 2002). The children can then brainstorm solutions to the problem. Each child can offer a solution. The teacher then facilitates a discussion of the proposed solutions. Next, the teacher asks the children to pick a solution that will work for everybody. All of the children have to agree on the solution for the solution to be used. This requires, at times, more negotiation and brainstorming. The children will also have the opportunity to talk about how they feel about the solution. This process presents experiences from other points of view, validates children's emotions, encourages them to channel emotions appropriately, and validates the individual in a group conflict. These strategies take time, but are well worth the life lessons children will learn from this process (Vance and Weaver, 2002). Most importantly, this process supports and models respect for each child in the classroom.

Relationships

Each of the principles mentioned in facilitating interpersonal and intrapersonal growth value the relationship between the child and his teacher. The relationship identifies and facilitates emotions, cognition, trust, autonomy, initiative, industry, and interaction. Relationships set the stage for the child's ability to identify feelings, control impulses, and appropriately channel emotions. The relationship between child and teacher has the most significant impact on cognition and learning (Greenspan, 1997). If the relationship is unhealthy, the child's cognitive development and ability to learn is greatly impaired (Greenspan, 1997). The child's emotional and social life is also at great risk (Erikson, 1963). There is not a single factor in education more important than the relationships the child has with her/his parents and teachers (Greenspan, 1997). The responsibility for taking relationships seriously supersedes any other educational goal. Relationships and emotions have a great influence on the development of all the intelligences.

Special Education and the Personal Intelligences

Minor challenges in the personal intelligences can present difficulties in the classroom. Significant challenges pose an even more difficult challenge. Meeting the child where they are, and accessing their strengths and interests, will serve as a starting point for addressing personal intelligence challenges (Greenspan, 1997; Armstrong, 2000). See Table 5.2 for personal intelligence strategies.

The Personal Intelligences and Culturally Appropriate Education

Intrapersonal intelligence creates the capacity to respect, accept, and empathize with other cultures. Intrapersonal and interpersonal antibias multicultural strategies include acknowledging and respecting a child's culture, understanding cultural practices and traditions, including relevant and meaningful cultural practices in the classroom, and decentering the traditional European-American emphasis in education.

For Joy, it would be important to understand the traditions and culture of her family. Through interacting with Joy's family, it is apparent that her family observes Chinese New Year. If her family did not celebrate Chinese New Year, it would not be appropriate to address it in the classroom simply because Joy is Chinese. It should be

TABLE 5.2 | *Special Education Strategies*

Name: Zach
Age: 3
Placement: Zach is three years old. He is currently in a regular preschool. Past preschools have discontinued his enrollment due to behavior problems.

Challenges:

Interpersonal:

■ Zach has a difficult time communicating his anger to other children. He becomes angry quickly and hits, bites, and kicks other children.
■ Zach does not make eye contact with his teachers. He frequently ignores his teachers and occasionally swears at them.

Intrapersonal:

■ Zach has difficulty managing his emotions.
■ Zach also has difficulty trying to identify his feelings. He refers to himself as angry and calm, no other feelings.

Strengths:

Bodily/Kinesthetic:

■ Zach has exhibited great bodily/kinesthetic strength. His gross- and fine-motor skills are above most peers.

Spatial:

■ Even though Zach is three, he engages in preschematic art representation. He often asks to draw.

Musical:

■ Zach comes into the classroom each morning singing. He expresses a love and interest in music.

Strategies:

Spatial:

■ Zach has an interest and strength in art. Helping Zach to express emotions through art might help him identify with them.
■ Zach can be asked to make an angry shape with crayons, a happy shape, a sad shape, a scared shape.
■ Zach can be asked to draw a picture of something that scares him, makes him laugh, makes him feel happy, and makes him feel sad.

Music:

■ Several music selections of varying tempos and genres can be played for Zach. A dancing game can be played. Zach will be asked to dance to the tempo. He will be encouraged to move faster, slower, and to stop. This game will help Zach manage his impulses.

Interpersonal:

■ Appropriate interpersonal skills will be modeled by his teacher.
■ Zach can be shadowed by a teacher during play. When a conflict arises, the teacher can step in before Zach begins to hit and model appropriate conflict resolution techniques. The teacher can ask Zach to identify his feelings or say, "I see you are feeling mad," etc. The shadowing must be constant to be effective. Intervening before Zach hurts a child will teach him the appropriate interpersonal skills.

TABLE 5.2 | *Continued*

- When Zach does hurt another child, encourage him to get a Band-Aid, the ice pack, or something to help the child feel better. Comfort the child who got hurt first before talking to Zach. Explain to Zach how that child must feel. Encourage the child who got hurt to tell Zach how that made him feel.

Intrapersonal:

- Read stories individually to Zach that communicate different feelings. Ask Zach how he thought the character in the story felt. Explain to Zach that sometimes you, as a teacher, feel sad, angry, etc., just like the character in the book.
- Use puppets to act out scenarios with Zach. Encourage Zach to solve the problem in a puppet story with his puppet.

addressed because her family enjoys and respects the holiday. Joy's community celebrates Chinese New Year together. Joy's class can be invited to participate in Chinese New Year celebrations in Joy's community. Her family may recommend community leaders and other individuals to come in and explain traditions and share celebrations.

It is important to integrate other aspects of Joy's daily cultural life into the curriculum in order to respect her personal intelligences. Joy's family eats traditional Chinese food with chopsticks. It would be important to offer chopsticks at every meal. Joy, as well as the other children, can choose to eat with chopsticks or forks. Chinese food selections should be available to Joy and the other children on a regular basis. Integrating Chinese food into the menu shows respect for Joy and her family.

Joy's mother has shared Joy's favorite Chinese lullaby. Joy's teacher can sing this lullaby to Joy at rest time. Chinese characters and art can be displayed in the classroom on a daily basis. Chinese music and stories can be integrated into the daily music and literature selection. These antibias multicultural strategies facilitate Joy's autonomy and initiative, and make her and her family feel welcome in the classroom community.

5.8 Journal Questions

Do you feel the personal intelligences are important to foster in a classroom? What will happen to society if the personal intelligences are neglected? What can happen if they are facilitated appropriately?

Summary of the Personal Intelligences

Negotiating, problem solving, sharing, accepting ideas, managing impulses, trust, autonomy, initiative, industry, and recognizing an emotionally safe environment are critical life skills that are necessary in each and every part of adult life. If time and attention are paid to these intelligences when children are young, they will have the opportunity to create an appropriate foundation for an emotionally healthy life. Their intrapersonal intelligence will benefit all aspects of their lives.

In considering the importance of addressing the personal intelligences in the classroom, the author looks to a quote from Karr-Morse and Wiley, the authors of *Ghosts from the Nursery,* "the child they [the adult] once were continues to live at the core of the adult they have become" (Karr-Morse and Wiley, 1997). The early childhood years significantly influence the child's growth and development. Intrapersonal and interpersonal intelligence must be purposefully addressed at the beginning of life and appropriately facilitated throughout the early childhood years.

 ## References

Armstrong, T. (2000) *Multiple intelligences in the classroom.* Alexandria, Va: Association of Curriculum Development.

Bluestein, J. (2001) *Creating emotionally healthy schools: A guide for educators and parents.* Deerfield Beach, FL: Health Communications Inc.

Chen, J., Ed. (1998) *Project spectrum: Early learning activities. Vol 2.* New York: Teachers College Press.

Elkind, D. (1988) *The hurried child.* Cambridge, MA: Perseus Publishing.

Erikson, E. (1963) *Childhood and society.* New York: W.W. Norton & Co.

Gardner, H. (1999) *Intelligences reframed: Multiple intelligences for the 21st century.* New York: Basic Books.

Gardner, H. (1993) *Frames of mind.* New York: Basic Books.

Goleman, D. (1995) *Emotional intelligence.* New York: Bantam Books.

Greenspan, S. (1997) *The growth of the mind and the endangered origins of intelligence.* Cambridge, MA: Perseus Books.

Hyson, M. (1994) *The emotional development of young children: Building an emotion-centered curriculum.* New York: Teachers College Press.

Joint Committee on National Health Education Standards (1995) *National health education standards: Achieving health literacy.* Atlanta: American Cancer Society.

Kamii, C. (1985) *Young children reinvent mathematics: Implications of Piaget's theory.* New York: Teachers College Press.

Karr-Morse, R., & Wiley, M. (1997) *Ghosts from the nursery: Tracing the roots of violence.* New York: The Atlantic Monthly Press.

Teele, S. (2001) *Rainbows of intelligence: Exploring how students learn.* Thousand Oaks, CA: Corwin Press.

Vance, E., & Weaver, P. (2002) *Class meetings: Young children solving problems together.* Washington, DC: NAEYC.

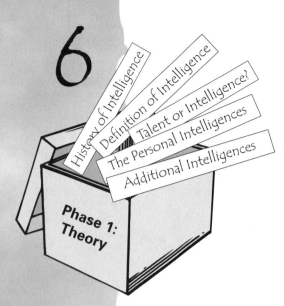

6

**Phase 1:
Theory**

History of Intelligence
Definition of Intelligence
Talent or Intelligence?
The Personal Intelligences
Additional Intelligences

Additional
Intelligences

Since the advent of the multiple intelligence theory presented in 1983 in *Frames of Mind* by Howard Gardner, additional intelligences have been presented, discussed, and challenged. Gardner (1983) suggested that more intelligences might exist and emphasized that the number of intelligences is not as important as looking at intelligence as possessing many different potentials. Intelligence cannot and should not be limited to linguistic and mathematical strengths. Intelligence involves a number of culturally important strengths, each adding meaning, relevance, and validation to the culture itself.

6.1

Journal Questions

Do you think any additional intelligences exist? Why do you think only seven were originally identified?

 ## Naturalist Intelligence

One of the new intelligences mentioned in *Intelligences Reframed* is naturalist intelligence (Gardner, 1999). This intelligence was not included in the original theory; however, Gardner formally announced the acceptance of naturalist intelligence in *Intelligences Reframed*. The naturalist intelligence involves the capacity to recognize and identify patterns and relationships in the natural environment, and the ability to recognize and take responsibility for the effect one has on the environment.

TABLE 6.1	*Naturalist Intelligence Careers/Interests*
Careers Associated with Naturalist Intelligence	Hobbies and Interests Associated with Naturalist Intelligence
Gardener Botanist Scientist Environmentalist Paleontologist Zoologist Veterinarian Meteorologist	Gardening Bird watching Landscaping Mountain climbing

In the NAEYC publication *Reaching Potentials,* science goals are presented by Kilmer and Hofman that are influenced by the Science Framework Addendum. Two of these goals clearly address naturalist intelligence: "to develop each child's innate curiosity about the world" and "to increase each child's knowledge about the natural world" (Kilmer and Hofman, 2001, p. 45). The third goal addresses naturalist and logical intelligence: "to broaden each child's procedural and thinking skills for investigating the world, solving problems, and making decisions" (Kilmer and Hofman, 2001, p. 45). Naturalist capacities are addressed and validated in national children's organizations and national science organizations.

Cultural Validation of Naturalist Intelligence

Cultural validation for the concept of naturalist intelligence exists as well. During the time of the earliest men and women, naturalist intelligence was essential for survival. In the present day, naturalist intelligence continues to play a vital role in all cultures. The natural environment is different from culture to culture and literate and nonliterate cultures must still demonstrate strengths in interpreting the natural environment to ensure survival. Natural phenomenons in countries around the world claim a significant number of lives. The ability to predict, interpret, and prepare for natural phenomena such as earthquakes, blizzards, floods, wildfires, and volcanic eruptions is highly valued in each culture. Literate cultures are also dependent upon the natural environment, but materialistic objects are part of a literate culture's natural world. These are objects such as cars, clothes, and so on that have become important in everyday life. Recognizing and interpreting materialistic objects could also be considered to be part of naturalistic intelligence.

WHY WAS NATURALIST INTELLIGENCE ADDED LATER? Many capacities attributed to naturalist intelligence were placed in various categories of logical, mathematical, and spatial intelligence. However, an overwhelming need to categorize these capacities as different or separate became apparent (Gardner, 1999). The hesitation to add the intelligence came, in part, from the inability to localize an area of the brain responsible for naturalist intelligence. This hesitation might be explained through two theories:

1. This part of the brain might be localized, but not found as of yet.
2. There might not be a localized area of the brain responsible for naturalist intelligence. This area of the brain has been so important for the survival of humankind that it is perhaps the most deeply integrated intelligence in the human brain.

As brain science continues to advance, we are able to get a clearer glimpse into the functions of the brain. With the advance of technology, Gardner (1999) expects to possibly find a locus of control for naturalist intelligence. Gardner (1999) suggests that the naturalist locus might exist in the part of the brain used in classification and recognition of objects. Finding this area of the brain has received very little research attention; researchers may not have found it due to lack of interest.

Another theory is that there is not a single locus for control of naturalist intelligence. Before there was an industrialized and literate world, there was a world much closer to, and dependent upon, nature. Naturalist intelligence was essential for survival and continues to be essential to survival. Early man and many contemporary nonliterate cultures were/are dependent upon their naturalist intelligence in order to survive. This part of the brain may continue to evolve and is now incorporating many of the materialistic objects of industrialized nations. The natural world as well as the materialistic world both contribute to the development of naturalist intelligence.

6.2

Journal Questions

Do you think naturalist intelligence should be considered as an intelligence? Do you think naturalist intelligence is valued in school? In society?

The integration of naturalist intelligence into the other intelligences is crucial for the development of the other intelligences. We use logic and reason to understand the natural world (logical/mathematical). Intrapersonal intelligence can connect us to ourselves and to the natural world. Nature can connect us to the spiritual world and guide our thoughts and actions (intrapersonal). Many of the refined motor movements have been developed through experience moving and surviving in the natural world (bodily/kinesthetic). The natural world is filled with a variety of colors, patterns, and contrasts. Art utilizes these colors, patterns, and contrasts and has a heavy reliance on the natural world.

There are even patterns in the skies and on the land to aid in the navigation of the earth, a developed spatial skill (spatial). There are many beautiful sounds and songs in

FIGURE 6.1 | Butterflies on Flowers

nature. The first musical instruments created by man were made to mimic sounds and songs of nature (musical). Children's first stories are often concerned with nature. Older children hear of struggles between man and nature in fairy tales (linguistic). Naturalist intelligence is intertwined in all areas of man's life and often offers a foundation to build upon other strengths.

 # Naturalist Intelligence and the Early Childhood Curriculum

The facilitation of naturalist intelligence is an important, but often overlooked component of the early childhood curriculum. Children, especially those in school and/or childcare, spend little time outdoors. This happens for a variety of reasons: children's lives are hurried (Elkind, 1989), they watch too much television, outdoor play is not valued by school, and it is simply too scary to allow even older children to play outdoors unsupervised (Kupetz and Twiest, 2002). However, the need to foster this intelligence is high. The facilitation of naturalist intelligence in the classroom can be encouraged under the guidance of three principles.

1. Naturalist intelligence develops in the natural world.
2. Naturalist intelligence involves interaction with natural properties, materials, and mediums (Steiner, 1998).
3. Naturalist intelligence develops in stages.

Natural Intelligence Develops in the Natural World

Natural intelligence develops in the context of the natural world. Children need experiences outdoors to appreciate, respect, and understand their natural environment. Many children no longer have the opportunity to play outdoors at home. Adults can remember outdoor play areas from their childhood. They played in the woods, a neighborhood park, a clubhouse, tree house, or the church parking lot. These places offered refuge, comfort, and kid-control, and are usually associated with happy memories (Elkind, 1989). Children today do not have this. They are sometimes scared to go outside by themselves and have good reason to be. Their physical safety is at risk in these same places that were considered safe by, and offered comfort to, their parents. Children who do have access to outdoor play environments do not always have the time to explore them. Organized sports, dance classes, and other adult-directed extracurricular events monopolize many children's lives (Elkind, 1989). This is why it is so important to create time for outdoor exploration. Children need time to investigate, compare, classify, observe, and communicate and form a relationship with the natural world. Books, movies, and manipulatives cannot possibly offer children the wealth of information that exploration in the natural world can. Scientists, biologists, zoologists, and mathematicians learn about their field from interacting with it. Young children are scientists, biologists, zoologists, and mathematicians. They deserve the same interaction with the environment.

6.3 Journal Activity

Develop a seasonal fairy or doll. It can be made with any materials you choose, but it must reflect one of the seasons. Use the doll to create a season display that would be inviting for young children to interact with.

BRINGING NATURE INSIDE THE CLASSROOM Natural materials can be brought into the classroom so children may have the opportunity to interact with them. Leeuwen and Moeskops (1990) suggest adding a nature corner. A nature corner allows the child to "follow the natural cycle of the year. Changes in the natural world are given expression indoors. The figures on the seasons table depict the essence of what is happening in nature" (Leeuwen and Moeskops, 1990, p. 7). A seasons table can encourage the child to pay closer attention to what is happening outdoors (Leeuwen and Moeskops, 1990). Leeuwen and Moeskops suggest covering the seasons table with a soft, inviting fabric. Nature materials can be presented along with teacher-made dolls and fairies that reflect the season.

Natural Properties, Form, and Materials

The traditional focus of arts education has concentrated on form development and emphasized the final product. The development of art is even viewed as stages of form development. Consequently, early childhood educators have focused and measured success and development in arts education by the forms children create. Form development may be more indicative of spatial and kinesthetic progress, rather than progress in art development.

However, art is not limited to forms alone. Historic and contemporary great artists are certainly not limited to forms. The interpretation and use of color, space, and materials along with the expression of emotions and ideas contribute to art development. Children need to be given the time and opportunity to explore their materials. Learning about color involves more than just naming a color. Color and placement of color conveys feelings, thoughts, and emotions. How two colors are placed together on paper can convey a multitude of meanings. Children should begin their exploration of color using one color. Inspiration for using and mixing colors may come from observing natural color relationships and contrasts in nature: how the sunset plays against the darkening sky, how a snowstorm can turn everything a pure, sparkling white, how rain clouds move swiftly through the sky, how fallen rose petals stand out against the dark rich soil, how the tops of green trees stand out against the clear blue sky, how tiger lilies stretch their warm orange heads to the sun, or how cosmos scatter their fern-like leaves with dazzling purple color.

Natural intelligence involves using and developing natural materials. Waldorf education is noted for its naturalistic approach to education (Steiner, 1998). Nature-made and nature-based materials fill the Waldorf classroom. No plastic or unnatural materials are present. The environment is filled with soft silks, materials from nature, homemade dolls and animals, tree blocks, and natural wood products and materials. Watercolors made from natural materials, beeswax crayons, modeling beeswax, sanded chunks of trees, homemade dolls and puppets, and so on are examples of natural materials that can be provided to children. Beeswax crayons provide the child with a very sensorial approach to color, space, and form. Modeling beeswax provides warmth and can soothe a child as they begin to explore with it. Natural watercolors provide a fluid and beautiful exploration of color. The primary colors should be explored first.

FIGURE 6.2

Children should be encouraged to discover how two colors react and blend and mix naturally with each other on wet watercolor paper. Rocks and tree blocks allow children to recreate and extend experiences witnessed in nature. These materials also allow them to create their own forms, rather than relying on adult-created forms. Cooking can also extend naturalist experiences. Children can grow wheat, harvest it, grind it into flour, make bread dough, shape the dough, then cook and eat the bread.

These Waldorf-inspired materials and experiences are important for all children. The materials help the child realize her naturalist potential and create a love and respect of the environment. The child realizes what resources are available in the natural environment and develops an understanding as to how to access these resources. Children must have the opportunity to manipulate and observe their natural environment in order to understand, respect, and interpret it.

Naturalist intelligence can be encouraged by the addition of natural materials in most areas of the classroom. Tree blocks can replace or be added to the block area.

Shells, starfish, pinecones, and stones can be added to the sand/water area to facilitate creative/expressive play. Natural objects can be made available for investigation under a microscope or magnifying glass in the science area. A garden can be created by the children inside or outside of the classroom. Miniature fairy gardens can be created by and for the children. In the outdoor play area, a sunflower house can be grown for children. A butterfly terrarium can be built for children who do not have the opportunity to see butterflies in nature. A nature corner or table can be established. Nature-inspired roles can be explored in the dramatic play area. The nature table helps the child to celebrate the seasonal changes in nature. Seasonal nature objects, dolls that represent nature and nature stories, and objects children bring from home can be included on the table.

Season changes can be celebrated with young children. Poetry can incite beautiful imagery associated with seasonal changes (Kupetz and Twiest, 2002). Children can create stories and listen to seasonal stories. Festivals that signify the change in a season can be held at the school. There are books that present factual and fantasy information about the seasons. The beauty of season changes can be brought out in stories, art, and music.

Symbol Development and Naturalist Intelligence

Naturalist intelligence does have a symbol system. The symbol system is related to specific fields. For example, meteorology, paleontology, and botany each have a specific symbol system. Particular weather patterns predict and symbolize current weather. Paleontologists interpret fossils, bones, and artifacts. Botanists classify, categorize, and recognize plants. The leaf, stem, and flower of a plant can communicate meanings relevant to botany. Meteorology, paleontology, and botany each have specific vocabulary and symbols that are indicative of their respective fields.

Children begin to explore nature through the senses. They smell flowers and freshly cut grass; watch the wind blow across the treetops; observe clouds; taste mint leaves picked from a garden; touch a sensitive plant, pinecone, or tree bark; and listen to birds, crickets, and bees.

Nature is also explored and interpreted on a physical level. Children engage in motor play in and with nature. They will run through grass; roll down a hill; pretend to fly like a butterfly, crawl like a kitten, or grow like a flower. Naturalist intelligence is represented through motor movements.

After children have perceived the natural world with their senses and interpreted the world physically, they begin to interpret and create symbols of the natural world.

Evidence of this lies within a variety of disciplines. A child will see a dark cloud and recognize that this symbol means rain is coming. The child will begin to draw flowers, trees, and the sun. The child will represent nature in the block area. Buildings might be built, then knocked down by a violent earthquake. The child will help build a snowman, or paint a bird feeder. The child may find a unique rock and identify it as a dinosaur fossil. Children will begin to use the vocabulary specific to the variety of fields that exist in naturalist intelligence. The vocabulary may be used nonsensically and many vocabulary words will be made up. Figure 6.3 demonstrates a child's first attempts at symbolizing nature.

The symbols will begin to become more creative and expressive. A theme will begin to emerge from the drawings, clay, blocks, etc. Children will pretend they are a seed growing into a beautiful flower. The children will incorporate natural themes into their play. For example, they may incorporate a snowstorm into their block area, or a thunderstorm that forces the picnic in the housekeeping area indoors, or ice fishing that becomes dangerous when a friend falls through the ice, or in a dinosaur dig on the playground.

FIGURE 6.3 | A Representation of Waterlillies by Monet.

Children will begin to make up explanations for natural phenomenon and believe they have some magical power over the weather or to make things grow. They will be able to plan a small garden, make up nature stories, and use music to symbolize sounds in nature. Figure 6.4 represents a sunflower house, built and tended to by five-year-olds.

The child's explanations for natural events become more believable (they may not be correct, but their explanations begin to make more sense). This occurs as children begin to differentiate between reality and fantasy. Imagination and fantasy, however, still play a big part in their interpretation of natural events. The child begins to see the relationship of rules in nature. For example, a child begins to understand that when something dies, it cannot come back. Rules for taking care of nature will begin to

FIGURE 6.4 |

emerge as well. They understand the importance of not littering and taking care of the environment (in programs where the environment is valued). As the child progresses to concrete operations, she begins to understand and is interested in recycling, conserving, and preserving the environment.

Naturalist Intelligence in a Natural World

Children should be encouraged to interact with the natural world on a daily basis. There are many man-made materials that aid a child's understanding of the natural world, but none are more important than the natural world itself. Interaction with the outdoors should never be limited solely to recess, but valued as an extensive learning opportunity that can be guided through gentle facilitation and a knowledgeable teacher. Large glass windows for observing need to be incorporated into every class-room. Natural light provides essential nutrients to the body, improves the mind, and elevates mood (Kupetz and Twiest, 2002). A large window invites a child to observe, a critical naturalist skill, when weather prohibits children from being outside. Field trips to zoos, museums, botanical gardens, science centers, and nature preserves allow children to see masters in these fields at work (Kupetz and Twiest, 2002). These kinds of experiences allow children to understand relationships and acquire information about their world. These experiences are invaluable learning opportunities, and should not be limited to end-of-the-year field trips. Children need to be questioned about their experience and invited to extend it in their classroom through drawings, stories, in-class museums, dance, dioramas, puppet plays, nature tables, and art experiences. Aesthetic development can be inspired with naturalistic materials.

Naturalist Intelligence and Special Education

In most of the other intelligences, challenges were easy to identify. Children are not referred for special education because of naturalist challenges. However, it is important to note that some children can demonstrate an extreme sensitivity to sounds, touch, or smells (Greenspan, 1997). These sensitivities may make outdoor time challenging. Some children are extremely sensitive to grass; others may be able to hear sounds barely heard by others. Bird calls may be deafening to some children. There are children who are extremely sensitive to natural light. Environmental allergens also pose a problem. Children with severe allergies or asthma may have a difficult time with the outdoors, animals, and/or natural materials that are brought indoors. Children with extreme sensitivities may avoid time outdoors altogether.

Naturalist strength can be used to help children deal with other intelligence challenges. The natural world may facilitate language, encourage motor exploration, demonstrate boundaries, and provide inspiration for aesthetic representation.

Table 6.2 offers a description of Ming. Her challenges, strengths, and strategies are addressed through the intelligences. Ming's sensitivity to touch and sound bring a unique challenge to the classroom, especially for outdoor play. This table will focus on her unique sensitivities and the characteristics that challenge her naturalist development.

6.4

Journal Question

How could you use naturalist intelligence to encourage language development?

Naturalist Intelligence and Culturally Appropriate Education

The natural world offers a place for children to appreciate, respect, and share their surroundings. The natural world can provide an entry point for language, games, and art.

Chinese poetry can be brought into the classroom during story or morning meetings. There is beautiful Chinese poetry that addresses the aesthetics of the natural world. Poems can be read in Chinese and English to all of the children. There are many Chinese fairy and folk tales that address natural phenomena. These stories can be read to all of the children and housed in the classroom literature area. It would also be important to include nature books with Chinese character identification.

TABLE 6.2 | *Special Education Strategies*

Name: Ming
Age: 6
Placement: Ming attended a preschool for children with Pervasive Developmental Disorder (PDD). She is currently enrolled in a regular kindergarten, with an aide, and does have a support specialist for learning and speech support. The support specialist provides services as a pull-out program.

Challenges:

Naturalist

Ming has an extreme sensitivity to touch. She does not like the touch or feel of grass on her legs. If she falls in the grass, she becomes extremely frightened.

Linguistic

Ming frequently engages in echolalia. She mimics the intonation, speech pattern, and words of others, and of favorite cartoons/movies.

Strengths:

Music

- Ming responds instantly to music. It has a calming effect on her. She enjoys the familiarity of the musical selection and it can serve as a motivating factor for addressing her sensitivities.

Strategies:

Naturalist

- A long pair of pants, gloves, and a long-sleeve sweatshirt with a zipper is on hand for Ming at all times. If it is time for outdoor play, Ming pulls on her pants, zips her sweatshirt, and puts on mittens. Her extreme sensitivity to touch causes this process to take more time. She is given a private spot in the center to pull her own clothes on slowly. Once outdoors, a teacher stays in close proximity to Ming in case she becomes uncomfortable. The outdoor space is in a grassy area. The grass is maintained constantly and cut grass is raked and bagged on a weekly basis. A large soft blanket is brought out for Ming. She approaches the outdoors by sitting on the blanket for a while until she is comfortable. She then can walk and play in the grass, but has the freedom to come back to the blanket play when needed.
- A large magnifying tripod is provided outside for Ming to use. Natural objects may be placed under the tripod for Ming to see. She does not have to touch the objects and the tripod makes her feel there is a comfortable boundary between her and the object.
- Naturalist objects are brought into the classroom and placed on the sensory table. Gloves and a tripod are available for Ming to use.
- Mittens and magnifying tripods are also available for other children to use as well.

Music

When Ming plays outside, a small portable CD player is placed on her blanket. When Ming exhibits stress outside she is brought over to the blanket and Ming's favorite music is played. The music has a calming effect on Ming. Music is also played during transition times indoors to signal the change from indoor to outdoor activities. If Ming demonstrates hesitation at outdoor time, she is encouraged to choose music and carry the CD player outside herself.

Summary of Naturalist Intelligence

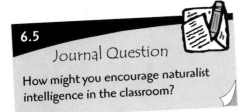

Naturalist intelligence is deeply integrated into every intelligence. Naturalist intelligence is essential for cultural survival. This intelligence can be brought into the classroom through stories, seasonal materials, nature walks, field trips, and the use of natural materials.

 # Existential Intelligence

Officially, Gardner has endorsed eight intelligences: linguistic, logical/mathematical, spatial, music, bodily/kinesthetic, interpersonal, intrapersonal, and naturalist. Gardner (1999) does hold the possibility that more intelligences may exist, but these additional intelligences are theoretical, and have not been endorsed as intelligences. The possibilities include an existential or spiritual intelligence, and a moral intelligence.

Addressing Spiritual Nature

Spiritual intelligence does not address the organized means of dealing with spiritual nature through religion. Spiritual intelligence addresses "spiritual concerns . . . in a more personal, idiosyncratic, or creative manner" (Gardner, 1999, p. 54). Gardner (1999) approaches spiritual intelligence through three venues: concern with existential issues, state of being, and effect on others. Existential issues deal with questions concerning the meaning of life. State of being approaches spiritual intelligence through "psychological states." These would include meditation, prayer, psychic ability, and a connection with spirituality (Gardner, 1999). The third approach is through a spiritual effect on others. Some individuals feel a stronger connection to the spiritual world and many times these individuals offer inspiration and hope to others. In examining these approaches, Gardner concludes that existential concerns provide the most cognitive approach to spirituality. Questions of existence can be addressed with or without religious influence. Gardner addresses spirituality through an intelligence he calls *existentialism*. Existentialism is "the capacity to locate oneself with respect to the furthest reaches of the cosmos—the infinite and the infinitesimal—and the related capacity to locate oneself with respect to such existential features of the human condition as the significance of life, the meaning of death, and the ultimate fate of the physical and the psychological worlds, and such profound experiences as love of another person or total immersion in a work of art" (Gardner, 1999, p. 60).

Existential intelligence is still very theoretical in nature. A careful examination and application of the criteria developed by Gardner to identify an intelligence has not, of yet, been carried out with existential intelligence.

Moral Intelligence

The idea of the existence of moral intelligence is intriguing. Gardner wrestled with the notion of a moral intelligence, but came to the conclusion that morality as an intelligence was not plausible (Gardner, 1999). A moral intelligence does not meet the intelligence requirements set forth by Gardner in *Frames of Mind*. Morality deals with the kind of person one is, not with the sophistication or cultural admiration of an individual's moral wisdom (Gardner, 1999). In *Intelligences Reframed,* Gardner (1999, p. 77) explains, "Morality is then properly a statement about personality, individuality, will, character and, in the happiest cases, about the highest realization of human nature." The application of intelligence is influenced by morality. Gardner (1999) explains that any of the intelligences can be applied in moral and immoral ways. For example, a skilled surgeon, possessing great bodily/kinesthetic strength, can purposely choose to murder a patient. The fact that he killed his patient was an immoral act. This immoral act does not take away from the surgeon's bodily/kinesthetic strength. A politician, with self-serving motives, can use his/her interpersonal strengths to manipulate voters or excuse immoral behavior. Morality, in conclusion, is not an intelligence, but can describe the application of intelligence.

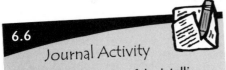

6.6

Journal Activity

Make yourself a chart of the intelligences. Include a symbol of the intelligence, a definition, and careers and interests that are associated for each intelligence.

Conclusion

This chapter concludes the theoretical phase of this early childhood text. Journal activity will encourage you to reflect on the information you have learned about the intelligences.

References

Elkind, D. (1989) *The hurried child.* Cambridge, MA: Perseus Publishing.

Gardner, H. (1983) *Frames of mind.* New York: Basic Books.

Gardner, H. (1999) Intelligences reframed: Multiple intelligences for the 21st century. New York: Basic Books.

Greenspan, S. (1997) *The growth of the mind and the endangered origins of intelligence.* Cambridge, MA: Perseus Books.

Kilmer, S., & Hofman, H. (2001) "Transforming science curriculum." *Reaching potentials: Transforming early childhood curriculum and assessment* (Vol. 2, pp. 43–62). Washington, DC: NAEYC.

Kupetz, B., & Twiest, M. (2002) "Nature, literature and young children: A natural combination." *Young Children* (Vol. 55, No. 1, p. 59).

Leeuwen, M., & Moeskops, J. (1990) *The nature corner: Celebrating the year's cycle with a seasonal tableau.* Netherlands: Floris Books.

Steiner, R. (1998) *Rhythms of learning: What Waldorf education offers children, parents, & teachers.* Hudson, NY: Anthroposophic Press.

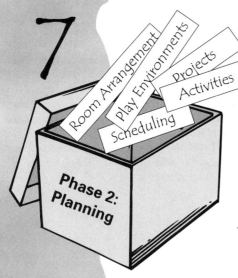

Phase 2: Planning

7

Facilitating the Intelligences with Activities and Projects

C hapter 7 begins the next phase of curriculum development—planning. Planning is one of the most challenging tasks for the early childhood teacher. The planning phase of curriculum development in this text provides:

1. Activities
2. Projects
3. Play environments
4. Scheduling, and
5. Room arrangement

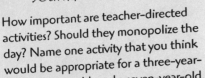

7.1

Journal Questions

How important are teacher-directed activities? Should they monopolize the day? Name one activity that you think would be appropriate for a three-year-old, five-year-old, and a seven-year-old.

A variety of teacher- and child-directed experiences are crucial in a developmentally appropriate environment. This text emphasizes the importance of the child's construction of knowledge. Therefore, child-initiated and collaborative experiences have a central role in the early childhood curriculum. Teacher-directed experiences are also important and do have value. A developmentally appropriate program does not ignore teacher-directed experiences, nor does such a program devalue the importance of teacher-directed experiences (Bredekamp and Copple, 1997). However, teacher-directed activities cannot consume the child's day. This text will categorize teacher-directed experiences as activities; child-initiated experiences as play; and collaborative experiences as projects.

Activities

Activities are not developed without considering the children's interests, needs, and developmental levels. The motivation for the activity comes from observing the child and creating an autonomous relationship with the child. The activities can present a developmentally appropriate skill, introduce or review a concept, extend *into* a play experience, or extend *from* a play experience. Regardless of the intention, the activity must be relevant to the child and presented in an appropriate way. Sometimes activities will have a very specific purpose. Many times the teacher will present the materials, generalize a purpose, and leave the exploration of the activity materials up to each individual child.

The purpose of the activity in the sample activity plans will take the form of an activity objective. The objective will attempt to generalize the purpose for the activity. Core intelligence concepts will also be listed on the activity plan. *The objective and the core concepts serve the function of communicating the teacher's expectations and generalizing the purpose of the experience. What the children will actually take from the experience will differ.* Unexpected concepts will be explored and mastered in the activity. Individual children will bring their individual strengths and challenges to the experience. This must be encouraged and expected. An interesting activity that has relevance to the child's life may encourage the child to ask a question or further explore a topic that he may not have thought of on his own.

The length of the activity should depend upon the interest of the children participating. The teacher-presentation part of the activity will depend upon the age of the children and their interest. Teacher-directed activities could be planned for one student, a small group, or a whole group.

When planning activities for young children, a written plan is useful and necessary. A written plan will help to:

- Clarify the teacher's purpose for providing the activity,
- Visualize the necessary materials,
- Examine the developmental rationale for the experience, and
- Clarify the procedure.

The following sample activity plans provide essential components for planning activities for young children. This lesson plan has been influenced by the activity plans suggested in Project Spectrums' Activity book (Chen, Krechevsky, and Viens, 1998) and the GOLD curriculum published by Louise Child Care (Schomburg, Smith, and Tittnich, 1986).

The sample activity plans provide ideas for activities that address each intelligence. This collection provides a starting point to help facilitate multiple-intelligence thinking and to facilitate appropriate activities for young children. Many ideas for activities will (and should) come from the children. It is extremely important to facilitate activities that are appropriate for each child. The National Association for the Education of Young Children (NAEYC) has created a publication, *Developmentally Appropriate Practices,* by Sue Bredekamp and Carol Copple (1997) that can serve as a guide in facilitating developmentally appropriate activities. Many of the following activities address a number of the intelligence areas even though they are located under just one intelligence heading. A single activity can address more than one intelligence.

Catapult

Logical/Mathematical
Ages 5–8

Activity Objective: The child will construct a catapult and measure the distance selected objects will travel.

Core Concepts:
- The child will explore and employ estimation strategies.
- The child will estimate and measure using various units.

Materials: Foam or wood blocks of varying lengths, 12" lengths of construction paper cut to look like feet, miniature animals, and people

Developmental Rationale: This activity was inspired by a group of kindergarten children playing in the block area. They constructed small catapults out of blocks and began to launch small figures across the classroom. The children began estimating how far their figures would go, and what types of blocks they should use. A safer place to explore this activity was cleared in the classroom. The children experimented using blocks of varying lengths. They estimated how far their figures would go and then measured the objects to see how close their estimates were. This is a wonderful example of how children let adults know what kinds of activities they are interested in and what laws of physics they are ready to investigate.

Procedure: Demonstrate how a catapult is made. Lay a small block on the floor. Balance a longer block across the smaller one lengthwise (so it looks like a seesaw). Place a small figure on the end of the longer block, closest to you. Smack the other end of the block with your hand to launch the figure. Have the children guess how far their figure traveled or would travel. Measure the distance using 12" feet. The children can record and compare their results. They can also discuss which launching techniques, blocks, and figures traveled the farthest, shortest, and so on.

Animal Tracks

Logical/Mathematical
Ages 5–7

Activity Objective: The child will identify an animal by the animal's tracks.

Core Concepts: The child will classify and compare objects.

Materials: Polaroid camera, nature-track cards, pictures of animals, notebook, bird feeder, birdseed, peanuts, and bread

Developmental Rationale: This experience could also fall under the naturalist category; however, it has been placed under logical/mathematical because of the activity's attention to problem solving. Children are curious and interested in their natural world. This activity allows the child to hypothesize, investigate, and come to a conclusion.

Procedure: In the winter, place a bird feeder, bread, and peanuts in a snowy area outside. Ask the children to guess what kind of animals they think will come to the feeder. They may draw pictures in a notebook of the animals they think will come. The following day, take the children outside to see the feeder. Ask the children what evidence they can find of the animals that may have come to the feeder. Many children will point out animal tracks and food fragments. Ask the children what we can use to identify the animals. Take pictures of the animals' prints using a Polaroid camera. Bring the pictures inside and lay them on the table. Ask the children to examine the tracks. What kind of animals could have

made the tracks? Have each child choose a picture to place in their notebook and draw a picture of the animal they think made the tracks.

Next, provide the children with animal-track cards. The cards will have animal tracks on one side and the animal that made the tracks on the other. The children can find the track they placed in their notebook and determine what animal made the track. Ask the children if their original hypothesis was correct. Then ask the children to draw their conclusion, what kind of animal made their track. If they are still uncertain, have them brainstorm methods for finding out what animal made the track.

Letter Box Treasure Hunts

Linguistic
Ages 5–6

Activity Objective: The child will explore a box containing objects that begin with the same sound.

Core Concepts:
- The child will begin to explore letter sounds.
- The child will begin to identify a few uppercase letters.

Materials: Small box with an uppercase letter on it

Developmental Rationale: The child can begin to explore letter sounds when they have mastered language-mediated play in most areas of development. This experience encourages the child to pay attention to sounds and to locate sounds in the environment. It offers an appropriate way to explore letter sound through manipulation of the contents in the box.

Procedure: Gather familiar objects that begin with the same sound and place them in a small box. Display the box (with a letter on the top) in the

classroom. The children are free to explore the box. The teacher can ask if there are any similarities among the objects in the box. The child can be encouraged to hunt for other objects in the room that begin with the same sound to put in the box.

Shaving Cream on Feet

Linguistic
Ages 4–5

Activity Objective: The children will describe what it is like to place their feet in shaving cream.

Core Concepts:
- The child will develop the skills necessary to communicate successfully.
- The child will develop a large vocabulary.
- The child will represent language creatively and expressively.
- The child will use adjectives in speech.

Materials: Shaving cream for sensitive skin, shower curtain, plastic drop cloth, plastic basin, rags, towels

Developmental Rationale: This activity allows the child to explore common materials in an unusual

way. This activity inspires the child to spontaneously verbalize the experience. This activity exposes and encourages children to use adjectives to describe experiences.

Procedure: The children (three to four maximum per group) take off their socks and shoes. The teacher lays a plastic drop cloth or an old shower curtain on the floor, and arranges chairs around the drop cloth. The children sit in the chairs and place their feet on the floor. Shaving cream is then squirted on and under their feet. The children put their feet in the cream and spread it around. Encourage them to talk about what they are doing and how the shaving cream feels. Encourage the children to use words to describe the feeling of the shaving cream. It is important to explain to the children that they are *not* to stand up and that they should keep the shaving cream to themselves. When each child is finished, place the water basin under

their feet. Have them place their feet in the basin and gently wash their feet and then dry them. Turn their chairs around so they can stand up on the floor and not in the shaving cream.

Museum Art

Bodily/Kinesthetic
Ages 5–8

Activity Objective: The child will represent a piece of artwork through manipulation of the body.

Core Concepts: The child will creatively manipulate the body to recreate experiences, represent objects in the environment, tell a story, convey feelings, and share information.

Materials: A large picture frame

Developmental Rationale: Art can be expressed and interpreted in a variety of ways. This experience allows the child to represent art through the

manipulation of the body and to communicate the interpretation to others.

Procedure: Plan a field trip to an art museum. Take a large picture frame on the field trip. After looking at specific pieces of artwork, invite a group of children or an individual child to represent the artwork by standing behind the picture frame and creatively moving the body and interacting with others to communicate the interpretation of the piece of art.

Charcoal Drawings

Bodily/Kinesthetic
Ages 6–8

Activity Objective: The child will use charcoal drawing techniques to create a picture.

Core Concept: The child will manipulate art media to represent an experience or idea.

Materials: Colored charcoal, brushes, paper

Developmental Rationale: As children work on the industry stage of development, they become interested in adult tools and roles. Sharing adult tools, techniques, and roles is very appropriate for children in this age group. This activity allows the adult to share an art technique, build kinesthetic

skill, and still allow for the child's creativity and individual expression.

Procedure: Introduce the child to colored charcoal. Talk about how the colored charcoal looks, feels, and moves on paper. Demonstrate how charcoal can be used to outline, shade, and blend. Demonstrate how the brush can help shape and blend the charcoal colors. Demonstrate how the tip and sides of the charcoal can be used to make different kinds of lines and shapes. Provide the children with a set of colored charcoal, brushes, and paper and allow them to experiment with the materials.

Writing Music

Musical
Ages 4–6

Activity Objective: The child will use symbols to represent music on staff paper.

Core Concepts:
- The child will represent ideas and the experience of music symbolically.
- The child will write and read music.

Materials: Enlarged blank staff paper, markers, child piano with colored keys

Developmental Rationale: Young children experiment with formal symbol systems through spontaneously creating symbols. This activity allows the child to create music symbols and begin to understand their function. The child is given the opportunity to create the symbol and attempt to musically "read" the symbol in context.

Procedure: Provide the child with enlarged staff paper and colored markers. Match the color of the markers with the color of the keys on the child-sized piano. Encourage the child to "write" her own music on the staff lines. The child can then use her music to play the piano. Encourage the child to play what she wrote.

The four-year-old child will scribble and mark a few music-like symbols. The child will bang on the keyboard at random while looking at the staff paper.

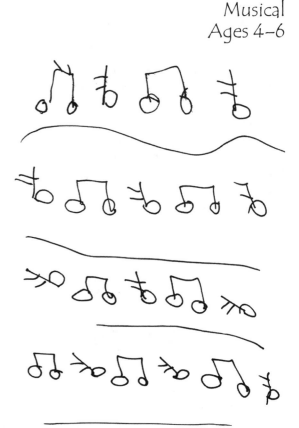

The five/six-year-old will create color-specific music-like symbols on the staff paper and play those notes (according to the note's color) on the piano.

Floor Piano

Activity Objective: The child will move up and down a floor piano and make the sounds that a piano would make.

Core Concepts:
- The child will demonstrate a familiarity with a variety of musical instruments.
- The child will identify a sound pattern.

Materials: Black and white construction paper, clear contact paper

Developmental Rationale: Musical intelligence needs to be investigated auditorily, physically, emotionally, and through words. This activity allows musical intelligence to be investigated through physical movement.

Procedure: Over a period of several weeks, play an actual piano or play piano music for the children. Talk about what it sounds like. Allow the children to play a piano or keyboard or to listen to piano music (such as Chopin). Tape black and white construction paper to a carpeted surface in a piano pattern. Cover with clear contact paper. Encourage the child to dance on the floor keyboard to the music. As the child's understanding of music increases, the child will move on the floor piano according to high/low notes. Names of notes can be put on the floor piano. The child can step on a note and another child can play the note on a real piano.

Mirror Images

Activity Objective: The child will observe his/her reflection in a mirror and paint what he/she sees.

Core Concepts:
- The child will perceive and interpret the environment through her senses.
- The child will create art representations of herself.
- The child will critically observe the spatial details of an object.

Materials: Full-length mirror, acrylic paints (that represent different skin tones, eye colors, feature colors, etc.), acetate, tape, stapler, poster board, thin paintbrushes

Developmental Rationale: The mirror activity provides the child an opportunity to creatively represent their self-image. This activity helps the

child understand and represent the image of the self and pay close attention to facial details.

Procedure: Spread a drop cloth on the floor under a supported full-length mirror. Tape a piece of acetate on the mirror directly in front of the child's reflection of his/her face. The child stands facing the mirror while the teacher asks the child questions about his/her reflection: "What color eyes do you have?" "How is your hair fixed today?" and so on.

Encourage the child to paint his/her face while watching it in the mirror. When the child is finished, gently pick up the acetate and place on a piece of white poster board. Staple the acetate to the poster board.

A Collection

Spatial
Ages 6–8

Activity Objective: The child will create a collection of objects and arrange them aesthetically.

Core Concepts:
■ The child will arrange objects in the environment for aesthetic purposes.
■ The child will display groupings of objects.
■ The child will arrange objects according to spatial features.
■ The child will classify objects.

Materials: Objects from nature that the child collects

Developmental Rationale: Children frequently observe, discuss, and interact with displays of objects that adults have designed. This experience provides the child the opportunity to create her own grouping based on aesthetic and spatial criteria.

Procedure: Plan a trip to a museum. Point out to the children the various collections of objects that are displayed at the museum. Ask the children why they think certain objects are grouped together. Facilitate a discussion concerning the purpose, meaning, and planning behind each display. After

the trip, invite the children to take a nature walk. Encourage the children to collect objects found along the walk. Bring the objects back to the classroom and encourage the children to talk about the objects they found. How would they classify the objects? Could specific groupings be made from these objects? How should the objects be displayed? The children can work in small groups to create a collection, then display and label their collection.

I Can Do it Myself!

Intrapersonal
Ages 3–5

Activity Objective: The child will be able to zip, button, lace, and tie.

Core Concept: The child will develop self-help skills.

Materials: Child's own clothes and coat

Developmental Rationale: Dressing oneself is a very important task that allows the child to feel secure and self-confident. This activity encourages the child to become more independent and develop necessary self-help skills.

Procedure: It is important to encourage the development of self-help skills in context in the classroom. When the child comes into the classroom in the morning, encourage the child to unzip or unbutton his/her own coat and hang it in the appropriate place. Before the child goes home, encourage the child to zip, button, or snap his/her own coat. If the child's shoe becomes untied, show the child how to tie their shoe and talk about what you are doing. Encourage the child to try it one step at a time. Each time the child uses the restroom, encourage the child to button, snap, or zip his/her own pants.

Family Portraits

Intrapersonal
Ages 5–8

Activity Objective: The child will paint a portrait of his/her family.

Core Concepts:
- The child will communicate information to peers through symbols.
- The child will be able to represent familial roles.

Materials: Paints, large/medium/small/fine-line paintbrushes, smocks, drop cloths, large easels, famous paintings of families, pictures of each child's family

Developmental Rationale: In order to understand and communicate the child's own role and responsibility in a family, the child needs to communicate other family member roles. If the roles in the child's family are confusing, talking about them can help identify and define them.

Procedure: Ask the children to bring in a picture of their family. Have each child in a large or small group talk about their family; who is in their family, what kinds of things each family member does, what each family member's job is. Encourage the child to identify his/her own role and responsibility. Talk about how each family is different and how special

and unique that is! Afterward, show the children some professional paintings of families. Display the professional paintings in the painting area. Talk about who is in the pictures. Invite each child to paint each family member. Display the child's paintings with the professional paintings in the painting area and/or in a center that reflects the uniqueness of each child.

Chair Bound

Interpersonal
Ages 4–8

Activity Objective: The child will experience activities in the classroom from a wheelchair.

Core Concepts:
- The child will experience activities from a uniquely challenged child's perspective.
- The child will respect another child's body and belongings.

Materials: Wheelchairs for each child

Developmental Rationale: The young child is developing empathy. (The seven-year-old will be able to feel and express empathy appropriately.) Empathy is learned through experience. This activity allows each child to experience the challenges and pleasures of being confined to a wheelchair.

Procedure: Contact a local children's hospital. Ask the hospital if they would be willing to let your class borrow wheelchairs for each student for a day. Provide each class member with a wheelchair. If there is not a child in the classroom who uses one, invite someone who uses one in to demonstrate how to use the chair. Encourage the individual to share her thoughts on being confined to a wheelchair. Have the children use the chair for all classroom activities for an entire class day. Provide a fun gross-motor experience for the children—chair volleyball, basketball, races, etc. Encourage the children to share their experiences and feelings about using the chair for the day.

Picture Puppets

Interpersonal
Ages 3–5

Activity Objective: The child will manipulate the puppets to take on the role of another child or teacher in the classroom.

Core Concepts:
- The child will understand and respect social and cultural diversity.
- The child will communicate information about others using symbols.
- The child will notice emotional distinctions and interpret moods.
- The child will interact with other children and adults empathetically.
- The child will communicate information to peers through dramatization.
- The child will be able to solve social conflicts appropriately.

Materials: Pictures of each child's face, Popsicle sticks, clear tape, large shoe box/cardboard box, construction paper, miniature life toys to represent different areas of the classroom

Developmental Rationale: This experience allows the child to interact with puppets that represent each child and teacher in the classroom. The experience communicates to the teacher the child's likes and dislikes, how she interprets her peers, how she thinks her peers see her, specific phrases used by peers and teachers, and what kinds of relationships the child has with peers and teachers.

Procedure: Cut out pictures of each child's face. Tape the face to a Popsicle stick. Use the box to make a small-scale classroom. Mark the different centers in the box by taking pictures of the centers in the classroom. Encourage the children to role-play using the puppets in the box. They will take on the roles of the other children in the classroom. Also include pictures of the teachers. It is interesting to see how the children perceive each teacher. This activity can be a way for the children to unknowingly evaluate the teachers.

 **Gardening**

Naturalistic
Ages 3–8

Activity Objective: The child will plan, plant, and take care of a garden.

Core Concepts:

- The child will recognize and take responsibility for the effect he/she has on the environment.
- The child will acquire knowledge about the natural world.
- The child will develop strategies for organizing and interpreting information from the natural world.
- The child will classify natural objects.
- The child will explain cause/effect relationships.
- The child will initiate changes to the environment.
- The child will observe and record information about the natural environment.

Materials: Outdoor space, worms, topsoil, plants/seeds/flowers (of the child's choice), watering cans, shovels, rakes, gloves, other gardening tools

Developmental Rationale: With the realization that one has an effect on the outside environment comes a new-found respect for it. This activity makes the child responsible for a small part of the environment around them.

Procedure: Invite a local gardener to come in to the classroom and talk to the children about what planting a garden involves. In the Spring, have the children draw a plan for the garden. Have the children measure the ground, clear away the grass, and turn over the soil. The children can then add topsoil. The children can vote on what kind of plants to have. Have a child write to the National Arbor Day Foundation for some inexpensive small trees. Ask parents for seed donations. Have the children follow their plan for where to plant the seeds and trees. Remind the children to read the directions and to measure how far apart the seeds and trees go. Have the children assign roles to take care of the

garden through the Spring, Summer, and Fall. If the children choose vegetables, be sure to have the children harvest, wash, and prepare the vegetables for a snack. They can share the snack with their parents and/or the gardener who spoke to them at the beginning of the activity. If outdoor space is not available, construct a large wooden box. Line the box with a large plastic drop cloth. Add a mixture of topsoil, potting soil, and peat moss. Add worms for soil aeration and a little corn meal to feed the worms. Sturdy, clear plastic can be used for one of the sides of the planting box. Cover the plastic with black paper. Plant seeds close to the plastic side of the box. Remove the paper periodically to check on worm tunnels and root growth. Be sure not to overwater the indoor garden. The children can experiment with their plants by blocking the sun from them, not watering them, planting them too close together, and so on. Each child can keep a picture log of the progress of the garden.

Ideas for Helping Children Plan Gardens: Planning a garden requires many skills. For younger children, tape small pictures of plants to tooth picks. Provide the child a flat tray of slightly wet sand. Instruct the child to arrange the plants in the sand. Provide a small area for young children to garden in. Using their model, help the children choose and plant the items as they are represented in their sand model.

If the children can represent forms schematically, encourage them to draw a plan for a garden. Talk about what types of plants might do well next to each other. Have the children share their plans and discuss/debate their ideas for the garden. The garden might follow a theme (such as a pizza garden with basil, oregano, and tomatoes; a vegetable garden; or butterfly garden). After the children agree on one plan they can choose roles for carrying out the plan to create their garden.

Fairy Gardens

Naturalistic
Ages 3–8

Activity Objective: The child will design, care for, and interact with a miniature fairy garden.

Core Concepts:

- The child will engage in all levels of play with the fairy gardens.
- The child will use natural objects in functional ways.
- The child will identify differences between natural and man-made objects.
- The child will care for a plant.
- The child will maintain a small garden.

Materials: At a local craft store, purchase miniature (doll-house-furniture-size) shovels, wheelbarrows, garden hats, benches, insects and small (or very small) animals, miniature bird houses, garden hats, garden tools, and a miniature fence.

Additional Materials Needed: Wood box approximately 20" × 12" × 12", potting soil, gravel, small pebbles, and miniature plants (baby tears, and elfin thyme work best) and small tree-like plants, miniature wishing wells, and fairies

Developmental Rationale: If space is not available for a large indoor or outdoor garden, a small fairy garden will offer the child a chance to interact with the natural environment. Miniature life toys allow the child to feel in control of events and experiences. Three-year-olds use the gardens for sensory and motor exploration. The three-year-old will feel powerful and in control over the manipulation of miniature life figures and tools. This activity will encourage the four/five-year-old to engage in various levels of symbolic play. The four/five-year-old will be able to plan a garden, play with natural materials, incorporate fantasy and fairy play into their play themes, and take care of the real plants in the garden. The older child will play with the materials as well, become more involved with creating miniature tools, houses, and materials (in the woodworking or art area). This experience will allow the older child to create elaborate themes, engage in language-mediated naturalist play, plan miniature gardens, maintain small indoor plants, and realize the effect she has on a contained environment.

Procedure: Plant the baby tears and thyme in the box. Surround the plants with a miniature fence. Plant the small trees and circle with gravel. You can add the miniature garden tools, a bird house, etc., to make a miniature back yard. Add fairies, tools, and flowers. Allow the children to also add materials. (Some children may prefer to set the entire garden up themselves.) The children may change the gardens to incorporate different themes and projects. For example, during a dinosaur project, the teacher can hide small bones or cardboard bones in the dirt in the miniature fairy gardens. Small ponds can be created with sticky foam fish. The children can make fishing rods (the sticky foam fish will stick to the strings of the fishing rods). Be creative with the garden and let the children interact with it.

Analyzing the Activities

7.2
Journal Activity

Pick an age group that you have access to. Design an activity for that age group based on the format suggested in this text. (You can do the activity with one child or a group of children that you have access to.) After planning the activity, gather the necessary materials and try the activity with the child/children. After you try the activity, complete an activity analysis of the experience.

Intelligence Area: _____

Age: _____

Name of Activity: _____

Activity Objective:

Core Concepts:

Materials:

Developmental Rationale:

Procedure:

After planning and presenting an activity for children, it is important to reflect upon the experience. The following form will guide the teacher in critically reviewing her activity and deciding what might be done differently if the activity is presented again.

Activity Analysis

Was the activity appropriate for the age of the children? Were the materials appropriate?

Was I prepared enough for the activity?

Did the children like the activity?

Was there anything the children needed to know before they took part in the activity?

Is there something I would do differently the next time I do the activity?

How long did the children engage in the activity?

Was the expected outcome achieved?

Were there unexpected concepts that were developed, introduced, or reinforced?

 # Summary

Teacher-directed experiences offer the child an opportunity to build core concepts in the intelligences, develop intelligence strengths, and work on challenges. The child needs an opportunity to try out skills learned during activities in contextual settings through play and project development. Collaborative experiences are necessary for the development of the intelligences. They provide children the opportunity to construct knowledge. Collaborative experiences often take the form of projects.

 Projects

As mentioned in Chapter 1, this text approaches early childhood curriculum with a constructivist methodology. Constructivism views children "as active constructors of knowledge" (Katz, 1999, p. 1). Subjecting children to teacher-directed instruction and activities all day does not provide time for children to explore and construct knowledge on their own. The activities mentioned earlier in the chapter are an important part of the child's day; however, they should never consume the entire day. The child needs time to inquire, investigate, construct, and manipulate. Play and projects provide the child appropriate methods of facilitating the construction of knowledge. They are necessities in a constructivist curriculum. Activities are teacher initiated, play is child initiated, projects are a collaboration (Edwards, Gandini, and Foreman, 1993). Children and teachers share responsibility in a project. Children generally choose the topic of study in a project. They may also choose several activities to investigate the project's topic. The children participate in research activities and interact with members in the community. Teachers plan activities, guide the project, arrange for field trips, and help plan the culminating event.

Projects are also extremely relevant to the multiple-intelligence theory. Children initiate activities and investigations that are interesting and appealing to their intelligence strengths. The child can choose how to express information in a project, again allowing him to use his intelligence strength. This section will focus on defining a project and explaining the process of a project, and will provide an example of the project process.

The Project Approach

Lillian Katz (1994, p. 1) explains that "a project is an in-depth investigation of a topic worth learning more about." The entire class, a small group, or an individual child can help create a project (Katz, 1994). This curriculum has stressed the importance of applying knowledge. This section of the text explains how projects encourage the child to discover and apply information in contextual settings.

Projects develop out of a three-step process (Katz, 1994). The first step, *Phase One,* is referred to by Katz (1994) as *"getting started."* During this phase, a topic is chosen. Sometimes the topic will originate from a particular activity or experience, a question, an interest, a challenge, or an idea. The child may initiate a topic after taking a field trip, hearing a story, attempting to solve a problem, or taking part in an activity or play experience. The teacher may initiate a topic after observing an interest, posing a question, or discovering an interest or challenge.

Topics that are child-initiated need to be approved and accepted by the teacher. Helm and Katz (2001) explain that a topic must be meaningful, relevant, able to be investigated safely; resources must be available; and it must respect the child's culture. The topic must be defined appropriately; if it is too broad, it will be difficult to investigate, too narrow and varying the investigative methods may not be possible.

After a topic is chosen, a brainstorming session takes place (Katz, 1994). The brainstorming session encourages discussion regarding the topic's content. The brainstorming session can take place on paper, a chalkboard, in journals, through video- or tape-recording, or through discussion. The children and teachers discuss exactly what they would like to get out of the project, in what direction they would like to see the project go, and the child's past experiences and knowledge of the topic (Katz, 1994). If the topic is appropriate and practical, and if the children's interest is high, the class creates a plan for investigation of the project. The plan may take the form of a visual web that will define children's concepts and understandings of the topic and provide areas worth investigating (Helm and Katz, 2001).

The second step, *Phase Two,* is referred to as *"field work"* (Katz, 1994). Phase Two requires the children and the teacher to review the web created in Phase One and plan field trips or for masters of the field to come into the classroom (Helm and Katz, 2001). The children are now ready for the investigation phase. The children and teachers investigate the topic through field trips, literature, exploration, and through people related to the topic. The child creates, models, observes, draws, records, experiments, discusses, and communicates her discoveries through many intelligences. The child communicates through play, art, math, dramatics, science, logic, nature, stories, songs, dance, and exhibits (Chard, 1992). Not every child works on every part of the project (only a handful of students at a time might even be involved or interested in the project). Each child explores the project through many domains. The child expresses her understanding of the topic through her intelligence strengths and interests. For example, if the children are investigating trees, one student might choose to express his knowledge about trees through creating a story, one through discussing the physical aspects of the tree, and one through creating an interpretative dance that communicates how the tree moves in a violent storm.

The third step, *Phase Three,* is referred to as *"culminating and debriefing events"* (Helm and Katz, 2001). This experience allows the child to communicate what she has learned in the project. The communication can occur in the form of reports, presentations, plays, festivals, dramatics, stories, or discussion. The communication will usually emanate from the child's intelligence strength.

In order to fully comprehend the depth and organization of a project, a sample project is provided. The sample includes teacher's notes, work samples, photographs, plans, and anecdotal records to fully illustrate the project.

Sample Project: A Dinosaur Museum

PHASE ONE—*GETTING STARTED* This project began with an unexpected discovery. Several preschool children were digging outside, looking for worms. One child dug up a long white object that resembled a bone. She picked it up and frantically jumped up and down. The other children asked to see it. One said, "Is that a dinosaur bone?" Another child said, "I think it's a rock." A third said, "I don't know, let's go see Miss Barb." Miss Barb examined the object. She provided the children with magnifying glasses and searched for dinosaur and fossil books in the classroom. The children spent the afternoon looking through books to see if they had found a fossil. The children determined they had found a fossil. The project involved six girls in the preschool class. Five of the girls were five and one was three.

The children began to ask questions:

How do bones get into museums?
How did this bone get into our earth?
How do people find big bones?

The teacher then asked the children if they would like to begin a dinosaur project. The children cheered, clapped, and jumped up and down.

The teacher asked, "What should our project focus on?"

"How about bones in a museum?"

"Bones in the dirt."

"Digging for bones."

Then one child jumped in the air and shouted, "Let's make our own museum." The children excitedly agreed.

The teacher wrote, "Dinosaur Museum" in the middle of a piece of poster board. She then drew a line down the center of the board and asked the children what they knew about a museum ("K"). She wrote their responses on one side. She then asked the children what they wanted and needed to learn about constructing a museum ("W"). She wrote their responses on the other side. (See Figure 7.1.)

The teacher then asked, "Where can we look for answers to our questions?"

"The museum." A field trip was planned to the museum. The teacher then met with the director to plan experiences and add play materials to the centers in the classroom to facilitate the dinosaur project.

PHASE TWO—*FIELD WORK* After reviewing the concept chart, the children decided to learn more about museums by visiting the local museum. The teacher also planned for a paleontologist to come into the classroom and talk to the children about preparing dinosaur exhibits.

FIGURE 7.1

K

Dinosaurs are big.
They are dead.
They are "stinked."
T-Rex is at the
museum.
Some eat meat.
Some are fast and
some are slow.

W

Where did they go?
Did people ever see
them?
Are there swimming
dinosaurs?
How do we make a
museum?
How do you find bones?
Can we dig bones up?
How do you make
a dinosaur?
Can we build a
dinosaur?

Field Trip At the museum, the children explored every part of the museum. Pictures were taken, drawings were made, and lots of discussion was facilitated. The children met with a docent who explained the process of excavating bones. The children were invited to participate in a dig set up in the museum.

The teacher reviewed key words that were presented in the museum; "paleontologist," "excavation," and "dig."

Photographs were processed that night and brought into the classroom the next day. The children were excited about the photographs.

"Look, look, look, there's the big bones, and the bones of the long-necked one."

After looking at pictures of the dig, one child exclaimed, "That's when we were pa-on-agists."

"No, paleogists."

"Paleontologists."

The teacher then announced, "Let's look at our pictures and determine what parts of the museum we are going to have in our classroom." The children discussed different parts of the museum and then decided what part of the museum they would work on.

A Dig A paleontologist came into the classroom and discussed the process of finding and preparing bones for an exhibit. The paleontologist brought the book, *Bones, Bones,*

We Look for Bones by Byron Barton. After reading the book, the paleontologist discussed the process.

"How did the paleontologists get the bones ready for the museum?" he asked.

"The children answered, "found," "dug," "brushed," "cleaned," "packed," "shipped," and "put together."

One child asked, "Where are places you would find bones?"

Several dig experiences (described below) were set up in the classroom for the children.

DIGGING FOR BONES IN SOIL

Materials: Dirt, a long, flat container, digging tools, brushes, and bleached chicken bones

Procedure: The teacher bleached several chicken bones and hid them in the dirt. The children dug through the dirt to find the bones.

DIGGING FOR BONES IN ICE

Materials: Water, deep tray, small dinosaurs, eggs, digging tools, fossils, shells, rocks, and bones

Digging for bones in soil

Procedure: Dinosaurs, eggs, fossils, shells, rocks, and bones were placed in a deep tray of water. The tray was frozen overnight. The children were provided with digging tools and safety goggles for chipping away at the ice to find fossils.

BONES, BONES, WE LOOK FOR BONES

Materials: Foam board cut into bone shapes, utility knife, brushes, and pieces of cloth

Procedure: The foam board was cut into several large bone-shaped pieces. Leg bones, tail bones, arm bones, claws, feet bones, a head bone, and a large rib (body) bone were cut. Four-inch slits were cut into the top and bottom of the bones to enable the children to put the bones together. The bones were hidden in the gross-motor room. The teacher reread, *Bones, Bones, We Look for Bones,* by Byron Barton. The teacher invited the children to go on a dig. The children pretended to climb down a mountain, cross a river, and enter a desert. The children searched the room for the hidden bones.

When they found a bone, they gently brushed the bones and cleaned them with cloths. After cleaning them, the children wrapped them in paper towels. The bones were carried back to the classroom and unwrapped. The bones were placed on the floor. The children began discussing what bone represented what part of the body. They began to try to fit the bones together.

They created a dinosaur that could stand up in the classroom. One girl ran over to the library and looked up a picture of a tyrannosaurus rex. "This is a T-Rex." She held the picture up for everyone to see. The children agreed. Another girl went to the art area and created a polka-dotted piece of paper. She brought the piece of paper over to the dinosaur and said, "Nobody knows what dinosaurs really looked like, I made him a cape." She inserted the cape into the back of the dinosaur's head.

Art and Play   Some of the children chose to represent dinosaurs through art and play. Dinosaurs were added to the block play area. One child picked up all of the dinosaurs and took them to the library area. She opened up an illustrated dinosaur dictionary. She then asked another student for help. Both girls located the model dinosaurs in the book. They then asked the teacher to write the names of the dinosaurs on stickers to put on the play dinosaurs. The teacher highlighted the names of the dinosaurs in the book and provided the children with stickers and markers. The children copied the names out of the book that corresponded with each dinosaur. They asked the teacher if they could display the dinosaur as a collection to let people know what certain dinosaurs are called.

During outdoor play, some of the children had noticed footprints in the mud. The children looked at the footprints and one asked if it was a fossil. The other child firmly stated that it was not a fossil; it was just bird footprints. The three-year-old walked over and put her foot on the prints. The other girls yelled at her and then one shouted, "Wait,

Bones, bones, we look for bones.

Look! She made a footprint." All of the children put their feet into the mud to make a footprint.

Back inside the classroom, the teacher read *Fossils* by Aliki. The teacher and children discussed the process of creating a fossil. Two students were undertaking the fossil part of the museum. They gathered together the play dinosaurs from the block area. The teacher provided brown clay and footprint cards. The children took turns creating footprints in the clay. The clay was allowed to harden.

One student put her foot in the clay and made a footprint. "These footprints we are making are too small. Look, they are smaller than mine."

The teacher asked, "How can we make the footprints the right size?" The children agreed to go back to the museum and measure the feet and footprints of selected dinosaurs in the museum. The children took the measurements back to the classroom and created footprint fossils of a more realistic size.

Dinosaur Babies Two girls were responsible for the dinosaur baby exhibit. At the museum, the children viewed a dinosaur nest, babies, and a mother hadrosaur. The

Nesting dinosaurs

girls wanted to create a nest in the classroom for the museum. They asked for hay and sticks. The teacher provided hay, sticks, and a straw wreath. The children filled the wreath with hay and sticks. One child retrieved plastic eggs from the housekeeping area to add to the nest. Miniature counting dinosaurs from the manipulative area were placed inside the eggs. The nest was available for play time. Pterodactyls were often seen stealing eggs during free play. The nest would also serve as an exhibit at the museum opening.

Dinosaur Models Three children took on the responsibility of creating dinosaur models in the classroom. The children chose several boxes that came with a computer order. They decided to construct a brontosaurus. They choose a long box for his neck, a short one for his head, a large one for the body, and four long boxes for his legs. They balanced the large box on the four smaller ones.

The legs kept falling over when they tried to work on other parts of the dinosaur. The teacher suggested using something to make the large box stick to the smaller one.

Choosing materials

Building a dinosaur

The children used glue—a lot of glue. They dumped glue into paint buckets and painted the glue on with large paint brushes.

They decided to make scales for the dinosaur. The scales were designed from scraps of foil and glued onto the dinosaur. The dinosaur was painted green. The color was chosen after the children looked at the color of the brontosaurs in a dinosaur book. "All of these brontosauruses are green, let's make ours green."

One student was captivated by the pterodactyl. She constructed a pterodactyl out of large arched paper scraps. She covered the scraps with glue and paint. She then poured sand on them. "This dinosaur looks like his wings are tough." She asked the teacher for help in hanging the dinosaur from the ceiling.

One student loved to growl and stomp around like a dinosaur. She decided to make a mask for her dinosaur movement and decided she was going to show people how dinosaurs moved in the class museum. She used paper plates "because they look like scales." She asked the teacher to staple the plates together after she folded them. She painted the plates and asked the teacher for help in adding a lace to tie the mask on.

During a free-play experience in the sand, one child was excited to find the cardboard cutouts of bones. She took gravel and placed it on a table. She then added a tree from the classroom and several play dinosaurs. She put the cutout dinosaur together and placed it on the gravel. "I made my own collection."

At the museum, the children had been fascinated by the television and the dinosaur movies. All of the children wanted a TV in their museum. The children decided they could make a TV out of a box. One student brought in a large boot box and a pipe cleaner. The teacher suggested using something as a screen. The children agreed on plastic. The teacher cut a slit in both slides of the box and helped a child fasten the plastic to the front of the box. The child who brought the pipe cleaner in put a hole in the top of the box and twisted the pipe cleaner for an antenna. The teacher asked what the TV should teach the people who watch it. Several ideas were discussed.

"Maybe it could be a cartoon."

"It could tell people about digs."

"It could tell people what happened to the dinosaurs."

The children agreed on drawing pictures of their theories about what happened to the dinosaurs. The pictures were drawn on a long sheet of fax paper. The paper was wound around a paper towel roll. The end of the paper was put through the slits, through the front of the box, then back through the other slit. The paper was then rewound on the other paper towel roll. This allowed the children to see all of their pictures. The children were disappointed that no sound was coming out of the box. The teacher asked, "How could we make sound for the TV?"

"We could say it ourselves."

"Tape our voices."

The children's voices were taped on a cassette tape and matched to their pictures. Each child explained what they thought happened to the dinosaurs.

PHASE THREE—*CULMINATING AND DEBRIEFING EVENTS*   The children decided their museum was complete and they could open it. The teacher asked how she thought people would know where to go in the museum.

"At the other museum, we had a map."

"Let's make a map of the museum."

A large piece of paper was placed on the floor. The teacher drew squares where each exhibit was in the classroom. Each child drew a picture of his/her exhibit and some used invented spelling to name their part of the museum. The maps were photocopied to distribute to parents.

The teacher asked, "How will people know to come here."

"Let's make birthday invitations."

"Birthday invitations, that's silly, let's make invitations to come to the museum."

Each child decided to make a separate invitation to their parent.

FIGURE 7.2 | Map of the Museum

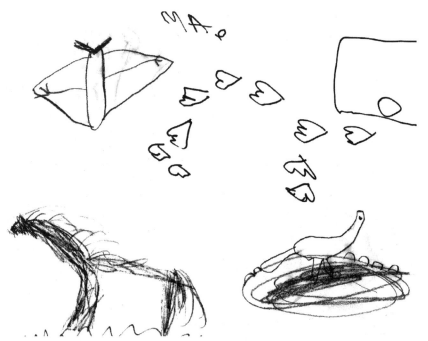

FIGURE 7.3 | Museum Invitations

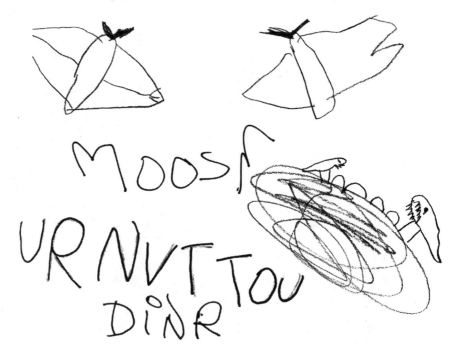

Museum Opening The invitations were sent out and a museum opening was scheduled. The children decided to create a video to tell people about the museum and their participation in it. Each child stood by their exhibit and was videotaped explaining the process and sharing information they had learned in the construction of the exhibit.

The teacher then asked, "What is our role going to be when people are invited to the museum?" Some children chose to stay by their exhibit to talk about it with visitors. Some chose to be in charge of the video, others to hand out maps. One child exclaimed, "All the museum workers had on red shirts, we have to have red shirts on for the opening." A note was sent home asking the children to wear red shirts to the opening.

The day of the museum opening finally arrived. The parents were greeted at the door by children who passed out maps. The children instructed the parents to find the TV and to sit down in front of it. A small group of children ran the video and then explained that the parents were free to visit the exhibits and ask questions. Parents circulated throughout the classroom. Children stationed at each exhibit explained their exhibit and answered questions.

After the opening, the teacher retrieved the concept map the children had made at the beginning of the project. She added a new category entitled "What we have learned." The children wrote down what they had learned about the experience.

Museum opening

   This project illustrates a collaborative experience. Some of the experiences were teacher-initiated, some child-initiated, and some planned by both.

   After the project ended, two children were observed playing in the art center. One child sat at a table, while one placed a box and green clay on the table. The child with the clay made a long green shape that she called diplodocus. She began to tell a story to the other child:

One day, a zillion years ago, a Diplodocus lived in a forest. It was time for her to have her babies. She built a nest in the forest and hid it in weeds. She laid her eggs. (As she said this, she made eggs and a nest out of clay.) *The eggs hatched and a baby dinosaur began to move around.* (She made a baby dinosaur out of the clay.) *The dinosaur grew, and soon was an adult.* (She placed the original dinosaur into the box again.) *Suddenly, a meteor shower began.* (She threw clay balls into the box.) *It killed the dinosaur.* (She placed the dinosaur on its side in the box.) *The world began to change. Many years later, a paleontologist was*

FIGURE 7.4 | Finishing the K-W-L Chart

L (What was learned - last part of KWL chart)

```
Dinosaurs are extinct. Maybe from a volcano, meteor,
because no food was left.

Their skin dies away and their bones are left.
Paleontologists find their bones, dig them up with brushes
and chisels, and carry them to museums.

Real bones aren't really in museums.  They make the bones
and put the real ones in safe places.

Dinosaurs lived in the water and on earth.  Some even flew
in the sky.
```

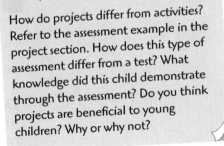

7.3

Journal Questions

How do projects differ from activities? Refer to the assessment example in the project section. How does this type of assessment differ from a test? What knowledge did this child demonstrate through the assessment? Do you think projects are beneficial to young children? Why or why not?

walking in the forest. He discovered some bones. (She made bones out of clay and scattered them through the box.) *The paleontologist took the bones back to his lab and put them together.* (She arranged the bones in a small plastic box and placed it into the large box.) *Now, kids can see that same dinosaur.* (She gathered plastic people and placed them inside the box to look at the bones.)

This experience was a beautiful assessment of what was learned during the project. She was able to express what she learned in an informal play experience.

 # Summary

Activities can offer a developmentally appropriate way of teaching children meaningful concepts. Projects offer a shared learning experience between the teacher and her students. Projects allow the child to construct knowledge and explore meaningful content. The next chapter focuses on play. Play involves child-initiated experiences that help the child construct knowledge and make sense of sensorial information.

References

Bredekamp, S., & Copple, C. (1997) *Developmentally appropriate practice in early childhood programs revised.* Washington, DC: NAEYC.

Chard, S. (1992) *The project approach: A practical guide for teachers.* Edmonton, Alberta: University of Alberta Printing Services.

Chen, J., ed. (1998) *Project spectrum: Early learning activities, Vol 2.* New York: Teachers College Press.

Edwards, C., Gandini, L., & Foreman G. (eds.) (1993) *The hundred languages of children.* Norwood, New Jersey: Albex Publishing Corporation.

Helm, J., & Katz, L. (2001) *Young investigators: The project approach in the early years.* New York: Teachers College Press.

Katz, L. (1994) *The project approach.* Eric Digest EDOPS946.

Katz, L. (1999) *Curriculum disputes in early childhood education.* ED436298.

Schomburg, R., Smith, M., & Tittnich, E. (1986) *Developing your curriculum.* Pittsburgh: Louise Child Care Center.

8

Room Arrangement
Play Environments
Projects
Activities
Scheduling

Phase 2: Planning

Play

8.1

Journal Questions

Write your definition of play.

What do you think is the value of play?

As an adult, what activities do you engage in that may be considered play?

What is the value of adult play experiences?

Is play crucial to the development of intelligence? Why or why not?

I Tried to Teach My Child with Books;
He Gave Me Only Puzzled Looks.
I Tried to Teach My Child with Words;
They Passed Him by Often Unheard.
Despairingly, I Turned Aside;
"How Shall I Teach This Child," I cried?
Into My Hand He Put the Key,
"Come," He Said, "Play with Me."

—Author Unknown

Play and the Early Childhood Curriculum

Standards, accountability, and testing are words that plagued the educational system in the first few years of the twenty-first century (Teele, 2000). With so much emphasis on standards, accountability, and testing, why should play even be considered in the early childhood classroom?

As the introduction to this text stated, no singular approach to early childhood education will work for every child. However, there is a constant of childhood that must be recognized: Children in all literate and nonliterate cultures play. Children play regardless of their

FIGURE 8.1 | Advocating for Play in the Primary Grades

© Sandra Stone, 1995. Reprinted with permission.

strengths, challenges, mental health, socioeconomic level, and parenting. Play demands respect and a place in the early childhood environment. Play is a crucial component to an appropriate early childhood classroom. Planned and unplanned content can be addressed through an appropriate play environment and can build a foundation for the intelligences.

Play and the Intelligences

Gardner emphasizes the importance of creating environments that facilitate a competency in each of the intelligences. This is especially crucial during the early childhood years. Young children should not be streamlined toward a particular domain because of an apparent intelligence strength. Rather, they should be given opportunities to build a foundation in each of the intelligences. When a child demonstrates a particular challenge or developmental delay in one of the intelligences, creating an environment that allows the child to use her strengths to build on the intelligence becomes crucial for developing a solid foundation. A foundation for the intelligence can be built through play experiences, teacher-directed activities, access to a variety of intelligence-specific material, appropriate scheduling, and purposeful planning of the environment. This chapter will focus on how to develop a foundation for the intelligences through play. In order to take advantage of the many benefits of providing play experience for young children, play must be recognized, defined, and understood from a developmental perspective.

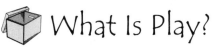 What Is Play?

Defining play is important to the understanding of the rest of this text. Play serves a very particular purpose in this curriculum and a complete understanding of the concept is crucial to the success of using this text with young children. Many theorists have defined play. Table 8.1 presents some prominent definitions.

Five Characteristics of Play

Fergus Hughes's (1995) definition of play summarizes the definitions in Table 8.1 and emphasizes five basic characteristics. Play is intrinsically motivated, freely chosen, pleasurable, nonliteral, and actively engaged in.

> *Intrinsically motivated*—The child is compelled or driven to engage in an experience. The child is not compelled to participate in the experience because of extrinsic rewards or from fear of punishment.
> *Freely chosen*—The child chooses what to do, when to do it, how to do it, and when to stop.
> *Pleasurable*—The child demonstrates contentment or pleasure from the experience.

TABLE 8.1 | *Definitions of Play*

Theorist	Definition of Play
Frederick Froebel	An expression of human development in childhood for it alone is the free expression of what is in a child's soul.
Jean Piaget	Play begins as soon as there is predominance to assimilation.
Sigmund Freud	The opposite of play is not what is serious, but what is real. Play serves the purpose of wish fulfillment and for the mastery of traumatic events.
Erik Erikson	Play provides model situations in which aspects of the past are re-lived, the present represented and renewed, and the future anticipated.
Lev Vygotsky	The child engages in an "imaginary, illusory world in which . . . unrealizable desires can be realized."
Maria Montessori	Play is the child's work.

Nonliteral—There is an expression of a thought or an experience in the activity the child has engaged in. There is some element of pretend.

Active engagement—The child is actively participating with his body and/or mind in the experience. The experience can be witnessed by another.

Identification and application of these characteristics allows the teacher to facilitate an environment that fosters the characteristics of play.

After determining the characteristics of play in Box 8.2, discuss the characteristics you identified with a friend or partner as you read the following discussions.

SCENARIO #1—DISCUSSION This experience was not freely chosen, not intrinsically motivated, and not pleasurable. The children were actively engaged and there was evidence of symbolism. This experience cannot be considered a true play experience for all of these children. The only child who exhibited true play was Jaleesa. She demonstrated all five characteristics as she went to the art center to make invitations to a party. However, this behavior was labeled as inappropriate by her teacher and quickly stopped. The children were not learning how to play and not really benefiting from this experience.

SCENARIO #2—DISCUSSION This experience was not pleasurable. The initial activity was freely chosen and intrinsically motivated, but the child was forced to end this experience too quickly and move on, making the next experience not freely chosen. The child was actively engaged in the task and beginning to use symbolism, but forced to stop before a true play experience began. In a timed experience such as this, children often do not even get out all of the materials they need. They simply get out enough materials to be easily cleaned up when the timer goes off. Because of the time limit, symbolism rarely emerges.

SCENARIO #3—DISCUSSION This experience was pleasurable, freely chosen, nonliteral, intrinsically motivated, and actively engaged the child in the experience. This experience was a true beneficial play experience for these children. The teacher facilitated when necessary in order to prolong the play scenario. The children were even allowed to continue their scenario after lunch. This type of experience is the hardest to facilitate and manage in a classroom. It is also the most rewarding.

 # Progression of Play

The nonliteral aspect of play is significant in defining play. It is through the development and use of symbols that "real-play" emerges (Piaget, 1962). The symbolism the child chooses to use can help determine when the child is ready for presentation of formal

8.2

Journal Activity

Following are three early childhood scenarios. Read each scenario carefully and identify which, if any, of the five characteristics are present.

Five Characteristics of Play (Hughes, 1995)

> Pleasurable
> Freely chosen
> Nonliteral
> Intrinsically motivated
> Active engagement

Scenario #1—Is This Play?

A preschool teacher is with a group of eight children. After a brief circle time, she announces that it is play time. She says, "Justin, Cory, go to the block center. Andrea, Jaleesa, go to the housekeeping center. Ralph, James, go to the discovery center. Felicity, Taylor, go to the art center." Cory turns to Justin and says, "I hate these stupid blocks, I want to paint." The rest of the children go to their center and begin to get out materials. Justin and Cory build a tower. Ralph and James get out magnifying glasses and look at the bees nest in the glass jar. Felicity and Taylor color pages out of a workbook. Andrea and Jaleesa begin to set the table for dinner. After a few minutes, Jaleesa wanders over to the art center and gets out a piece of paper. She announces that she needs to send out invitations for her party. The teacher walks over to her and gently says, "Jaleesa, you are in the housekeeping area right now, put the paper down and go back to your center." Jaleesa groans and walks back to the housekeeping center.

Scenario #2— Is This Play?

A group of eight preschoolers are engaged in circle time with their teacher. At the end of circle time, the teacher says, "Okay, now it's play time." She calls the children one at a time to play.

"Justin, pick a center." She pauses until Justin is in a center. "Cory, pick a center." She continues this until all children are in a center. She places a timer on a bookshelf and sets it for 15 minutes. "I'm setting the timer, when it dings, you have two minutes to clean up and move to another center." Justin hurriedly knocks all the blocks off the shelf. He begins to build an elaborate castle. He uses all the blocks in the center. He begins to choose people, animals, and dinosaurs. He strategically places them in and around his castle. Justin then begins to manipulate and talk to the people in his castle. RINGGGGGGGGGGGGG!! The timer goes off. Justin angrily kicks at his castle. "I wasn't finished," he yells. The teacher says, "Justin, we go through this every day. The timer went off, clean up and move to another center." Justin throws the toys on the shelf and moves to another center.

Scenario #3—Is This Play?

A group of eight preschoolers were having circle time with their teacher. The teacher announces, "Let's think about which centers we would like to begin in today." She lets the children talk about this for a few minutes. Justin announces, "I want to play with the blocks. Me and Cory want to build a castle." She listens to other children talk about their center. She then says, "Justin, where would you like to begin?" "BLOCKS!!!" He jumps up and skips over to the block area. The teacher then continues this by asking each child where he or she would like to begin. Justin, Cory, and Taylor begin to play in the block area. Justin and Cory say to Taylor, "Tay, we are going to build a castle, we need a lot of the blocks." Taylor asks, "Can I help?" "Yep, here, make the bridge to get into it." Justin, Cory, and Taylor work together to build an elaborate castle. They are talking about their castle as they are building it. After it is finished, they begin to get out people, animals,

8.2

continued

and dinosaurs. Taylor announces she is the queen. Justin announces he is the king. Cory says he is the king. They argue over this for a few minutes. The teacher walks over and asks what the problem is. Cory and Justin explain that they want to be the king. The teacher suggests that there might be two kinds of kings, one for the front of the castle and one for the back. The children agree. The teacher provides 1½ hours of uninterrupted play. Some children stay in the same center, some move from center to center. Ten minutes before clean up, the teacher warns that clean up is coming. She then rings a clean-up bell. Justin, Cory, and Taylor are still playing with their castle. The teacher walks over and reminds them it is clean-up time. "We weren't finished." The teacher explains that it is lunch time. "Clean up the blocks that you are not using for your castle. You can leave the castle up and finish after lunch." The children agree.

(adult) symbol systems (Schomburg, 1996). Play begins with sensory and motor experiences and progresses through various stages of symbolic representation (Piaget, 1962). The child progresses through play stages as a result of interaction and experience with materials, people, and her environment. The GOLD (Goal-Oriented Learning Directed) curriculum of Louise Child Care offers clearly defined levels of play based on Piaget's theory of symbolic development (Schomburg, Smith, and Tittnich, 1986). The levels are sensory, motor, level I representation, level II representation, and level III representation.

Sensory

The first stage of play involves the senses. The child touches, tastes, smells, hears, and looks at objects and people in their environment (Schomburg, Smith, and Tittnich, 1986). Infants learn about their environment primarily by using sensory exploration; however, all children (and even adults) will engage in sensory play. This is especially true when new materials are brought into the room. For example, if new glue, art materials, a pet, sand table, or dress-up clothes are brought into the room, the child will explore the materials with the senses before engaging in any other type of play. Sensory play is developed by providing experiences that stimulate the senses and allow for sensory organization of materials in the environment. This stage can also be referred to as the scribbling stage. The intentionality of this stage is simply for the sensorial experience (Schomburg, 1996).

The simplicity of the intentionality cannot be devalued. Sensory stimulation is an absolutely necessary experience for brain development (Hannaford, 1995). Sensory experiences coordinate brain functioning and create synapses. Sensory experiences are necessary for the development of higher-level brain functioning.

Motor Play

Thorough sensory exploration of materials leads to the development of motor play. This stage is characterized by movement. The child moves her body and/or materials. The intentionality of the experience is centered on movement (Schomburg, 1996). This stage can also be referred to as the functional play stage (Stone, 1985). The child utilizes motor movements to manipulate the toys and tools in very functional ways. For example, the child will make a car drive or an airplane fly, and will fill and dump cups full of sand.

Level I Representation

The motor movements in the second stage will lead to more purposeful use of materials and the creation of a symbol or the engagement in the nonliteral aspects of play. This stage is also referred to as the cognitive/manipulative stage of play. This stage characterizes the beginning of the nonliteral or pretend characteristic of a true play experience. The child will engage in experiences, including fine-motor and organizational experiences that contribute to mental organization and use of symbols. Children begin to construct objects out of blocks, sand, puzzles, drawings, paintings, and so on, and begin to name these objects. The child will pretend a block is a telephone or pretend to be mom cooking dinner. The child recognizes and acknowledges the symbols, although the adult may not always recognize the symbol (Schomburg, 1996).

Level II Representation

This stage is also referred to as the creative/expressive or dramatic play stage (Stone, 1985). The child begins to express thoughts, ideas, and feelings through the verbal and nonverbal use of symbolism. The child's symbol becomes a theme or storyline (Schomburg, 1996). The child's theme will emerge in a drawing, in role-play, or will develop in play with miniature life toys. The theme/storyline will have a sequence and last for a significant period of time (Schomburg, 1996).

Level III Representation

This level of play is often referred to as language-mediated or games with rules. Sophisticated use of language symbolism is characteristic of this stage of play. Words are used in place of actions or materials (Schomburg, 1996). Children will say "Let's pretend we went to the beach," pretend to count imaginary money, and/or develop and stick to rules of a game or play theme. This level of play is the most sophisticated and can help indicate when a child is ready for formal symbol systems (Schomburg, 1996).

8.3

Journal Activity

Read the following scenario and decide which play levels the children are engaged in. Consult with a friend if necessary.

Andrea and Rosie are at the sand table. Rosie fills up containers of sand and dumps them repeatedly. Andrea puts her hands in the sand and lets them run through her fingers. She then rubs her hands together and tells Rosie the sand is rough and soft. Kathy and Joy run to the sand table. There are seashells in the sand table. Kathy says, "Joy, let's pretend we are at the beach. I love the beach. We can find the seashells on the beach." Kathy and Joy bury their seashells in the sand. Kathy puts her index finger in the sand and screams, "Ouch, a crab bit me, help!" Joy giggles and smashes the sand with her fingers. "Don't worry, I killed it." Janet, Jen, and Colleen bring their cars over to the sandbox. They begin to make roads in the sand with their cars. As they do this, they make engine and horn noises. Denise and Brenda bring their cars, people, and trees to the sandbox. "Oh no," says Denise, "your guy is falling into the sand, he's getting covered up." Denise pushes a small figure into the sand and covers him up. Brenda grabs a shovel and digs the figure out. "You almost got sucked into the quicksand." Debbie and Kathy come over to the sandbox. Debbie says, "Let's build a castle." They begin to make wet sand blocks and stack them into a shape of a building. Kathy says, "Debbie, we have to make a tower." They both begin to work with the sand to make a tower shape.

What kind of play is Andrea involved in?

What kind of play is Rosie involved in?

What kind of play are Kathy and Joy involved in?

What kind of play are Jen, Janet, and Colleen involved in?

What kind of play are Denise and Brenda involved in?

What kind of play are Debbie and Kathy involved in?

This level of play requires fewer props. Props can be taken out of the play areas. Children will begin to create their own props and use language and imagery as props.

Play Stages at the Water Table

The following examples illustrate the various levels of play at the water table. The interaction with materials and the language used by the child often indicate the level of play the child is engaged in.

Sensory—Provide no materials at the water table except water. Add food coloring, ice, warm water, carbonated water, and scents to the water to enrich the sensory play of the water. The children will smell, taste, touch, listen to, and observe the colors, scents, and temperatures of the different kinds of waters available.

Motor—Provide measuring cups and other objects for dumping and filling the water. The children will engage in the motor movements of dumping and filling.

8.4
Journal Questions

Observe a child playing in the block area of a preschool classroom.

Was there evidence of sensory play?

Motor play?

Level I Representation?

Level II Representation?

Level III Representation?

Cognitive/Manipulative—Provide boats in the water. The children will begin to recognize and use the boat symbols to manipulate and name in the water. The children will use the boats very functionally.

Creative/Expressive—Add boat docks, boats, fish, sea animals, seashells, starfish, people, and small fishing poles to the water. The children will begin to develop a theme to their water play.

Language-mediated—The children will expand on their theme, begin to talk about water play experiences that happened at home (such as bathing, fishing, swimming) and incorporate them into their play. They will begin to say things like, "Let's pretend we are at the beach and you were buried in the sand when a crab came along . . ."

Social Levels of Play

The developmental progression of play emphasized the interaction the child has with materials, his own body, and the environment. Interactions with peers focus on the social aspects of play. Parten (1932) suggests children progress through social stages of play. Social stages of play include: onlooker, solitary, parallel, associative, and cooperative.

Onlooker Play

Onlooker play suggests the child takes a passive role in the experience. The child stands back and observes other children playing. Children of all ages can and do engage in onlooker play (Parten, 1932).

Solitary Play

In solitary play, the child plays alone. There is no interaction with peers or adults; however, the child may talk to himself or his play materials (Parten, 1932).

Parallel Play

In parallel play, the child plays next to someone who has similar materials. For example, two children may be playing with trucks. They will each make truck noises and drive their trucks through the play area; however, they do not speak to or acknowledge each other (Parten, 1932).

Associative Play

Associative play involves the interaction between children. The children playing with the trucks may ask each other questions, share ideas, and carry on a conversation about their play materials.

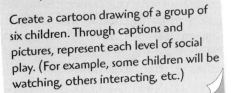

8.5

Journal Activity

Create a cartoon drawing of a group of six children. Through captions and pictures, represent each level of social play. (For example, some children will be watching, others interacting, etc.)

Cooperative Play

In cooperative play, the children are able to negotiate roles, themes, and materials. The children share and accept other children's ideas and actions (Parten, 1932).

Each social level of play has value and is important in developing creativity and social skills (Parten, 1932).

The Teacher's Role During Play

Lev Vygotsky (1978) explains that learning occurs through social interaction. Social interaction is an absolutely necessary part of learning that takes a child from one level of learning to the next. The process of using interaction to develop higher level thinking skills is referred to as the Zone of Proximal Development. Vygotsky (1978, p. 86) explained the Zone of Proximal Development as "the distance between the actual developmental level as determined by independent problem solving and the level of potential development as determined through problem solving under adult guidance or in collaboration with more capable peers."

How does this relate to play? Socialization is a necessary part of learning (Vygotsky, 1978). After careful observation, the teacher decides at what moment it is appropriate to interact with the student. The motivation for the interaction extends from the desire to help the child's play skills evolve. Interaction can help the child move from one play level to the next, or move from one social play level to the next.

If the teacher notices that a five-year-old's play consistently exists in the Level I (cognitive/manipulative) stage, the teacher can help the child move into Level II (creative/expressive) play. This can be done through suggesting or providing props, asking questions, and helping the child establish a theme. The teacher initiates an interaction, moves the play to a different level, and then backs away. Backing away is important. The child's play may continue at that level without the support or interaction of her teacher.

Social interaction can also help a child move from one level of social play to the next. For example, two three-year-old children are playing in the block area. They are playing next to each other and both are building a tall tower. The children are playing with similar materials; however, they are not interacting or even acknowledging that the other child is present. The children are engaging in parallel play. The teacher may come over and ask the children to tell her about what they are creating. After listening to each child, she may point out that both of them are working on the same project. One child may have difficulty getting the top of the tower to stand. The teacher can ask the other child how she got her tower to stand. She can encourage this child to give suggestions to the other child, or offer blocks and other materials. The teacher will attempt to create a dialogue, and inspire the children to ask one another for materials or ideas. The teacher is attempting to engage the children in associative play. The teacher will step back after the children begin to engage in associative play and will observe where the associative play takes the children.

 # Center Play

Play must be approached with careful planning and knowledge of play stages. Play materials need to be organized into specific areas. (The areas of the classroom are typically referred to as centers.) Center play has been approached in a number of ways. Some programs rotate children into very specific teacher-directed centers in order to accomplish a teacher-created goal. This type of approach to center play is not consistent with the play information presented in this chapter. Play must be intrinsically motivated, freely chosen, nonliteral, actively engaged, and pleasurable (Hughes, 1994).

Play centers that address one or more of the intelligences will be presented in this chapter. A description, a photographic example, suggested materials, an example of play levels, and a list explaining which intelligences are addressed by the center will be provided for each sample play center.

Several materials should be included in each play center. The materials are organized according to the play level the materials may encourage. It is important to note that it is *not* expected that you provide all of the suggested materials. The number and variety of materials made available to children should depend upon the space available,

BOX 8.6 | *Functions of Center Play*

The type of center play described in this chapter will:

■ Reflect the five characteristics included in our definition of play,

■ Encourage the developmental progression through play stages, and

■ Facilitate the eight intelligences.

the number of children that typically use the center, the shelving available, the age and level of play the children engage in, and the interests of the children at the center. Many of the materials suggested are inexpensive and can be made, found at garage sales, or purchased at dollar stores. Some materials and the Montessori equipment mentioned are expensive. They can be purchased through fundraisers, donated by parents, purchased through grants, and some of the equipment can be made. It is recommended that the equipment and furniture should be of good quality and it must meet local safety guidelines. The quantity is not as important as the quality of the materials.

The materials should be organized, labeled, and visually accessible to the children. Shelves can be labeled using pictures, outlines of the objects, or words (depending upon the age/level of the children using the materials). The individual play centers need to be clearly defined. Signs and pictures indicating the name/purpose of the play center should be hung at the child's eye level. Shelving, furniture, or low movable walls should separate the centers. An effort should be made to create enough space for the children who choose the specific play center to be able to play in it (instead of limiting the number of children allowed in the center—if at all possible). This can be done by creating enough physical space for each center and by providing enough interesting choices in each of the centers. With interesting choices in each center, the size of the group at play in each will be smaller.

Ideally, the play environment should be large enough to accommodate many play center choices—small group, large group, and individual workspaces. However, this is not always possible. If space is very limited, alternate play centers. Provide a couple of play centers in the morning, and then provide different centers in the afternoon. Use shelves that have wheels and can close and lock for quick room arranging. These shelves can be closed and pushed aside for large group time. Large containers with center materials in them can be kept under tables. These containers can be opened and the materials presented on the table for center time. Another option is to have double shelves in each play area. One shelf might have materials for one play center, while the other shelf has materials for a different play center. One shelf can be covered with material while the other shelf is in use. These strategies will allow children to have access to a wider variety of materials, without cluttering the environment.

Time Considerations

The child should be provided with enough play center time to choose a center, take out and organize all of the relevant materials, set the materials up, create and develop a theme with the materials, and put the materials away. Children may change centers as frequently as they need to. The time frame should allow for and accept the child's play center decisions. At least 1½ to 2 hours of uninterrupted playtime should be provided in

8.7

Journal Questions

Why do you think children need the suggested length of time to play? Why is it important to give children enough time to play?

a full-day schedule. In a half-day schedule, at least 1 hour, but preferably 1½ hours should be provided.

The Teacher's Role

The teacher's role is extremely significant during play-center time. This is *not* the time to take care of paperwork or other classroom maintenance tasks. This is a time of observation, facilitation, and conflict management. The teacher should carefully observe the children interacting with materials and peers. Observation includes observing and recording the child's tasks, accomplishments, successes, and challenges. The teacher should make anecdotal notes concerning how the child uses materials, how the child interacts, what the child's interests are, and any other relevant and/or interesting observations. The anecdotal notes can be jotted down quickly, filed away, and analyzed during a more convenient time. The teacher can use center time to decide which centers are working and which need restructuring.

The play centers are meant to inspire children to manipulate, symbolize, create, express, and give meaning to play materials. The meanings children create need to be reflected upon by observant teachers. Teachers then need to respond to these meanings by analyzing individual children's strengths and interests. Teachers also need to be observant of children's weaker areas and be prepared to help them deal with these weaknesses.

Facilitation can and should occur during this time of the child's day. The teacher can facilitate progression in a play stage with suggestions, conversation, questions, or by adding or taking away materials (Vygotsky, 1978). The teacher can facilitate appropriate peer interaction through conflict resolution. The teacher must have excellent observation skills and know her/his students well enough to anticipate when struggles between children will emerge. The teacher can encourage a child to follow through and complete a task or the teacher can demonstrate a particular technique or use of a material. This is a very busy time of the day for the teacher and the children.

The sample play centers that follow address many of the intelligence areas. The number of play centers that should be made available to a specific classroom will vary according to the size of the classroom, number of children, teacher/child ratio, and availability of materials. The number of play centers will vary, but there should always be enough play centers to address each of the intelligence areas and the interests of the children. This does not mean that eight play centers (one for each intelligence) must be provided. Many play centers address more than one of the intelligences.

The sample play centers presented in this text include extensive materials lists. Not every material suggested should be included in the play center at one time. The materials can change as the interests and development of the children change. Materials can

change to reflect a theme or incorporate material relevant to a class project. The material list shortens in the language-mediated level of play. The child may use materials from the creative/expressive suggestions and will begin to substitute language for props. It is important to begin to take away specific props once the children have engaged in creative/expressive play for a period of time. The exclusion of props will encourage the child to use her imagination and invent props on her own. This does not mean that one day all the props are taken out of the center, but it does mean that props can begin to be taken out as play progresses.

Sensory Exploration

Play begins with sensory exploration. Sensory perception and discrimination is crucial for development of all the intelligences. A sensory exploration station is appropriate for all ages in all classrooms. The child must develop the senses before engaging in other types of play. The sensory exploration will involve all of the senses and integrate motor play. The materials can change to fit the interests, ages, and needs of the children in the classroom. The sensory exploration station can be a play center with specific materials that address each of the senses or can have an experience, which promotes the use of the five senses to explore it. For example, a light table or nature table would encourage sensory exploration.

Sensory Exploration Center

To encourage *touch,* provide materials such as: different textures of sandpaper, kinetic cylinders, tactile dominoes, Lauri puzzles, surprise bags filled with familiar objects, weighted bars, Braille books, and material scraps.

To encourage *taste,* include: foods that represent different cultures, edible flowers, seeds, foods of different tastes and textures.

To encourage *sight,* provide: color slides, color wheel, transparent colors (to blend to make new colors), Monet paintings, puzzles, bubbles, prisms, and a large window.

To encourage *listening,* include: shakers, rattles, rain stick, tape player, recorder, Montessori bells, taped bird calls or animal noises.

To encourage *smell,* provide: salt/pepper shakers filled with different spices and smells, perfumed cards, and real flowers.

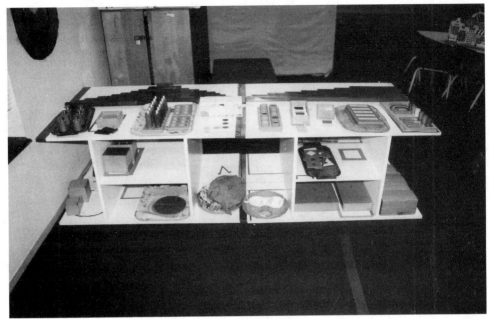

Sensory play center

 # Sample Play Centers

Housekeeping Center

The importance of "a place like home" (commonly known as the housekeeping or dramatic play area) was not realized for me until a powerful incident took place in the classroom. Jayne (name has been changed) played in the housekeeping area every day in my kindergarten classroom. Jayne was sweet, compliant (a little too compliant at times), and eager to please. Her insistence about playing in the housekeeping area concerned me a little. I thought about ways of encouraging her into other areas of the classroom, but she seemed compelled to begin her play in the housekeeping area. I noticed that when she was in the housekeeping area, she was more assertive than at any other time during the day. Jayne would assign her peers roles and expect them to follow their role dutifully. If the "father" did not follow her expectations or if the "baby" cried too much, she seemed bothered and uncomfortable. One morning, as Jayne entered the housekeeping area a quick rage built up. In a matter of seconds, Jayne knocked over the shelves, threw dishes on the floor, threw clothes on the floor and screamed. The behaviors were quite uncharacteristic of Jayne. I took Jayne aside and she sobbed. She then told me her father had beat her mother severely enough to break her

Housekeeping center

mother's arm and bruise her ribs. Her father smashed the windows in the house and was escorted out of the house by the police.

I realized the importance of the housekeeping area for Jayne. This was her chance, her time to make things right. This was her chance to interact with familial roles in a safe, secure environment. This was her place to make things like they were supposed to be. In this play area she felt comfort and control over the uncontrollable situations in her life. The housekeeping area in the classroom allowed Jayne to develop her intrapersonal skills through expression in a safe, predictable environment.

HOUSEKEEPING AND PLAY DEVELOPMENT   This area is beneficial for children in Jayne's situation as well as for children who have more stable home lives. The housekeeping area allows the child to act and interact with familial and community roles. They experiment with dialogue, dialects, and vocabulary. This area can be comforting for children who simply miss their parents. In addition, children are exposed to other children's family traditions and culture through the experiences they bring with them to the housekeeping area.

Sometimes the housekeeping area is referred to as the dramatic play area. This area may take on different themes. While experimenting with dramatic play themes is important for young children, there must always be a place like home. The theme play can take place in the housekeeping area with the change of a few props, or in a separate area of the classroom. The housekeeping area needs to be well organized and provide space for children to move around freely, try on clothes, and interact. Large, open space should be avoided. Room to move freely is important, but furniture should be arranged so children can interact in an intimate group without the temptation to run through the housekeeping area. The area needs to have adequate light and materials need to be accessible to children. Hanging clothes on hooks or hangers encourages children to put their materials away responsibly and allows children visual access to all available materials. Every material in the center should have a proper place that is clearly labeled. The labeling can be done by taking pictures of materials and taping the picture to a shelf or by providing the children with outlines of the materials on the appropriate shelf or bin.

The housekeeping area offers opportunities for children to exhibit play stages and provides the potential for developmental growth. Specific materials do not guarantee the child will exhibit a specific stage of play; however, specific materials can encourage a specific play stage.<TBLIND NUM="2" ID="TB.08.002"/>

HOUSEKEEPING AND THE INTELLIGENCES   Play centers help the child develop a variety of intelligences. The housekeeping center encourages development in most of the intelligences.

The housekeeping area encourages *linguistic* development as the child:

- Experiments with dialogue, dialect, and the vocabulary of various familial and community roles;
- Uses language to communicate ideas, thoughts, and to initiate interactions; and
- Describes actions, verbally solves problems, and poses questions to peers.

The housekeeping area encourages *logical/mathematical* development as the child:

- Uses logic to solve problems; and
- Sequences events in her dramatic play theme.

The housekeeping area encourages *spatial* development as the child:

- Realizes how her body moves in space in the dramatic play area and around others; and
- Chooses clothes that may fit him.
The housekeeping area encourages *interpersonal* development as the child:

- Experiments with familial, community, and gender roles;
- Works out problems in play themes; and
- Negotiates ideas and accepts other's ideas in the play theme.

TABLE 8.2 | *Housekeeping and Play Development*

To Encourage This Play Stage:	Provide the Following Materials:	This Is What Play in This Stage Will Look Like:
Sensory	Dress-up clothes of different textures Flower vases/flowers	The child will feel the different types of clothing. The child will look at flower arrangements, etc. The child will explore materials with the senses.
Motor	Dress-up clothes that zipper, button, Velcro, snap, and slip on Hats, mittens, shoes Butterfly/fairy wings Brooms, dustpans, dusters, sponges, iron/iron board, rags to fold, shoes, and shoe polish	The child will attempt to dress her/himself. The child will sweep the floor, use a dustpan, dust, polish shoes, arrange flowers, try on mittens, shoes, and hats. The child will mimic body movements of familial and community roles. The child will use materials in functional ways.
Level I Representation (Cognitive/Manipulative)	Familial and community props and dress-up clothes Sink, table, refrigerator, baby dolls, keys, mirror, doll beds, doll high chairs, food, food boxes, baby food, flowers, place mats	The child will pretend with props in this center. The child will take on a specific role. The child will pretend to feed her baby, walk the dog, or answer the telephone.
Level II Representation (Creative/Expressive)	Silks, large squares of material Tools, tool belt, large boxes Fireman hats, hose scraps, and large cardboard boxes Flippers, goggles, beach blankets, sunglasses Sleeping bags, sticks, marshmallows Money, cash register, food boxes, grocery bags Shoes, shoe boxes, benches Butterfly wings, fairy wands, flowers, blankets (for pretend chrysalis) Curlers, pretend hairdryers and curling irons, panty hose braids (braid panty hose and attach the braids to headbands)	A theme will begin to emerge in the child's play. The child will ask for nonavailable props. The child will gather props from other areas to extend their dramatic play theme. They will experiment with different genders and different roles.

TABLE 8.2	*continued*	

To Encourage This Play Stage:	Provide the Following Materials:	This Is What Play in This Stage Will Look Like:
Level II Representation (Creative/Expressive)	Baby dolls, diaper bags, diapers, bottles, cradle, baby food jars, spoons, blankets Kitchen timer, chef hats, rolling pins, cookie cutters, aprons, cooking utensils	
Level III Representation (Language-Mediated)	The child will begin to use fewer props. The need for the materials in the previous box diminishes as he replaces props with language.	The child will use role-appropriate vocabulary and language. The child will use his imagination more frequently for creation of imaginary play props. The child will say, "Let's pretend," count out imaginary money, or create elaborate theme-specific props. The child will describe events related to the dramatic play theme. The child will respect and take part in role-related play.

The housekeeping area encourages *intrapersonal* development as the child:

■ Begins to recognize and empathize with other's needs and wants for materials and turns;
■ Communicates her own needs and wants;
■ Works on impulse control; and
■ Reacts to other's feelings and impulses.

The housekeeping area encourages *bodily/kinesthetic* development as the child:

■ Incorporates gestures and body movements that symbolize familial, community, and gender roles; and
■ Uses gestures and body language to communicate.

Art Center

Springtime was approaching. As I looked around the hallways and walls of the classroom, I saw many winter projects, paintings, and drawings that hung on the wall. In my own selfish yearning for Spring, I longed for the halls and walls to be filled with signs of spring flowers. I took the children outside to see the first spring flowers, a few daffodils. I picked one and brought it back into the classroom. The children and I looked the flower up in a botany book to discover the name of the flower. I asked my three-, four-, and five-year-old children if they would like to paint the daffodil. One of my three-year-olds squealed yes, picked up a paintbrush and proceeded to actually paint the daffodil flower itself. Another child covered her entire paper with yellow, green, and blue. (As I looked at it, it looked more like a green and yellow blob than the springtime daffodils I had imagined covering the hallway.) Faithe painted her picture blue several times. When I asked her to tell me about her picture, she said it was blue. She then added the word sky, blue sky. Jackie painted a dog (that resembled more of a gremlin than a dog). I encouraged the children to take the pictures home.

On teacher appreciation day, a parent had given me a beautiful red rose. I was touched and immediately found a vase, poured water into it and placed the rose in it. The children were excited at the sight of the rose. I placed the rose in the middle of a long table. The children sat around the rose, admiring and talking about it. They touched and smelled the flower. I had beeswax crayons in my classroom and noticed the crayons were sitting directly in the sun. I moved the crayons, placing them on the table so they would not melt. One of the children, Jackie, asked for a piece of paper. She took the slightly warm crayons and began drawing on the paper. She turned the crayons and experimented with the lines and shapes each side of the crayon produced. She looked at the rose and began to use the side of the crayon to create a rose on her paper. The rose was beautiful and the crayon stroke she used presented a very lifelike re-creation of the rose. The other children became very interested and asked her to show them her technique. Jackie demonstrated her technique to several children. The other children began to create roses. I secretly wanted to keep these pictures but they were too precious to their creators. Reluctantly, I let the children take the pictures home.

ART AND PLAY DEVELOPMENT   The motivation for art comes from within the child. Preschoolers are dealing with autonomy and initiative. They are often not responsive or interested in teacher-directed experiences. This is especially true with art. When art is forced or extrinsically motivated, it may lack meaning, expressiveness, or detail; or the art may reflect external expectations; or the child may simply express her initiative by purposefully creating anything but what was asked.

When the motivation and purpose for the creation comes from within the child, the artwork emanates meaning and purpose. The child's purpose may be to re-create an experience, share an idea, communicate a feeling or mood, experiment with materials, or simply to experience the physical sensations and movements of art materials. The meaning and purpose is up to the child. When children have free access to materials in an art center, they have the opportunity to create meaning and purpose.

The art center of the classroom should be made available to children on a daily basis. It is important to remember that children need to have a choice in this center.

They need to decide what materials they need to explore, create with, or communicate with. A teacher-directed craft or activity does not belong in the art center. Seasonal or theme-related materials can certainly be added to the art center. Techniques can be demonstrated to the child in this center, but specific step-by-step teacher-directed activities do not allow the child to experience the necessary stages of art development and art play. Teacher-directed art experiences could be carefully planned and offered during the activity times in the schedule. Participation in the art center should be voluntary.

A variety of materials need to be available to children and should be displayed in an aesthetically pleasing way. Materials can be stored in glass or clear plastic jars, and clearly labeled baskets. As discussed in the section on naturalist intelligence, natural materials should dominate the art area. Modeling beeswax, clay, natural watercolors, season materials, and child-suggested materials should be arranged and available to young children.

Symbols children create through art have significant meaning. The symbol can communicate a mood, feeling, remembrance, or signal a specific stage of development. Children will use materials differently at different stages of play development.

ART AND THE INTELLIGENCES   The art center creates a safe atmosphere where children can construct and communicate representations of their environment. Their constructions and representations reflect a variety of domains and facilitate a foundation in many intelligence areas. The art center encourages *linguistic* development as the child:

- Learns vocabulary associated with the arts;
- Tells a story or tells about the object she created; and
- Writes about his painting, drawing, or sculpture.

The art center encourages *logical/mathematical* development as the child:

- Creates patterns, mixes colors, sorts objects, and chooses art materials; and
- Solves problems related to the creation of the art project.

The art center encourages *spatial* development as the child:

- Learns the boundaries of his materials;
- Creates forms and represents her view of the world;
- Organizes materials; and
- Explores the sensory aspects of her materials.

The art center encourages *musical* development as the child:

- Creates a musical instrument or a sound maker; and
- Creates art in response to a musical genre.

TABLE 8.3 | *Art and Play Development*

To Encourage This Play Stage:	Provide the Following Materials:	This Is What Play in This Stage Will Look Like:
Sensory	Sand painting, glue, feathers, sandpaper, felt, colored rice, marshmallow cream, glitter, bubble wrap, foam paint, jello, pudding, fudgesicle painting Famous artwork displayed at child's eye level	The child will feel the materials. The child may pour glue or paint on his hands, bury his hands in rice, finger paint, run his fingers across the different textured materials, and bring soft materials to his face. The child will engage in disordered, random scribbling. The scribbling marks may even go off the page.
Motor	Finger paints, scissors, hole punchers, metal insets, stencils, large and small paintbrushes, paints, sponges, paint rollers, dabbers, beeswax crayons, modeling beeswax, collage materials, paper for ripping	The child explores the art materials in a physical way. The child does not create or attempt to create any kind of symbol, the child enjoys the motor movements involved in the art experiences. The child will poke her fingers in play dough, rub the modeling beeswax to feel the warmth, experiment with scissors and hole punchers, and will tear paper. The child will engage in controlled scribbling.
Level I Representation (Cognitive/Manipulative)	Colored pencils, clay, paint, white drawing paper, easel painting, play dough, crayons, markers, art books	The child will begin to create and name forms. The forms will begin to become recognizable (from an adult perspective). The child becomes interested in the symbols she can create. The child begins the preschematic art stage.

The art center encourages *naturalist* intelligence as the child:

- Represents objects in nature through art materials; and
- Uses natural materials such as beeswax, weeds, pine cones, etc., to create art.

The art center encourages *interpersonal* development as the child:

- Shares techniques and materials with other children;
- Waits for her turn to use a particular material; and
- Communicates ideas and collaborates with other children to create an art project.

TABLE 8.3 | *continued*

To Encourage This Play Stage:	Provide the Following Materials:	This Is What Play in This Stage Will Look Like:
Level II Representation (Creative/Expressive)	Fine black markers; acetate; oil pastels; clay tools; acrylic paints; salt ceramic; jewelry beads; paper of various shapes, sizes, textures and colors; mirror; eye dropper; flowers Famous pieces of artwork Music of various genres	A theme begins to emerge in the artwork. The pictures begin to have a baseline, and a theme is present in the creation. The child has her own idea for using art tools and experiments with shape, size, color, and effect. She can create stories from looking at artwork that is full of imagery and fantasy. The child will be able to creatively describe a piece of artwork. The child will create art in response to music.
Level III Representation (Language-Mediated)	Art games	The child becomes very interested in the product she creates. She accepts and is interested in adult art tools. She prefers to use art tools in field-specific ways. Her interpretation of her artwork becomes more realistic and tailored to the objects represented. Her pictures have a definite theme or *schema*. She engages in schematic art presentation. The child will be able to tell a story about a piece of artwork, discuss the possible motivation or intention of the artwork, and identify thoughts, emotions, and feelings the artwork evokes.

The art center encourages *intrapersonal* development as the child:

- Expresses emotions, thoughts, and ideas through art;
- Interprets mood, emotion, or an intention through an artwork; and
- Respects her own physical and material boundaries in the art area.

The art center encourages *bodily/kinesthetic* development as the child:

- Manipulates art tools;
- Learns and utilizes appropriate artist's techniques; and
- Incorporates bodily and kinesthetic movements into the production of the artwork.

Block Play

While teaching in a kindergarten classroom, I had a small group of children who engaged in block play daily. One afternoon, while working with a small group of children on a project, I noticed small people and animals flying over the shelves in the block area. As I approached the block area, I observed a group of boys building catapults with the blocks. They proceeded to launch small people and animals into the air with their catapults. My first reaction was to immediately stop the play (for safety reasons). I paused and observed the children engaged in this task. I noticed they were very interested in the catapult structure itself, and how it could be improved to launch the animals a greater distance. Many of the other children in the class stopped to watch the catapults as well. The room itself was much to small to allow this type of play to continue. I invited the class to choose some blocks for a catapult and to also choose people and animals of different shapes and sizes. I gathered measuring tools (a yardstick, measuring tape, a ruler, and feet). The feet were exactly twelve inches long and were used to measure long distances in the classroom. I took the class to a small gymnasium and asked them to line up at a baseline on the gym floor. The children were encouraged to build different types of catapults in small groups and to try launching different objects of varying sizes and shapes.

The children were encouraged to hypothesize about what type of catapult would launch an object the farthest, which object could be launched the farthest, which shapes were more effective, etc. After experimenting with the catapult structure, the children began predicting

Block center

how far their object would fly through the air. Some children wrote their predictions down, while some said them verbally. The children then chose a measurement tool to see if their predictions were correct. The unexpected catapult project lasted over an hour. Many children came in the next day with drawings and ideas for different kinds of catapults.

BLOCKS AND PLAY DEVELOPMENT   The block area can be an unexpected source of activities, play, and experimentation with all of the intelligences. The possibilities the block area holds are limitless. A skilled teacher can take advantage of the many "teachable moments" that occur in the block area. Having a variety of blocks and manipulatives is important in order to inspire creativity, problem solving, and architecture. Organization is also extremely important in this area. Blocks can be sorted on shelves by color, shape, and/or size. Block materials should be visibly accessible to children so they have an idea of what materials are available to work with.

BLOCKS AND THE INTELLIGENCES   Blocks offer a unique medium to develop each of the intelligences. If space and materials are limited and/or the facilitation of the intelligences in the classroom is just beginning, blocks offer an excellent starting point.

Blocks encourage *linguistic* development as the child:

- Uses vocabulary and dialogue related to block building;
- Shares information, communicates ideas, and asks for help;
- Works out conflicts verbally; and
- Engages in story plots and dramatizations.

Blocks encourage *logical/mathematical* development as the child:

- Experiments with balance, patterning, cause/effect, measurement, classification, and sorting; and
- Poses questions, makes a plan, and solves problems.

Blocks encourage *spatial* development as the child:

- Experiments with form, symmetry, visual balance, size, shape, patterns; and
- Makes a visual plan for block building.

Blocks encourage *musical* development as the child:

- Creates sounds through manipulating various sizes and textures of blocks.

Blocks encourage *naturalist* development as the child:

- Represents structures in nature through block play;
- Incorporates objects of nature in block play;
- Re-creates natural disasters and phenomena through block play; and
- Manipulates natural blocks.

TABLE 8.4 | *Blocks and Play Development*

To Encourage This Play Stage:	Provide the Following Materials:	This Is What Play in This Stage Will Look Like:
Sensory	Blocks of different sizes, shapes, and textures Homemade blocks with rice or stones inside Natural tree blocks	The child will look at, touch, and listen to the different sizes, shapes, textures, and sounds of blocks. The child will line blocks up.
Motor	Milk container blocks (½ gallon milk containers covered with contact paper), foam blocks, soft blocks, hollow blocks, cars, airplanes Wrapping paper, carpet roads	The child will stack blocks up, knock them over, and repeat this process over and over again. The child may wrap and unwrap blocks in paper. The child will make an airplane fly, a truck drive, and people move. The child will organize blocks. The child will stack hollow blocks to make steps or for sitting.
Level I Representation (Cognitive/Manipulative)	People, animals, dinosaurs, trains, train track, cardboard tubes, street maps	The child will begin building a block structure and naming it. The child will begin to become interested in not only the creation of the block structure, but also the function of it. The child will name the block structure she creates. The child will make patterns with blocks and be able to sort them according to color, shape, size, etc. The child will construct a maze for the class hamster or a map of the classroom. The child will begin building with an idea in mind.
Level II Representation (Creative/Expressive)	Seasonal materials, fairies, gnomes, dolls Miniature tools, rocks, dump trucks A small patch of grass, miniature garden tools Trucks, miniature shovels, cotton balls	After creating a structure, the child will begin to interact with it. A theme will begin to emerge with the structure. The child will use props related to the structure.

TABLE 8.4	*continued*	
To Encourage This Play Stage:	**Provide the Following Materials:**	**This Is What Play in This Stage Will Look Like:**
Level III Representation (Language-Mediated)	Block games	The child will be able to tell a story about his play or structure. The child will talk about why and how he built certain aspects of his structure. The child will use language in the place of some props.

Blocks encourage *interpersonal* development as the child:

- Works out conflicts, negotiates building plans, and problem solves with peers; and
- Shares materials, takes turns, and begins to empathize.

Blocks encourage *intrapersonal* development as the child:

- Recognizes and accepts her contribution to a group structure;
- Manages impulses; and
- Expresses herself through block play.

Blocks encourage *bodily/kinesthetic* development as the child:

- Manipulates small, large, and hollow blocks; and
- Respects material and bodily boundaries.

Music Center

For an example of the importance of music, reread the example with Jacob at the end of Chapter 2.

MUSIC AND PLAY DEVELOPMENT Music has a powerful influence on all aspects of our lives. This influence extends to the classroom. Many times, music is only presented to children through a teacher-directed activity. Children are not left with play materials to explore during play center time in the classroom.

One obstacle that must be overcome is the noise created in the music center. While noise is an integral part of the active early childhood classroom, an excessive amount of noise may interfere with other children's thought processes. The music center must be carefully placed to minimize distraction to other areas of the classroom. Surround the area with shelving or thick material to absorb some of the sound.

Music center

Provide a variety of materials in the center and change the materials based on the needs and interests of the children in the classroom. The following are groups of materials that could be made available in the music center at different times.

1. The music center could consist of a floor piano (see the Activities section of Chapter 7), classical music CDs or a piano, large paper floor staffs, and large paper notes.

2. The music center could incorporate materials for making instruments, such as coffee cans, oatmeal containers, rice, beans, spoons, rubber bands, scraps of material, and construction paper.

3. Materials could be provided that would inspire children to create their own music, such as songbooks, blank staff paper, black markers, and pens.

4. Instruments could be made available according to type, such as percussion instruments, woodwinds (recorders), etc.

5. Instruments that reflect a particular culture could be available.

6. Art materials could be made available that would encourage children to respond to certain musical genres. For example, watercolor painting to Mozart, or drawing to "Peter and the Wolf."

7. Recordings of music and a space large enough to dance should be available. The music can represent different genres, tempos, and rhythms.

It's important to note once again that music is not solely a teacher-directed experience. The child must have the opportunity to explore and create with musical materials on a daily basis. Music is an essential part of the child's daily play environment.

MUSIC AND THE INTELLIGENCES   In Chapter 4, the validity of music as an intelligence was discussed. Music should be approached in the classroom with the same respect and appreciation as the other intelligences. A music center, however, should not be restricted solely to musical intelligence. A music center addresses additional intelligences and, as presented in Jacob's story, can be an essential tool in symbol development.

A music center encourages *linguistic* development as the child:

- Repeats or makes up words to a song;
- Tells a story through songs; and
- Develops an awareness of the use and function of written symbols.

A music center encourages *logical/mathematical* development as the child:

- Recognizes time signatures;
- Distinguishes the time meaning of each note;
- Recognizes, claps, and symbolizes rhythm;
- Learns musical sequences and patterns; and
- Solves problems in a musical context.

A music center encourages *spatial* development as the child:

- Arranges notes on a scale;
- Increases body awareness through movement and dance; and
- Recognizes and names different musical symbols.

A music center encourages *bodily/kinesthetic* development as the child:

- Responds physically to music;
- Dances;
- Manipulates musical instruments; and
- Uses his body to create sounds.

A music center encourages *musical* development as the child:

- Manipulates the variety of instruments available;
- Creates sound from an object;
- Recognizes, dances, and responds to different musical genres;
- Experiments with, writes, and reads the musical notation system;
- Recognizes, repeats, and creates rhythms, tempos, and melodies; and
- Narrates her play with song.

TABLE 8.5 | *Music and Play Development*

To Encourage This Play Stage:	Provide the Following Materials:	This Is What Play in This Stage Will Look Like:
Sensory	Music of different genres, tuning forks, instruments, bells	The child will listen to a variety of music. The child will move randomly to the music. The child will listen to rhymes, songs, and fingerplays.
Motor	Music, simple instruments, homemade floor piano (see the Activities section of Chapter 7), streamers, drums	The child will move more purposefully to the music and exhibit a sense of rhythm and beat. The child will move faster or slower, depending upon the tempo of the music. The child will perform the motions of recognized fingerplays.
Level I Representation (Cognitive/Manipulative)	Blank staff paper, music books, felt board notes and staff Floor staff and paper notes Watercolor paints, oil pastels, crayons, modeling wax, modeling clay	The child will recognize the difference in musical genres. The child will be able to repeat fingerplays, songs, and rhymes. The child will begin to scribble or make purposeful marks on staff paper and say she is writing her own music. The child will paint or draw in response to music. The child will use instruments functionally; can beat a drum, shake bells, etc. The child will begin to create dance poses and call it ballet or tap.
Level II Representation (Creative/Expressive)	Blank staff paper, watercolor paints, oil pastels, materials for child-made instruments, bubbles	The child will write music and play an instrument more creatively. The child will create his own instrument and pretend to write his own music. The child will communicate feelings and themes through dance and instrument play. The child will make up names to musical notes and signs. The child can pretend to be a feather floating, a raindrop, or an animal. The child's understanding of musical genres begins to increase. The child is able to identify the genre when listening to a short piece of music.
Level III Representation (Language-Mediated)		

TABLE 8.5 | *continued*

To Encourage This Play Stage:	Provide the Following Materials:	This Is What Play in This Stage Will Look Like:
Level III Representation (Language-Mediated)	Interval or pentatonic flute Musical games Tape recorder	The child will make up her own song and can record it on a tape recorder. The child will incorporate formal notes into her music writing. The child will be able to begin to play an instrument such as the interval or pentatonic flute. The child will begin to recognize the formal rules to musical genres and begin to identify formal names of notes and signs.

A music center encourages *naturalist* development as the child:

- Identifies and recreates sounds in nature;
- Finds rhythm and melody in nature sounds; and
- Represents nature through music.

A music center encourages *interpersonal* development as the child:

- Listens and observes music and dance from other cultures;
- Communicates information through music;
- Performs and plays in a group;
- Appreciates and shares musical interests with others; and
- Interprets meaning from musical selections.

A music center encourages *intrapersonal* development as the child:

- Manages impulses while dancing and/or listening to music;
- Relates music to a particular mood or emotion;
- Responds physically and/or emotionally to music; and
- Communicates feelings, emotions, and meaning through musical compositions.

Library and Publishing Center

One of my three-year-old's favorite stories was "Why Mosquitoes Buzz in People's Ears." I thought it was unusual for a three-year-old to express such enthusiasm for this story. She looked at the pictures, talked about the poor owl's baby, and delighted in the sequence of the

Literature and story center

story. At the local library, I was excited to discover a movie entitled Why Mosquitoes Buzz in People's Ears. *I brought it home and put it into the VCR. When it started, my daughter frowned. She ran up to her room and retrieved the book. She turned the TV off and sat down on the floor. "I want you to read it, Mommy."*

LIBRARY/PUBLISHING CENTER AND PLAY DEVELOPMENT   Stories are an integral part of life. Many times children watch classics (and other programs) on television instead of reading them. Reading, or being read to, requires an active brain. Watching television requires a passive brain (Healy, 1990). Television should not have a central role in the education of young children. People should play the central role and the main source of stories.

The literature center should be comfortable, well-lit, and inviting. The literature center should have other materials available besides good-quality books. Story cubes, story tapes, and puppets should be included, as well as a variety of props. For example, a basket, red cape, and flowers can be made available along with a copy of *Little Red Riding Hood;* a baby, child, and adult gorilla can be made available along with a copy of *Little Gorilla* by Ruth Bornstein; three bowls could be available with *The Three Bears;*

TABLE 8.6 | *Library/Publishing Center and Play Development*

To Encourage This Play Stage:	Provide the Following Materials:	This Is What Play in This Stage Would Look Like:
Sensory	Touchy feely books Story, song, and rhyme cassettes	The child will listen to songs, rhymes, and stories about herself. The child will look at pages in a book. The child will touch "feely" books.
Motor	Books	The child will move like the characters in a book and turn pages in a book. The child will respond physically to a story.
Level I Representation (Cognitive/Manipulative)	Books with props, story cubes	The child will be able to retell a story or "read" a memorized story. The child will retell a story using story props. The child will be able to find pictures corresponding to stories on story cubes.
Level II Representation (Creative/Expressive)	Puppets, dolls, miniature life toys, child-made books and puppets	The child will add her own creativity to familiar stories. The child may make up a different ending or add new characters to stories. The child will use invented spelling and symbols to write about her drawings. She will begin to tell stories about her pictures. The child will use props or puppets to tell an elaborate story with a beginning, middle, and an end.
Level III Representation (Language-Mediated)	Materials to create books, such as paper, puppets, stamp pads, pictures, stapler, hole puncher, blank books	The child will write her own stories using drawings, invented spelling, and symbols. The child will also read stories. The child does this by recalling a memorized story, using picture clues to tell a story, or by making up a story. The child knows the function of print, can recognize and identify where print is used in a story, and attempts to create print.

or miniature characters or dress-up clothes corresponding to other favorite stories can be available. Child-made, teacher-made, or commercial puppets can be available alone or with books. Props can also be made available for children to retell or create their own stories (without books).

Children need the opportunity to create their own stories so materials should be available for that purpose. The children could also illustrate spoken stories. In addition, time and space should be available for the child to curl up with a teacher and be read to.

Many times, children are introduced to literacy through flash cards and direct instruction of letters/letter sounds. While recognition of letters and sounds is an important component of reading, those skills do not have to be taught directly, especially to young children. A more appropriate way to introduce children to language and literacy is through a purposeful, well-planned play environment.

LIBRARY/PUBLISHING CENTER AND THE INTELLIGENCES The library/publishing center appropriately addresses many aspects of linguistic intelligence. In this play center, children can investigate language on their terms with their particular interests. However, the library/publishing center is not solely limited to the development of linguistic intelligence.

The library/publishing center encourages *linguistic* development as the child:

- Reads, creates, retells, interprets, illustrates, and writes his own stories;
- Verbally responds to others' stories;
- Shares experiences relevant to the stories shared and read in the classroom;
- Listens to stories;
- Develops his own linguistic symbols;
- Utilizes symbols, grammar, and print in meaningful ways;
- Discovers the varying functions of print;
- Uses invented spelling to express her understanding of phonetics; and
- Recognizes sentence structure and grammar rules.

The library/publishing center encourages *logical/mathematical* development as the child:

- Sequences stories, reads about math and science concepts; and
- Reads about scientific phenomena.

The library/publishing center encourages *spatial* development as the child:

- Illustrates her own stories;
- Creates visual symbols to represent stories, characters, and/or letters;
- Uses pictures to tell a story;
- Visualizes a story; and
- Incorporates word-shape clues and visual patterns into his decoding skills.

The library/publishing center encourages *musical* development as the child:

- Reads/writes song books;
- Creates poems; and
- Reads stories related to music.

The library/publishing center encourages *naturalist* development as the child:

- Reads/listens to stories about nature; and
- Represents nature or experiences in nature through drawing/writing.

The library/publishing center encourages *interpersonal* development as the child:

- Listens to and shares stories;
- Expresses and interprets emotions of others through stories;
- Listens to stories from other cultures;
- Accepts others' ideas into his stories;
- Incorporates other characters' points of views in her stories; and
- Discovers that two characters can react completely differently to the same situation.

The library/publishing center encourages *intrapersonal* development as the child:

- Expresses and interprets his own emotions through stories; and
- Writes and draws in her journal.

The library/publishing center encourages *bodily/kinesthetic* development as the child:

- Uses gestures to tell a story; and
- Manipulates the props and puppets to tell a story.

Puppets

Five-year-old Brenda had a difficult young life. She was the daughter of a cocaine-addicted mother and a father with mental illness. She was taken away from her parents within months of her birth. She never lived with a foster family for more than one year. At five she was angry, confused, had little trust in anyone, and exhibited signs of emotional and attachment disorders. Her behavior could be so erratic that friendships were difficult for her to form. She had great difficulty relating to peers or forming attachments. She desperately wished to be accepted by her peers. It was difficult for her to talk about her feelings of rejection and desire for acceptance.

Brenda began to take an interest in the puppet corner of the classroom. Brenda would often choose a cute, soft puppy puppet to play with. While using the puppet, she would tell me how angry, sad, or lonely the puppy was. She would ask the other children if they liked the puppet; if they thought the puppy was pretty. Brenda would become excited when the children

Puppet center

would pet the puppy or when a child told the puppy they liked it or thought it was pretty. The puppy became an extension of Brenda. She used the puppy to gain peer acceptance and to communicate difficult feelings and thoughts. It opened up an extremely vital method of communicating and a way for Brenda to begin to find some healing in the difficult life she led.

PUPPETS AND PLAY DEVELOPMENT   Puppets offer a nonthreatening medium to express emotions, experiment with language, and encourage expression. A puppet theater can be used occasionally, but the emphasis should not be on the performance. The performance aspect of puppetry may discourage some children from using the materials. Instead, informal stories and play offer a greater benefit to all children.

PUPPETS AND THE INTELLIGENCES   Puppets involve the voice, movement, song, and communication and help develop many of the intelligences. There are a variety of reasons for using puppets in the classroom. They can be used to communicate information, share a story, teach a concept, share a song, or communicate personal information.

TABLE 8.7 | *Puppets and Play Development*

To Encourage This Play Stage:	Provide the Following Materials:	This Is What Play in This Stage Would Look Like:
Sensory	Puppets of different sizes, shapes, and textures	The child will feel and look at the puppets.
Motor	Puppets with large mouths, legs, and arms	The child will make the puppet move, dance, walk, open/close its mouth, etc.
Level I Representation (Cognitive/Manipulative)	Animal puppets Puppet families	The child will begin to pretend with the puppets. The child will makes a dog puppet bark, a mother bird puppet feed her baby bird puppets, etc.
Level II Representation (Creative/Expressive)	Dragon, witches, wizards, kings, queens, princesses, and prince puppets Puppets with disabilities, glasses, abnormalities Materials to create puppets	The child will tell a story with the puppets. The story will have a theme, but will not necessarily make sense. The child will use the puppets to explain a concept or talk about feelings. The child will use the puppets to talk to other children.
Level III Representation (Language-Mediated)	Materials to create puppets, scripts, props, and scenery	The child will use the puppets to tell elaborate stories with a beginning, middle, and end. The child's story will have a logical sequence of events and will often solve a moral dilemma related to the child's life. The child will be able to coordinate a puppet show with peers, write a script, create scenery, create props, and create his own puppets.

Puppets encourage *linguistic* development as the child:

- Tells stories;
- Develops vocabulary; and
- Communicates feelings, shares events, and develops language by communicating with the puppets.

Puppets encourage *logical/mathematical* development as the child:

- Sequences events; and
- Is presented with logical/mathematical information through puppets.

Puppets encourage *spatial* development as the child:

■ Negotiates stage space in puppet play; and
■ Manipulates puppets in the environment.

Puppets encourage *musical* development as the child:

■ Uses the puppet to tell a finger play, sing a song, or move to music.

Puppets encourage *naturalist* development as the child:

■ Listens to or creates puppet stories with animal and/or nature themes;
■ Incorporates natural events into story lines; and
■ Uses natural materials to create puppets or for story props.

Puppets encourage *interpersonal* development as the child:

■ Negotiates a puppet play theme with other children;
■ Talks to other children through the puppets;
■ Plans and coordinates a puppet show with other children;
■ Solves problems through puppet stories;
■ Relates to other children through the use of a puppet; and
■ Uses a puppet that represents a different race, culture, or disability.

Puppets encourage *intrapersonal* development as the child:

■ Expresses emotions, stories, ideas, and feelings through puppets.

Puppets encourage *bodily/kinesthetic* development as the child:

■ Manipulates the puppet to communicate a role; and
■ Respects body boundaries with the puppets.

Logic/Math Center

One night at dinner, my five-year-old daughter was drinking juice out of a juice box made of foil. My husband blew into the straw of an empty juice box and inflated it. My daughter laughed and sucked the air back out of it. She then blew air to inflate it again. With a puzzled look on her face she said, "Mom, why doesn't this float. I am blowing air into it like a balloon, it should float." I began a lengthy explanation about gases and the differences between helium and the air we breathe. She looked at me and laughed. "Mom, that's silly. Watch this." She took a napkin, looked up, and placed the napkin on her face. She blew the napkin up in the air and it floated back to the ground. "See Mom, you don't have to have helium to make something float. I just used my air and my air isn't helium." She then looked at me and stated very

Math and logic center

matter-of-factly, "I got it. I know why it doesn't float. You know how when you put a hole in the balloon with a fork or something and the air gets out. It doesn't float anymore. Well, there is a hole in my juice box for the straw. Of course that's why it doesn't float."

LOGIC/MATH AND PLAY DEVELOPMENT Young children use fantasy and imagination to make sense of and explain logical and mathematical events. This precausal reasoning allows the child to draw conclusions rooted in fantasy and limited life experience. As the child reaches the age of seven or eight, they begin to demonstrate the concrete operational stage of development. Their ability to reason becomes more focused and purposeful. They take what life experiences they do have and offer conclusions that sound more believable. Children can explore reasoning in the logical/mathematical play center of the classroom.

The logical/mathematical center in the classroom should focus on problem solving and number concepts. Materials that offer an appropriate challenge and the opportunity to explore number should be available in this center. Children should have the space to work comfortably in small groups in this center. Debate and discussion over possible conclusions, algorithms, and techniques are important in the development of logical/mathematical thinking.

TABLE 8.8 | *Logic/Math and Play Development*

To Encourage This Play Stage:	Provide the Following Materials:	This Is What Play in This Stage Would Look Like:
Sensory	Natural materials, fish tank, class pet, plants	The child will explore the materials with her senses.
Motor	Small stacking blocks, rice pouring, liquid pouring, nuts and bolts, folding rags	The child refines small motor movements through the manipulation of small materials.
Level I Representation (Cognitive/Manipulative)	Button sorting, bead stringing, sequence cards, measuring units, patterning blocks, picture schedule	The child will classify, count, categorize, sequence, and measure materials. The children will begin to establish relationships between cause and effect. The child will use one-to-one correspondence.
Level II Representation (Creative/Expressive)	Measuring units, number rods	The child will make up mathematical terms and numbers. The child will make up possible causes for problems in the classroom. The causes will include fantasy and imagination. The child will pretend to read the time on a clock.
Level III Representation (Language-Mediated)	Card games such as war, fish Measuring sticks, rulers	The child will take part in number games and respect the rules of the game. The child will use mathematical vocabulary. The child will explain logical events. The child will establish cause/effect relationships.

LOGIC/MATH AND INTELLIGENCE   The logic and math center facilitates a strong foundation for logical/mathematical development. Through the play and manipulation of the materials housed in this center, the other intelligences are addressed as well.

The logic/math center encourages *linguistic* development as the child:

- Develops mathematical vocabulary; and
- Verbalizes problem-solving strategies.

The logic/math center encourages *logical/mathematical* development as the child:

- Explores, creates, and solves problems with materials;
- Develops number concepts, sequencing, and one-to-one correspondence;

- Manipulates numbers; and
- Discovers the properties of materials.

The logic/math center encourages *spatial* development as the child:

- Develops spatial ordering skills;
- Problem-solves spatial tasks; and
- Recognizes the appropriate placement of logical and mathematical symbols.

The logic/math center encourages *naturalist* intelligence as the child:

- Interprets, predicts, and explores natural events in logical terms.

The logic/math center encourages *interpersonal* development as the child:

- Negotiates solutions to problems and engages other children's help.

The logic/math center encourages *intrapersonal* development as the child:

- Manages impulses, channels emotions appropriately, and develops frustration tolerance.

The logic/math center encourages *bodily/kinesthetic* development as the child:

- Develops fine-motor skills to manipulate logical/mathematical materials.

Reflective Center

Andrea had wealthy parents and was involved in many activities. She attended kindergarten, dance class, Brownies, soccer, classes at the science center, art classes in the museum, and second-language classes. Andrea was overwhelmed by the amount of activities she participated in. At times, Andrea confessed she wanted to hide from everything. At five years old, she recognized she needed a break.

Brittany had been in foster care since she was a couple of months old. She has never been with a family for more than a year. She was a "crack baby." She has a psychotic father who repeatedly requests to see her and then cancels. She has received counseling, therapy, and intensive behavior modification therapy. The therapist recommended evaluating and judging every behavior Brittany engages in and immediately rewarding or punishing her. At times, Brittany was overwhelmed with her life situation and the constant evaluation of her every action. She fantasized about retreating into a place of her own where she could be alone.

REFLECTION AND PLAY DEVELOPMENT Both of these children benefited from the reflective center in the classroom. They needed to get away from the hurriedness, expectations, stress, and pressure of their daily routine. The reflective center allowed

TABLE 8.9 | *Reflective Center*

To Encourage This Play Stage:	Provide the Following Materials:	This Is What Play in This Stage Would Look Like:
Sensory	Colored bottles of water/oil, fish tank, lava lamps Softened natural light Colored cellophane on windows (to create a small stained glass effect) Silks, blankets, pillows, large stuffed animals, beanbag chairs Tape of nature sounds, soothing classical music Mirrors	The child will lie down, observe the softened visual effects, listen to the soothing music, watch the fish swim.
Motor	Table-top mirrors, pictures of children's faces Rocking chairs	The child will rock in the rocking chair. The child will practice making faces in the mirror.
Level I Representation (Cognitive/Manipulative)	Cardboard box Emotion cards Family albums Personal cubby	The child will understand the purpose of the reflective center. The child will recognize the need to go into the reflective center. The child will recognize the need to be alone. The child will name the emotions on the emotion cards. The child will name the emotion the child is feeling at a given moment. The child will look at pictures of the child's family. The child will retrieve a personal object from her cubby for comfort.
Level II Representation (Creative/Expressive)	Journals, crayons	The child will draw a picture of how they feel or how something made them feel. They will draw about experiences they have had or are anticipating.

TABLE 8.9 | *continued*

Level III Representation (Language-Mediated)	Portfolios	The child will explain why he is feeling a particular way. The child will brainstorm solutions to peer problems. The child will discuss motivations for particular behaviors. The child will tell or create a story about a child who is dealing with a similar situation. The child will discuss his/her progress while looking back at work samples contained in his/her portfolio.

these children time to relax, regain control, put problems out of their mind, or reflect on problems in journals. For at least part of their day, they had a private place to refuel.

Materials should be available in this center that allow children to engage in various play levels. The play materials will not involve active, aggressive play. This should be a quiet center in the room that respects the child's need for quiet play and time to be alone.

REFLECTION AND THE INTELLIGENCES   The reflective center in the early childhood classroom is often neglected. However, the importance of it cannot be stressed enough. In order to fully explore and develop intrapersonal intelligence, the child must be given the opportunity to reflect and record thoughts, reactions, and interpretations of the day's events.

The reflective center encourages *linguistic* development as the child:

■   Verbalizes thoughts, feelings, and emotions;
■   Communicates the need to use the reflective center; and
■   Writes in her journal.

The reflective center encourages *intrapersonal* development as the child:

■   Recognizes the need for the reflective center;
■   Works on his journal in the center;
■   Reflects on experiences;
■   Recognizes the benefits of relaxation; and
■   Identifies, recognizes, and symbolizes feelings and reactions.

The reflective center encourages *bodily/kinesthetic* development as the child:

■   Recognizes the body's need for a break; and
■   Manages bodily impulses.

Spatial Center

Four-year-old Jamal was constantly stepping on and touching other children. He would walk right over block structures and other projects. When confronted, he would have no idea he had walked over other children's play materials. At circle time, he laid on other children as he spread out his body. His intentions were not to bother the other children. His teacher recognized that Jamal did not have a clear sense of body boundaries. She decided to bring a large mirror into the classroom. She encouraged Jamal and the other children to watch their movements in the mirror. She gave them streamers and other materials and instructed them to move the streamers to cause certain effects in the mirror. At circle time, she used colored tape to make bubbles around the circle. She explained to Jamal that he was to keep his body inside his special bubble during circle time. These experiences helped Jamal develop body boundaries and transfer his awareness of body boundaries into his play.

SPATIAL CENTER AND PLAY DEVELOPMENT   Play in the spatial center of the classroom can encourage body and materials boundaries, encourage the development of the senses, and help the child find his/her place in the classroom, community, and the world.

Spatial center

TABLE 8.10 | *Spatial Center and Play Development*

To Encourage This Play Stage:	Provide the Following Materials:	This Is What Play in This Stage Would Look Like:
Sensory	Braille book; smelling bottles; color palettes; objects of different textures, weights, smells, and sounds	The child will run his hands across a Braille book, find objects that look/smell/feel/sound/taste the same.
Motor	Metal insets, knobless cylinders	The child will stack materials such as knobless cylinders or cubes. The child will trace the metal insets. The child will bump into other children and not have an understanding of body or materials boundaries.
Level I Representation (Cognitive/Manipulative)	Binomial cubes, trinomial cubes, pink tower, geometric solids, puzzles, maps, globes, red rods, gears, objects hidden in a box/bag, star charts, pictures of the night sky, old clocks, radios, computers, flowers, vases Mirror	The child will identify shapes, build a maze with the red rods, find their state on a globe, identify objects hidden in a box through touch, complete the binomial/trinomial cubes, build the pink towers, identify the geometric solids, complete a puzzle, or arrange gears so they will turn. The child will identify a constellation. The child will arrange flowers in a vase. The child will take apart an old clock or radio. The child will begin to understand where their body begins and ends. They will realize materials boundaries.
Level II Representation (Creative/Expressive)	Small fairy gardens, sand gardens, groupings of objects and small shelves	The child will creatively draw her own map of the school or of the way to her house, etc. The child will arrange gears creatively, but functionally. The child will make up her own constellation. The child will group related objects and create a visual display of these objects. The child will design a small garden. The child will create a purposeful flower arrangement. The child will invent creative explanations for the function of the different parts of the radio, etc.

TABLE 8.10	*continued*	
Level III Representation (Language-Mediated)	Chess, checkers	The child will observe the rules and be able to play games that require spatial skills, such as checkers, chess, or other board games. The child will identify constellations and explain why the constellation has a particular name. The child will create names of constellations she discovers or creates. The child will create a more accurate map of the school or the way to her house. The child will be able to give verbal directions to accurately get from one familiar location to another (from the front door to the bathroom, from the sand area to her cubby). The child will discuss appropriate plans for a garden, explaining why particular plants or objects should be placed in a particular area. The child will talk about the function of the parts of the equipment she takes apart. The child will put the equipment back together. The child will let another child know when their body or material boundaries have been violated through words.

SPATIAL CENTER AND THE INTELLIGENCES The spatial center will target materials necessary for the development of a foundation for spatial intelligence. In addition to developing spatial intelligence, manipulation of these materials will encourage development in other intelligences.

The spatial center will encourage *linguistic* development as the child:

- Uses and develops vocabulary related to spatial concepts; and
- Discusses plans for spatial tasks.

The spatial center will encourage *logical/mathematical* development as the child:

- Classifies, categorizes, and compares materials.

The spatial center encourages *spatial* development as the child:

- Manipulates objects and purposefully places objects in her environment;
- Discovers physical characteristics in objects;
- Discovers where his body is in space;
- Mentally recreates his environment;
- Creates a map of her environment;
- Identifies and creates shapes; and
- Creates an arrangement or grouping.

The spatial center encourages *naturalist* development as the child:

- Prepares and arranges objects in his natural environment; and
- Manipulates, discusses, and recognizes spatial properties of materials.

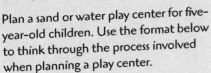

8.9

Journal Questions

Plan a sand or water play center for five-year-old children. Use the format below to think through the process involved when planning a play center.

Name of play center (sand or water):

Materials:

Developmental rationale (Why would this play center be important and relevant to five-year-old children?):

Draw a sketch of how the play center might be set up:

What intelligences does the play center address?

What would sensory play look like in this center?

What would motor play look like in this center?

What would level I representational play look like in this center?

What would level II representational play look like in this center?

What would level III representational play look like in this center?

The spatial center encourages *interpersonal* development as the child:

- Discovers her physical place in the world; and
- Negotiates, takes turns, shares, and interacts with other children in the play center.

The spatial center encourages *bodily/kinesthetic* development as the child:

- Develops appropriate motor skills through the purposeful manipulation of the materials.

 # Summary

Planning for play spaces takes careful consideration of the developmental levels, interests, strengths, and challenges of each child in the classroom. Children build concepts, construct knowledge, communicate information, and share emotions during play experiences. A carefully planned play environment encourages choice, peer interaction, and interaction with developmentally appropriate materials.

Providing time for activities, projects, and play requires careful planning skills and it is essential for the early childhood teacher to master them. The next chapter will provide strategies for planning sufficient time for play, projects, and activities, and address additional scheduling and environment concerns.

References

Hannaford, C. (1995) *Smart moves: Why learning is not all in your head.* Arlington, VA: Great Ocean Publishers.

Healy, J. (1990) *Endangered minds: Why children don't think and what we can do about it.* New York: Touchstone.

Hughes, F. (1995) *Children, play, and development.* Boston: Allyn & Bacon.

Kamii, C. (1985) *Young children reinvent mathematics: Implications of Piaget's theory.* New York: Teachers College Press.

Parten, M. (1932) Social participation among preschool children. *Journal of Abnormal and Social Psychology, 27,* 243–269.

Piaget, J. (1962) *Play, dreams and imitation in childhood.* New York: W. W. Norton & Co.

Schomburg, R., Smith, M., & Tittnich, E. (1986) *Developing your curriculum.* Pittsburgh: Louise Child Care Center.

Schomburg, R. (1996) "Using symbolic play abilities to assess academic readiness." *Play, Policy, & Practice Caucus.* Washington, DC: NAEYC.

Stone, S. (1995) "Wanted: Advocates for play in the primary grades." *Young Children.* (Sept. 1995, vol. 50, No. 6, pp. 45–54).

Stone, S. (1985) *Playing: A kid's curriculum.* Glenview, IL: Good Year Books.

Teele, S. (2000) *Rainbows of intelligence.* Thousand Oaks, CA: Corwin Press.

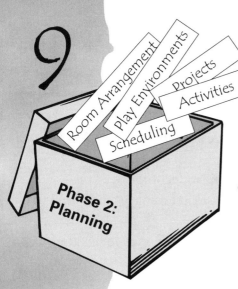

9

Room Arrangement
Play Environments
Projects
Activities
Scheduling

Phase 2:
Planning

Planning Spaces and Time

Scheduling

Time. It seems there is a constant yearning for more time in contemporary America. This is especially true in the school system. There is never enough time to cover all the content or meet parental, administrative, and societal schooling expectations.

9.1

Journal Questions

What goals do you think a schedule can address?

Interview an early childhood teacher (preschool to second grade). Ask them to write down their schedule. Or create a schedule for a specific age group.

What does the schedule tell you about the classroom? What is valued or worth spending time on in this classroom?

Managing time is a precious skill. Managing time wisely can lead to better health, less stress, and a better life. If each part of the child's day is clearly understood, recognized, and attended to, the day will go more smoothly and the child will get more out of it. Creating an appropriate schedule communicates that children are valued and respected in the classroom.

Appropriate scheduling offers many benefits. It can address many goals of the early childhood curriculum, facilitate the development of the intelligences, and communicate the value of the child's time.

227

An appropriate schedule:

- Provides children with a flow that respects their natural body rhythms;
- Balances and provides both active and quiet experiences;
- Encourages self-reflection;
- Develops self-control and relaxation techniques;
- Utilizes every opportunity to develop morality and attend to all of the intelligences;
- Prepares children for managing their time as older children and as adults;
- Provides purpose and meaning to the child's day;
- Provides children time alone and time with the group;
- Balances teacher-directed/child-directed/collaborative experiences;
- Provides children with strategies they can use to cope with transitions and allows them to transition well from one activity to the next; and
- Is realistic.

Each part of the child's day is significant—from arrival to departure. Each part of the day should offer an opportunity to form relationships, facilitate interactions, model, assess, build content, and construct knowledge.

Arrival

The child's arrival and the greeting from her teacher can address intrapersonal and interpersonal skills, as well as communicate that she is a valued member of the classroom community. The greeting the child receives communicates a message. If a teacher is hurried, doesn't bother (or is unable) to look at the child, and is busy engaging in other tasks, the child may feel that she is not valued and has to wait for the attention and consideration of her teacher. However, if the teacher looks the child in the eyes, greets her upon entering the classroom, and makes her feel that her presence is welcomed and necessary, the child will feel valued and respected. Children, especially young children, have much to say to their teacher upon entering the classroom. Usually this process only takes a few minutes. If the dialogue is overwhelming (or prevents the teacher from welcoming other students) the teacher can greet each child independently and encourage the child to create a drawing or journal entry to communicate what is on her mind. The drawings, if necessary, can be shared during the morning meetings.

In the author's experience, there are many tasks the teacher must take care of in the morning. However, the children are of no lesser importance than these tasks. If the teacher is lucky enough to co-teach or has an aide, the aide or one teacher can take care of the greetings. The other teacher can take care of other morning tasks. If the teacher does not have morning help, some morning tasks can be shared with the children.

For example, attendance and lunch-choice duties can be shared with the children. If children need to choose a lunch (for the cafeteria lunch count), the choices can be drawn on a blackboard in pictures or letters (or both). The child can choose a picture of herself, or pick out her written name, and place her picture/name under the picture of the lunch she chooses. The children, if able and appropriate, can take part in tallying the lunch count. This activity involves choice, math skills, symbol/letter recognition, and enforces routine.

Attendance can also be taken by the children using a similar method. Each child can have a picture of him/herself with his/her name written on it. The children can find their picture and place it on the "present" board. Many math and language activities can extend from the attendance and lunch experiences (Kamii, 1985).

Other arrival activities can include close-ended play, classroom responsibilities, and journal work. Close-ended play experiences involve tasks that have a specific purpose. These tasks might include using puzzles, peg-boards, sorting materials, stacking materials, and beads. Classroom responsibilities can include tasks such as watering plants, wiping off tables, setting up materials, feeding animals, and getting materials organized for project work. Free play (utilizing all play areas) is cautioned during this time of the day. The time and attention required in observing, facilitating, and maintaining the play environment may be difficult when trying to greet each child and take care of arrival responsibilities.

Children may also take part in journal writing during arrival time. Each child can have his own notebook or sketch pad. Children can draw pictures or write about anything—experiences they have had, tasks they would like to accomplish, problems they are having, fears or concerns. The teacher can circulate and ask the child if they would like to talk about their drawing. The children might also have the opportunity to share their journal entries during morning meetings. Whether to share journal entries is completely up to the child. The journal experience develops intrapersonal intelligence.

9.2

Journal Question

How do you think greeting each child can affect the day?

Morning Meeting/Sharing

At morning meetings the teacher can share expectations, communicate important information, offer a formal greeting, and discuss the day's plans. This formal greeting invites all the children to participate. The same greeting is used each day. The greeting can take the form of a prayer (if allowed), song, dance, or fingerplay. The next part of the morning meeting can be sharing. Children can talk about their journals, share family events, or talk about an item they brought to school that day. The teacher also takes part in the sharing. If a lengthy sharing has taken place, children may need an active song or dance and need time to stretch.

Next, calendar time can take place. Calendar time is traditionally used in classrooms to work on number recognition, patterning, and counting. This is appropriate for older children (first and second grade). Young children need experiences to develop the concept behind using a calendar. They need to understand why a calendar is used and what it represents. Younger children can talk about the season and keep track of days through event planning. A blank weekly calendar should be present at the beginning of each week. The teacher and/or children can draw pictures of one event/activity that will take place each day. Children can talk about how many days until a special event, or what day of the week that event will occur. However, this kind of calendar experience may be more meaningful for younger children than reciting the month, date, and day of the week.

The morning meeting can end with children sharing their plans for the day: what play centers they intend to play in, what projects they are involved in, and so on.

The length of the morning meeting should depend on the age and group size of the children. Plan on the morning meeting taking as long as the children seem comfortable sitting and talking. Older children should be able to take part in the morning meeting for longer times.

9.3

Journal Questions

Did the schedule you wrote or received address morning meeting time? What kind of goals do morning meeting times address?

By having a formal sharing time, children begin to learn about other children, cultures, and families. Class meetings provide a safe way of sharing personal information, accomplishments, and acknowledgments, and can build a sense of community (Vance and Weaver, 2002). Children also begin to learn about other points of view and about respect for other children. This opening activity also encourages the growth of interpersonal and intrapersonal intelligence.

Meal Times

All early childhood programs have meal or snack times. This part of the day can encourage interpersonal and intrapersonal development, develop and/or communicate morals, help children deal with transitions, and provide experience with different cultures. Meal time is an important event in a child's life, especially meals away from home.

Meal or snack times can sometimes be chaotic. However, with appropriate planning and attention to meal or snack times, teachers can take full advantage of the countless ways meal times can address cognitive, physical, and emotional needs. Carol Garboden Murray introduces twelve strategies that help to nourish all aspects of development during meal times (Murray, 2000). The following strategies, presented in "Learning about Children's Social and Emotional Needs at Snack Time—Nourishing the Body, Mind, and Spirit of Each Child," can motivate teachers to make changes in the emotional climate, physical arrangement, and the flow of snack times in order to create an enriching, soothing, important time for children to satisfy their physical and emotional hungers. Many of the strategies can also be applied to meal (breakfast/lunch/dinner) times as well.

1. Choose a small-group or whole-group snack routine
2. Organize snack trays
3. Plan a transition ritual before snack
4. Define each child's personal space
5. Sit at eye level with children
6. Teach genuine respect and care by modeling social skills
7. Teach independence in small steps
8. Offer food choices to strengthen self-identity
9. Observe and reflect
10. Let spontaneous conversation flow
11. Teach concepts at snack time
12. Don't sacrifice spontaneous child-generated language for teacher topics

These strategies are taken from Murray, 2000.

Murray suggests whole-group snack times for half-day programs. This type of approach to snack respects the time limit reality of a half-day program. The whole-group snack times provide for all of the children to eat at the same time. This approach takes great organization, routine, and planning. Children sit at tables with one adult. (If there are two adults, then there can be two tables of children, and so on.)

Small-group snack time is suggested for full-day programs and for groups of children who find the transition to snack difficult or are dealing with significant emotional or physical challenges. For small-group snack, the food is set up as a center (similar to a block center, dramatic play center, etc.). The snack center should be private, cozy, and away from distractions. An adult should be available to children when they participate in the snack center. The children choose when to eat snack. Some children come to school hungry, others are not hungry until later in the day. The small-group approach allows children to eat when they are hungry (Murray, 2000).

Organizing snack trays in advance helps to eliminate confusion and relieves some stress often associated with snack times. Before children arrive, snack trays can be prepared with the necessary utensils, silverware, napkins, food, drinks, and plates. At snack time, the trays can be easily retrieved and wait time is minimal (Murray, 2000).

Perhaps the most significant obstacle associated with snack is the transition to it. However, transition techniques can successfully overcome the obstacle. Murray suggests engaging the children in a presnack activity. This activity lets children know snack is next and involves them in snack preparation. Washing tables, spreading out tablecloths, setting the table, choosing and making flower arrangements, and arranging and preparing the snack are effective transition presnack activities. A familiar song, fingerplay, or rhyme can also signify snack time (Murray, 2000). Meal times and rest times often remind the child of activities that go on in the home. This may increase the child's tension in the transition to meal times. Pictures of the child's family can be attached to the placemats. Materials that can help children act out meal themes in the dramatic play area should be available. Families can occasionally be invited to take part in meal times with children.

Children need an appropriate amount of space and time to eat snack. In some kindergarten programs, snack is expected to last only a few minutes, with minimal involvement from the teacher. Snack often takes place at the child's desk in these programs. Hurrying snack and minimizing social interaction during snack may cause unnecessary stress and indigestion. Children require the appropriate space and time to begin and finish their snack. This time must allow for and encourage social interaction. Children must also feel they have a personal space at the snack table. This space can be provided through child-made placemats or familiar seating (Murray, 2000).

While sharing snack with children, it is important for teachers to sit at eye level with their group of children. This encourages interaction and promotes respects. Teachers can then model appropriate self-help, social, and emotional skills (Murray, 2000).

Children are expected to use good manners when eating with their families or a group of peers. It's necessary to have an appropriate role model to inspire good social habits and behavior. Teachers must use good manners and exhibit positive social skills in order to encourage and acknowledge those qualities in children (Murray, 2000).

Independence is an important goal of meal time. At the beginning of the program, younger children will require more assistance in preparing and serving snack. Gradually they will become more socially and physically able to take over the serving and preparation of snacks (Murray, 2000).

Snack choices should reflect an understanding of good nutrition. A healthy snack choice can help stabilize blood sugar, which can improve or maintain a healthy mood. Children who feel good and who are satisfied will often engage in tasks more deeply and behave more appropriately (Murray, 2000).

Snack choices should reflect the culture of the children in the classroom. Teachers need to communicate with the families to find out what kinds of food the child eats at home. These food choices can be available weekly to all children.

While being physically and emotionally available to children at snack time, teachers should also observe and reflect upon social and emotional behaviors children exhibit during snack. Teachers can mentally assess social skills, notice friendships, recognize if children are excluded, and reflect upon the morals, manners, and socialization information offered (Murray, 2000).

When managing a large group of children, there is often little time to witness or take part in a lengthy conversation with children. Snack time offers the perfect opportunity to let children converse, observe how they respond to one another, and see how children make sense of their world. It's important to let the children take the responsibility for the content addressed during snack time. This is not a time for teachers to converse with each other, but to facilitate a discussion between and with the children (Murray, 2000).

Snack time can also provide teachers a time to review or introduce concepts. Math, science, language, logic, and personal skills can all be creatively addressed during the preparation, serving, and eating of snack (Murray, 2000).

While engaging children in concepts occasionally at snack time, it is important not to monopolize the conversation with teacher topics. Children need to be able to converse freely and bring up topics that are of interest and importance to them (Murray, 2000).

Cleanup of snack can present an additional transition problem. Teachers have many tasks to attend to while cleaning up and children's needs are usually put on hold for a little while. Children can help with the responsibility of cleanup time.

Children can be invited to take part in cleaning up snack. Children can dispose of their garbage, clean the tables, fold napkins/placemats, sweep the floor, remove lunch dishes, and even help to wash dishes. It's important for children to recognize the responsibilities that are attributed to meal preparation and cleanup.

The nutritional value of snack and meal times is also of critical importance. The American lifestyle is full of fast-food meals with little time to enjoy meals as a family.

The school/center environment can offer the one meal that may be relaxed and nutritionally sound. Nutrition has more benefits than the obvious health-related ones. Poor protein intake has been related to low academic performance (ASFSA, 1989). One of the most significant documented vitamin deficiencies in American children is iron (Parker, 1989). The ERIC Digest on Nutrition and Learning reports that "Iron deficiencies and anemia can lead to shortened attention span, irritability, fatigue, and difficulty with concentration." Poor nutrition can lead to skeletal, muscular, and systems problems in children. It is crucial for normal growth and development that children receive the proper nutrition. Fresh fruits and vegetables, whole grains, protein, milk (soy, rice, etc., if needed), and plenty of water (Hannaford, 1995) should be available to children at snack and meal times. Teachers also need to communicate the importance of healthy food choices to parents (ED369579).

9.4
Journal Questions
Think back to the box you bring to the classroom. What past experiences and feelings about meal times do you bring to the classroom? Do you feel meal times are important for young children? Why or why not?

Guided Fantasy Stories/Relaxation Techniques

The transition to quiet time can be difficult for some children. Some children are uncomfortable sleeping away from home, some do not wish to give up their exploratory nature for fear of missing something, some children do not have the self-control to quiet their bodies, while others simply cannot relax. Being able to relax is difficult, even for adults. With all of the content expectations of many early childhood programs, relaxation seems more of a luxury than a necessity. Nothing could be farther from the truth. Relaxation is an important skill that is necessary for developing self-control. Relaxation is an intrapersonal skill that can help children manage their impulses, be better able to take turns, transition more easily, and recognize their personal limitations.

Before relaxation can occur, children must practice letting go of anxieties and fears. Children need to know they are accepted and forgiven for daily conflicts and mistakes before they are truly able to relax (Darian, 1994). Adults can assure children of their feelings and acceptance of children before rest times. Visualization stories and songs can help children let go of anxieties, relax their bodies, and surrender to rest or sleep.

Visualization stories can include guided fantasy stories. Children of all ages can benefit from guided fantasies (Edwards, 1990). Guided fantasy stories are rehearsed stories that allow the children to creatively conjure mental images while the teacher takes the child on an imaginary journey (Edwards, 1990). The child must be in a comfortable position inside or outside. The child closes her eyes and allows her mind to create images related to the story. Breathing exercises are usually encouraged at the

9.5
Journal Activity

Write your own guided fantasy story. Create a story that allows children to visualize a special place and encourages children to relax.

beginning of the fantasy. At the end, it is important to slowly allow the child to mentally return to the classroom. The child should be given time to reflect on the images created during the guided fantasy. This can provide the child with images to help her drift off into sleep, or keep her mind occupied during rest time. Edwards (1990) cautions teachers to always read through the guided fantasy, rehearse it, and discover what images the fantasy brings to the teacher's mind.

Outdoor Play/Gross-Motor Play

Unfortunately, in contemporary America many children have lost touch with nature. There used to be sacred outdoor spaces that children felt close to or felt they had ownership of. Most children today do not have access to forests, the woods, tree houses, or gardens, and many times do not even have a backyard. With hurried schedules and hurried lives, time for enjoying the outdoors is often forgotten and/or devalued. However, because we are part of nature it is vital that we participate in nature.

There are some diseases that could be avoided in some cases by providing children with adequate nutrition and access to sunlight and the outdoors. For example, there are a growing number of children who suffer from vitamin deficiencies that lead to diseases such as rickets. Rickets can be prevented with adequate amounts of vitamin D, which is necessary for normal bone growth in young children. The skin synthesizes vitamin D with exposure to sunlight (Merck Manual Online).

The outdoors also offers children a relationship with and respect for nature, science, math, weather, language, and spatial concepts. The outdoors is a resource of beauty, wonderment, and respect.

Children should be given a daily opportunity to attend to gardens and bird feeders, observe weather patterns and changes, and interact with insects and animals. Children do not need expensive outdoor equipment but they do need time and space to interact physically with nature. They need to be able to touch, taste, smell, observe, and listen to the sights and sounds of nature.

9.6
Journal Activity

Create an appropriate outdoor adventure for four-year-olds.

If there is no access to outdoor space, every effort should be made to bring the outdoors inside. Hang bird feeders outside the window, plant an indoor garden, open windows, allow as much natural light to enter the classroom as possible, and observe weather and nature patterns from open windows. Also, if outdoor space is inaccessible, children should have an opportunity to engage in gross-motor play indoors. They need to have access to the appropriate space to move large muscles and work on the coordination of physical tasks and strength. Outdoor play should be available to children on a daily basis, except in extreme weather conditions.

Rest/Nap Time

It is necessary to provide a rest or nap time in early childhood programs. Most preschoolers will need to sleep sometime during the afternoon. Kindergarten, first-, and second-grade children also need a rest, or a break from the day's activities.

Rest or nap time should always begin with relaxation exercises, as mentioned in the previous section. Music can be used as part of the relaxation exercises, but must be carefully chosen. Many programs use classical music or nature sounds to lull children to sleep. Some classical music is too exciting or stimulating to allow children to relax. Nature sounds, which contain unfamiliar animal sounds or thunderstorms, may frighten children and not allow for relaxation either. The music must be calm, soothing, and familiar. Many children will need to have the music turned off after they are relaxed. Some children have a powerful physical reaction to sound and will not be able to give in to sleep while the music is being played.

The classroom environment during nap or rest time should be soothing and have minimal light. Children should have their own familiar blankets and be encouraged to use the animals or dolls they sleep with at home. Ideally, there should be a separate place in the center that is away from distraction and stimulating materials for nap time. Often, this is difficult to do in a school or center. Many times shelves are pushed aside and children nap in the middle of the play area. There are several things that can be done to offer a softer, less stimulating feel to the play area for nap time. Shelves can be covered with silks or other soft materials. Blankets or sleeping bags can be laid out on the floor before the children's sleeping mats are put down. A pleasant-smelling candle can be lit (if allowed) or a bottle of watered-down perfume, vanilla, lavender, or other calming scent can be misted in the air before nap time. Many preschool children benefit from having their back rubbed or their hair stroked. This individual attention further allows them to feel safe, needed, and relaxed. Older children can be individually talked to in whispers before rest time.

It's important to minimize distractions during nap time. Encourage other teachers not to disturb the class during this time.

For children who are having difficulty with nap time, a small photo album of their family can be available on their mats for them to look through before resting.

It's important for teachers to take a moment and rest as well. Unfortunately, many tasks usually need to

9.7

Journal Questions

Why do you think rest time is important? Why is a quiet part of the day so important to young children?

be completed during rest or nap time. A teacher should allow herself at least fifteen minutes to relax with the children after she has attended to their rest-time needs. This will allow the teacher to relax and recharge as well.

Cleanup

An overwhelming task for the early childhood teacher is keeping the room clean and materials well organized. When the teacher respects and cares for materials, children will follow his example. Giving time and respect for cleanup is important. Children learn responsibility, time management, and self-control during a well-organized cleanup. Children should be gently warned individually that cleanup time is approaching and asked to complete whatever tasks they are working on. Cleanup time can begin with a song, gesture, or sound. Children should be responsible for the area they were playing in when cleanup time began. Five-, six-, and seven-year-olds can have an area of the room they responsible for. They can wash tables, sweep the floors, straighten shelves, find missing pieces to puzzles, and so on. Cleanup time is a whole-class effort

and can create a sense of community, responsibility, and respect for the environment. It can also offer an opportunity to build problem-solving skills. Children can measure amounts of sand that spilled during play time, devise more efficient cleanup methods, predict and measure cleanup times, and chart cleanup-time responsibilities. Cleanup time also offers children an opportunity to work out conflicts and challenges children to work cooperatively.

Play

Play is an important and valuable part of the child's day. Play experiences must be planned during times where the teacher is fully attuned to and aware of the children's actions. Play offers an opportunity to develop all the intelligences, form relationships, work on strengths, and address challenges. Play also offers an opportunity for the child to construct knowledge, take initiative, and develop industry. Play must incorporate the five characteristics presented in Chapter 8. In order to do this, play needs time to develop. An uninterrupted block of time must be dedicated to play. An hour or two may be necessary to plan, initiate, follow through, and clean up a play experience. Play should not be compromised for remedial work or specials. All children benefit from time dedicated toward exploration and investigation.

The teacher should not take care of administrative duties during play time. The teacher has a variety of roles during play: She may observe, facilitate, assess, plan, take anecdotal records, and maintain the organization and safety of the play environment.

9.8

Journal Questions

Look at the schedule you wrote or received. Is there time provided for play? Is play valued in this classroom?

Project Time

It's important to include project time in a child's day. This is a time for collaborative efforts between children and teachers to create and apply an understanding of a significant discovery or interest.

Project time can be offered in conjunction with play. Children can choose to work on their project during play.

The significance of planning for project time is that it allows the teacher to be environmentally, physically, and cognitively ready to respond to the child's needs and questions during project work.

Project time integrates many intelligence areas and allows children to utilize and recognize their intelligence strengths. Project time also strengthens interpersonal development and allows for personal reflection and personal criticism.

Journal Time

Journal time encourages self-reflection and allows children to create symbols; to communicate feelings, problems, successes, and worries; and begin to interpret moods and intentions. Three-year-olds may not have an interest in or be ready to create a picture journal. It's generally more appropriate to begin journals when children start to engage in preschematic art representation. This usually occurs around the age of four.

The journals seem to work best for four- and five-year-olds if they are spiral-bound and contain good-quality paper. Children can be encouraged to draw pictures of events, feelings, and experiences that they wish to communicate. Children who use invented spelling can begin to write about their pictures. Older children can write and/or draw in their journals.

Journals can be completed during or after project work, when children arrive in the morning, after play time, after a significant event in family or school life, or before rest time. The journals should be available to the children to use any time there is choice time.

Children can choose to share their journal entries with teachers, other children, or not at all. Journals encourage intrapersonal development and provide the teacher with clues concerning the feelings and intentions of students. Occasionally, the teacher may find a very significant concern represented in the journal. It's important to respond to the concern and get the child any services that are necessary to address the concern.

Activities

Teacher-directed activities are an important part of the child's day. However, too often these experiences monopolize the child's day. It is important to balance child-directed, teacher-directed, and collaborative experiences in the child's schedule. The use of developmentally appropriate activities is often said to ignore teacher-directed learning (Kostelnik, 1992). This is simply not true. Teacher-directed activities are an unavoidable and necessary component to a child's day. Younger children will require shorter teacher-directed activities, while older children will be able to attend to and engage in longer and more frequent teacher-directed activities. The activities generally should last as long as the children are interested.

The activities should be designed to develop one or more of the intelligence areas. Teachers should seek out each other's strengths in preparing intelligence-specific activities. (Examples of activities were provided in Chapter 7.) Developmentally appropriate activities should be designed with respect to the child's age, development, and interest. Activities challenge children, but it's a challenge that, with effort, they can meet (Bredekamp and Copple, 1997).

Transitions

Perhaps the most perplexing challenge for the early childhood educator is achieving smooth transitions. Transitions are a significant part of the day that deserve the same attention and respect that other parts of the day receive. When children's needs during transition times are tended to, children will be better able to make transitions in life. Being able to successfully transition from one experience to the next involves intrapersonal intelligence.

When children are engaged in a task, their focus is not on missing their parents or worrying about what's coming next. During transition times, the concentration on tasks is broken. Children think about their parents, home, and other parts of the day. This adds to the difficulty children have in making successful transitions.

Despite the challenge transitions pose to early childhood educators and children, they are a necessary part of the day. There are techniques that can ease the stress associated with this part of the day.

Picture calendar. Teachers can draw or post photographs of children engaging in different parts of the day. The photographs/drawings can be arranged in the sequence the day will occur so children can see what's going to happen next.

Signal the transition with a song/gesture/sound. Children can generally transition more smoothly when they have something to focus on. Participating in a familiar song or seeing a gesture that signals a change can help children to focus on a task and provide the expectation for the next experience. A bell or other musical instrument can also signal the change.

Reminders. Children can be gently reminded that in five minutes they will have to clean up, or that five minutes is left before lunch.

Responsibility. Children can be responsible for particular tasks during transition times. For example, while waiting for lunch children can wash tables, put out placemats, or arrange flowers. Before nap time, children can cover shelves with silks, find their doll or stuffed animal, or look through family picture albums.

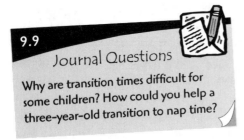

9.9

Journal Questions

Why are transition times difficult for some children? How could you help a three-year-old transition to nap time?

Teachers must observe children and make mental notes of those who need specific transition techniques. Sometimes the transition techniques are used with whole groups, and sometimes just one or two children need help with the transition.

Plan, Do, Review

High Scope (Maher and Brickman, 2001) includes a specific method when initiating activities and facilitating play experiences. Before any experience is initiated, the adult encourages the child to plan or set goals (depending on the age). In this curriculum, the planning would take part during the morning meeting. The child would discuss her plans for the day, what materials she might use, and any problem-solving strategies she might employ. After the play experience, the child is encouraged to review what has happened. She can talk about the accomplishments and challenges of the experience, the problem-solving techniques she used, her emotional reactions, or she can summarize her experience. This process validates the meaning of the experiences and encourages intrapersonal development through goal setting and reflection.

Communicating the Importance of the Schedule

The following brief explanation of scheduling can be used to communicate the importance of each part of the day to parents and other staff members.

EXPLANATION OF SCHEDULING

Arrival: The arrival of the children is a critical and important part of the day. It is important to welcome each child into the classroom and ask them informally how they are doing. Children bring a lot of experiences and emotions into the classroom and this time allows them to talk to each other about home and school experiences. Set aside a few cooperative and individual activities that the children can work on during this time. Some children may choose to be alone and work in their journals or by themselves. This choice should be respected. Greeting the children gives you an opportunity to really know and understand your students and helps to facilitate the development of interpersonal and intrapersonal intelligence.

Sharing: By allowing a formal sharing time, children begin to learn about other children, cultures, and families. They also begin to learn about other points of view and about respect for other children. This opening activity also encourages the growth of interpersonal and intrapersonal intelligence.

Outdoor/Gross-Motor Play: Children need to have experiences outdoors. The outdoors opens up a whole new world of activities and special phenomena. As long as the weather permits, a special time to be outdoors should be included. This time can be used for exploring the outdoors, observing, and playing in small groups. If the weather is too cold or rainy, indoor gross-motor play should be encouraged. This activity encourages the growth of bodily/kinesthetic intelligence and can facilitate the growth of other intelligences as well.

Snack: Snack is also an important part of the children's day. It can allow the children to feel responsible by giving them the opportunity to set the table, fix and arrange the snack, and clean up. They may also be allowed to practice following a recipe and measuring. Snack gives the children a chance to socialize and work on appropriate table manners. The children can set out placemats or a tablecloth, napkins, utensils, flowers, and pour their own drink. This can help them develop logical/mathematical, interpersonal, intrapersonal, and kinesthetic intelligence.

Centers: This special time of the day allows the children to work independently or in small groups in centers that recognize each of the intelligence areas. The centers should be introduced by a teacher and can be changed periodically to meet the needs of the children. There should be limits as to the number of children and materials in the center. Physical boundaries for the centers need to be established as well.

Cleanup: Children need to take the responsibility for cleaning up. However, there should be an appropriate time for cleaning up; children should not be expected to put materials away the minute they appear to be done with them. They may be working out an issue and sometimes need materials from several centers in order to work the issue through. Before the official cleanup time, signal the children that cleanup may be starting soon. Allow flexibility for the official cleanup time. Some children may need to save a project so that they can work on it for several days or so they can show it to their parents. Negotiate a space and time limit with the children if this occurs.

Lunch: Children can set up and clean up their own lunch. It is important for children to choose their own places to sit and to have time to socialize. After lunch, provide a space for the children to go to talk with other children of various ages. This helps to facilitate interpersonal and intrapersonal intelligence.

Guided Fantasy Story: Guided fantasy stories allow the child to visualize experiences. They can also help the child self-reflect and relax before resting. This helps develop intrapersonal, spatial, and linguistic intelligence.

Rest Time: Rest time gives the child the opportunity to sleep or relax after a morning of hard work. Rest time should not be stressful. Provide the children with soft music, a quiet, homey atmosphere, and allow them to bring blankets and stuffed animals from home.

Specific Intelligence Activity: This time of the day provides the child with a group activity that intentionally develops a specific intelligence. Younger children need shorter and fewer group-activity times. Older children can have longer and more group-activity times. This is a good time to have specialists in each of the intelligences come into the classroom to work with children on specific skills, processes, and introduce careers.

Project Time: This is a time that allows children to develop, plan for, and work on special projects. Specialists can also be helpful during this time to take small groups of children and help them develop their part of the project. Projects can be initiated by the teacher or child.

Journal Time: To develop intrapersonal intelligence, a special time for reflecting and self-evaluation is important. A journal time at the end and beginning of each day gives the child a chance to express and reflect on experiences with their words and/or pictures.

Sample Schedules

Following are sample schedules that can be used with full- and half-day programs. Schedules for three-year-olds, four- and five-year-olds, kindergarten, first grade (six-year-olds), and second grade (seven-year-olds) are provided.

Three-year-olds have their own schedule because threes are such a unique age group. The three-year-old is dealing with the monumental transition from toddlerhood to early childhood. Many three-year-olds will appropriately demonstrate toddler behaviors and toddler development. It is important to recognize the variance that will exist in a group of three-year-olds. That is why it is suggested that three-year-olds have their own classroom.

The times are only given to suggest the length of an experience. Children's interest and development are different. The schedule will need personal adjustments to make it most beneficial and appropriate for each group of children.

SAMPLE SCHEDULE FOR 3-YEAR-OLDS (FULL DAY)

6:30–7:30 *Arrival*
7:30–8:00 *Breakfast*
8:00–8:15 *Morning meeting*
8:15–9:00 *Outdoor play*
9:00–9:30 *Snack*
9:30–11:00 *Free-choice play*
11:00–11:20 *Cleanup*
11:20–11:40 *Story/songs/sharing*
11:40–12:00 *Lunch preparation (setting table, washing table, washing hands, etc.)*

12:00–12:45 *Lunch*
12:45–1:00 *Rest time preparation*
1:00–1:15 *Guided storytelling/relaxation strategies*
1:15–3:00 *Nap time*
3:00–3:30 *Snack*
3:30–4:00 *Activity*
4:00–5:00 *Play/project work*
5:00 *Departure*

SAMPLE SCHEDULE FOR 3-YEAR-OLDS (HALF DAY)

8:30–9:00 *Arrival*
9:00–9:15 *Morning meeting*
9:15–9:45 *Outdoor play*
9:45–10:10 *Activity*
10:10–11:30 *Play (snack incorporated into a play center)*
11:30–11:45 *Cleanup*
11:45–12:00 *Guided fantasy/relaxation strategies*
12:00 *Departure*

SAMPLE SCHEDULE FOR 4- OR 5-YEAR-OLDS (FULL DAY)

6:30–7:30 *Arrival*
7:30–8:00 *Breakfast*
8:00–8:20 *Morning meeting*
8:20–9:00 *Outdoor play*
9:00–9:30 *Snack*
9:30–10:00 *Activity*
10:00–11:30 *Play*
11:30–12:00 *Cleanup/sharing time*
12:00–12:45 *Lunch*
12:45–1:00 *Guided fantasy/relaxation strategies*
1:00–2:30 *Nap time*
2:30–3:00 *Activity*
3:00–3:30 *Snack*
3:30–4:30 *Project work/play (afternoon snack provided in play centers)*
4:30–4:45 *Journals*
4:45–5:00 *Meeting/sharing*

SAMPLE SCHEDULE FOR 4- OR 5-YEAR-OLDS (HALF DAY)

7:30–8:00 *Arrival*
8:00–8:20 *Morning meeting*
8:20–9:00 *Outdoor play*
9:00–9:30 *Activity*

9:30–11:00 *Play (snack incorporated into a play center)*
11:00–11:15 *Cleanup*
11:15–11:30 *Journals*
11:30 *Departure*

KINDERGARTEN SCHEDULE (FULL DAY)

7:30–8:00 *Arrival/greetings*
8:00–8:30 *Morning meeting*
8:30–9:15 *Outdoor play*
9:15–9:45 *Activity*
9:45–10:15 *Snack*
10:15–11:45 *Play*
11:45–12:00 *Cleanup/sharing time*
12:00–12:30 *Lunch*
12:30–1:00 *Gross-motor play*
1:00–1:15 *Guided fantasy/relaxation strategies*
1:15–2:00 *Rest time*
2:00–2:30 *Activity*
2:30–3:15 *Project work/play (afternoon snack provided in play centers)*
3:15–3:30 *Cleanup/journals*
3:30 *Departure*

KINDERGARTEN SCHEDULE (HALF DAY)

7:30–8:00 *Arrival*
8:00–8:30 *Morning meeting*
8:30–9:00 *Outdoor play*
9:00–9:40 *Activity*
9:40–11:15 *Play (snack incorporated into a play center)*
11:15–11:30 *Cleanup/journals*
11:30–11:45 *Guided storytelling/relaxation strategies*
11:45 *Departure*

FIRST GRADE/6-YEAR-OLD SCHEDULE

7:30–8:00 *Arrival/greetings*
8:00–8:30 *Morning meeting*
8:30–9:00 *Activity*
9:00–10:00 *Outdoor play*
10:00–10:30 *Activity*
10:30–11:45 *Play (snack offered in a play center)*
11:45–12:00 *Cleanup*
12:00–12:30 *Lunch*

12:30–1:00 *Gross-motor play*
1:00–1:15 *Guided fantasy/relaxation strategies*
1:15–1:30 *Rest time*
1:30–2:30 *Project work/play*
2:30–3:00 *Activity*
3:00–3:30 *Cleanup/journals*
3:30 *Departure*

SECOND GRADE/7-YEAR-OLD SCHEDULE

7:30–8:00 *Arrival*
8:00–8:45 *Morning meeting*
8:45–9:30 *Activity*
9:30–10:30 *Outdoor play*
10:30–11:15 *Activity*
11:15–11:30 *Cleanup*
11:30–12:15 *Lunch*
12:15–1:00 *Gross-motor play*
1:00–1:20 *Guided fantasy/relaxation strategies*
1:20–2:00 *Activity*
2:00–3:00 *Project work/play*
3:00–3:30 *Cleanup/journal writing*
3:30 *Departure*

Summary

Each part of the day has significance and meaning and requires time and planning. Instead of hurrying through the day in order to squeeze in content, provide time for children to construct knowledge through play, choice, projects, and journal work. Allow the child to feel valued by greeting and attending to the child during transition times. Provide quiet times during the day to encourage reflection and help manage impulses. The schedule communicates values, provides structure, encourages reflection, and develops the intelligences. The child's physical environment can as well.

9.10

Journal Question

Look back at the schedule you wrote/received. How might you change the schedule to reflect the information contained in this chapter?

Environment

The proper environment invites interaction and encourages intelligence development. The environment can have a tremendous influence on the mood, development, interest,

9.11

Journal Questions

Visit a preschool, kindergarten, or primary classroom. Sketch the room arrangement.

Think for a moment about a place you love to be; a place that excites you, surprises you, interests you, awakens you, relaxes you, encourages you, and inspires you.

Write down what it is about that place that makes you feel that way.

Think for a moment about a place you hate to be; a place that frustrates you, angers you, depresses you, bores you, discourages you.

Write down what it is about that place that makes you feel that way.

What are the differences between these two places? What makes the place you love so loveable? What makes the place you hate so unbearable?

and production of children. As adults, we recognize the importance and influence of our own living and working space and we need to recognize that the environment has the same effect on the child. We need to respect and nurture the child's space.

The environment plays a crucial role in the education and growth of young children. Loris Malaguzzi, former director of the Reggio Emilia early childhood schools in Italy, stated that the environment is the child's third teacher. The environment communicates mood, intentions, perceptions, and meaning (Edwards, Gandini, and Forman, 1993). The environment is a continuation and affirmation of the child's culture and curriculum. Presenting the environment well is the teacher's greatest curricular asset. A well-prepared environment offers the child security, strength, trust, self-esteem, consistency, boundaries, and self-control (Montessori, 1965). A well-prepared environment also offers a child comfort, safety, and cultural affirmation; encourages interaction and communication; and beauty (Edwards, Gandini, and Forman, 1993). The environment can also encourage responsibility, strength, and creativity, and promotes nurturance, imagination, and cognition (Steiner, 1998). The environment protects children from the harmful influences of the adult world (Steiner, 1998; Edwards, 1995). An effective environment supports the philosophy of the curriculum.

This curriculum's philosophy is rooted in an understanding of play, multiple-intelligence theory, and child development. The environment must reflect this. The environment should allow for playful exploration of each intelligence. Space; intelligence-specific materials; a presentation and selection of materials that promote the five levels of play; room to move the body purposefully and safely; materials that reflect the developmental age and needs of the children involved; access to natural light; comfortable seating and working areas; and a design that allows for independent, small-group, and large-group work are fundamental components of a multiple-intelligence environment.

Promoting Intelligence Development with the Environment

Equal emphasis should be placed on all intelligences in the multiple-intelligence classroom. The environment needs to reflect and demonstrate this equal emphasis by devoting space, materials, and presentations representative of each intelligence. The music area of the classroom must allow for noise and movement, yet not be distracting to the rest of the classroom. The environment must include equipment and space for large- and small-body movements to encourage bodily/kinesthetic development. Access to natural light, natural materials, the outdoors, animals, and plants promotes naturalist intelligence. To encourage interpersonal and intrapersonal intelligence the environment must provide places for children to experience tranquility, softness, and reflection; space for small- and large-group interaction; places to be alone; and materials and furniture arrangement that encourage conversation, play, and cooperation. Access to a variety of art mediums, large and small blocks, maps and globes, as well as appropriate organization of the environment encourages the development of spatial intelligence. The environment must provide places for storytelling, reading, puppet play, and role-play to encourage linguistic intelligence. An effective multiple-intelligence environment offers problem-solving challenges, encourages children to hypothesize, experiment, and evaluate in order to develop logical/mathematical intelligence. Thought, value, respect, and understanding of child development and culture must emanate from every aspect of the physical environment.

The physical environment itself should consist of play areas, small- and large-group work areas, a welcoming/departing area, rest area, and toileting area.

Play and the Environment

Play areas can be created to invite intrinsic exploration of each intelligence and give the teacher easy access to intelligence-specific materials. Chapter 8 provides examples of individual play areas along with intelligence-specific play materials and suggestions. The play centers suggested can serve as a starting point for teachers implementing a multiple-intelligence curriculum. As teachers develop comfort and familiarity with their children and the curriculum, they can use their own creativity to further develop, expand, and create new play centers. Play centers suggested are blocks (spatial, interpersonal, intrapersonal, logical/mathematical, naturalist, linguistic, bodily/kinesthetic), community (personal intelligences, spatial), dramatic play (personal intelligences), problem solving (logical/mathematical), library/publishing (linguistic), creative arts (spatial, bodily/kinesthetic), sand/water (logical/mathematical, spatial), woodworking (spatial, bodily/kinesthetic), practical life (bodily/kinesthetic, spatial, interpersonal), sensory (logical/mathematical, naturalist), sound and movement (music, bodily/kinesthetic), story circle (linguistic, interpersonal), puppet play (linguistic, bodily/kinesthetic, naturalist, interpersonal, intrapersonal), reflection (intrapersonal), and the world around us (naturalist). A teacher using the curriculum for the first time might implement the block, housekeeping, music, reflective, naturalist, and library areas initially. After the teacher has developed a further understanding and familiarity with the curriculum, additional play areas from the suggested list can be introduced or innovative ones can be created.

Work Space

The environment necessitates appropriate space for children to work alone, and in small and large groups. A large appliance box can provide a child privacy to work alone. Allowing a child to use individual rolled carpets can clearly communicate his need for space to investigate materials independently. Accessible small round tables can provide small-group spaces. Small throw rugs can be rolled out for small-group work and can then be put away easily. A large uncluttered carpeted area can provide large-group space. Two half-circle small-group tables can be combined for large-group work. Large-group work can also take place outdoors.

Welcome and Departure Area

The welcome and departure area of the room is vitally important to the success of each day. Children, parents, and teachers need an inviting, warm, soft, and special place in which to begin and end their day. This space should be small and intimate. Pictures of each child and their family can be used as wallpaper for this area. The child's culture should be represented in this area with pictures, shared information, magazines, artwork, and music. Children may have their own personal space, cubbies, or lockers in this area. Teachers may use this area as an informational exchange with parents. Intelligence information, development tips, strategies, and classroom information can be presented here. A fish tank, soft lighting, soft music, live plants, and comfortable chairs or couches offer warmth and slow the pace of hectic days.

This area should be designated specifically for greetings and departures. Teachers need to look each child in the eyes and greet them. Teachers can point out an interesting event or goal of the day and communicate to the child how happy they are to have the opportunity to be with them that day.

This should also be a place for parents to say goodbye in the morning and reunite with their child after a long day. It is not a place to bring up discipline problems or other concerns. Meeting and conference times can better facilitate those concerns.

Some children may need a few moments alone with their parents or a teacher in this area before joining the classroom. When appropriately planned, this area facilitates intrapersonal and interpersonal development.

Rest Area

The rest area of the classroom can be a separate space apart from the play areas, or the play areas can be manipulated to incorporate the resting place. Lights need to be dimmed; comfortable cots or mats with temperature appropriate blankets and pillows should be provided. Soothing colors, textures, sounds, and plants can be added to ease the transition from wakefulness to rest. Familiar blankets, dolls, or stuffed animals must be easily available to the children in this area. If this area is shared with play space, cover the shelves with soft, flowing fabric. This indicates the materials are not to be used and contributes to the tranquil nature of rest time.

Throughout the day, a small area of the room can be offered to children who need to rest earlier or later than the scheduled rest time. This area can be as simple as a box with blankets or it can be a small partitioned area with blankets and pillows.

The rest area should be away from distraction, noises, and out of view of the arrival and departure area.

Toileting Area

The toileting areas should be readily accessible to children at any time of day. It should be clean, and fully stocked with soap, towels, toilet paper, and nonallergenic hand lotion.

Achieving Environmental Balance

As a general environment rule, active and calm areas should be placed at opposite ends of the classroom. Wet and dry areas should also be placed at opposite ends of the class-

9.12

Journal Question

Look back at the room arrangement you drew. How can you change the room arrangement to reflect the information presented in this section?

room. Children and teachers should be able to move freely throughout the classroom; however, dividers and furniture should be strategically placed to prevent distraction and inappropriate motor play, and provide accessibility to all children.

FIGURE 9.1

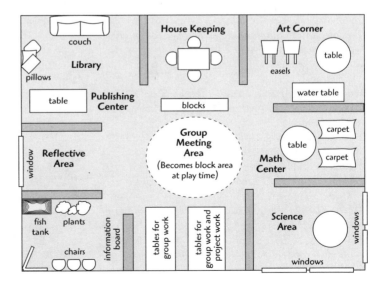

Summary

The environment can offer limits, structure, beauty, consistency, and intelligence development. The teacher's role is to create an environment that responds to the children's needs and interests and to keep the environment organized and safe. Sample room arrangements follow. First is a photograph of a preschool classroom. There is room for the entire class to meet, for small-group work, and individual choice. Children can move freely, the environment is organized and areas of the classroom are well-defined. Figure 9.1 addresses the kindergarten classroom.

Conclusion

This chapter concludes the planning phase of curriculum development. The next chapter will look at the third phase: curricular implications.

References

American School Food Service Association (ASFSA). (1989) Impact of hunger and malnutrition on student achievement. *School Food Service Research Review*, 13 (1, Spring): 17–21.

Bredekamp, S., & Copple, C. (Eds) (1996) *Developmentally appropriate practice in early childhood programs* (Revised Edition). Washington, DC: National Association for the Education of Young Children.

Darian, S. (1994) *Seven times the sun: Guiding your child through the rhythms of the day.* Marshall, WI: Gilead Press.

Edwards, C., Gandini, L., & Forman, G. Eds (1993) *The hundred languages of children.* Norwood, NJ: Alblex Publishing Corporation.

Edwards, L. (1990) *Affective development and the creative arts.* New York: Merrill Publishing Company.

ED369579 1994-06-00 *Children's nutrition and learning.* ERIC Digest.

Hannaford, C. (1995) *Smart moves: Why learning is not all in your head.* Arlington, VA: Great Ocean Publishers.

Kostelnik, M. J. "Myths associated with developmentally appropriate programs." *Young Children* (May, 1992): 17–23.

Maher, J., & Brickman, N. (2001) *Language and literacy: High/scope preschool key experiences.* Ypsilanti, MI: High Scope Press.

Merck Manual Online. *Vitamin deficiency and dependency.* http://www.merck.com/pubs/mmanual/section1/chapter3/3d.htm

Montessori, M. (1965) *Dr. Montessori's own handbook.* New York: Shocken Books.

Murray, C. "Learning about children's social and emotional needs at snack time" *Young Children.* (March 2000, Vol. 55, No. 2, pp. 43–52).

Parker, L. (1989) *The relationship between nutrition and learning: A school employee's guide to information and action.* Washington, DC: NAEYC.

Steiner, R. (1998) *Rhythms of learning: What Waldorf education offers children, parents, and teachers.* Hudson, NY: Anthroposophic Press.

Vance, E. & Weaver, P. (2002) *Class meetings: Young children solving problems together.* Washington, DC: NAEYC.

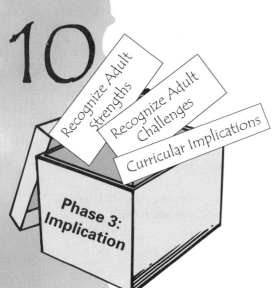

Phase 3:
Curricular Implications

Curricular Implications

T his chapter addresses Phase 3 of curriculum development: curricular implications (Bredekamp & Rosegrant, 1999). This implication phase of curriculum development offers strategies for:

1. Implementing the theory and the planning information presented in the first nine chapters.
2. Assessing adult intelligence strengths and challenges.
3. Utilizing play experiences to reach intelligence-specific goals.

10.1
Journal Questions
(After completing Figure 10.1)
Were your strengths in intelligences what you expected? Do you have a strength that was not represented in this assessment?

What strengths do you have that you can bring to the classroom? What gifts can you share with the children you teach? For example, if you have a naturalist strength and enjoy gardening, you can share your gardening interests and skills with the children.

Recognizing Adult Strengths and Challenges

The first step in implementing the multiple intelligence theory is understanding how the theory applies to you as an adult, and as a teacher. Recognizing your own strengths and challenges allows you to become a more competent, capable teacher. The following assessment helps to identify the strengths and challenges you possess. This assessment is by no means an IQ test or an

FIGURE 10.1 | Adult Multiple Intelligence Assessment

Place an "X" next to the statements that describe you and your interests.

_____ 1) I love to read and I am good at it.
_____ 2) I believe that there is a rational explanation for everything.
_____ 3) I enjoy and am good at putting together puzzles.
_____ 4) I frequently participate in and am good at sports.
_____ 5) I play an instrument.
_____ 6) Friends, family, and coworkers frequently ask me for advice.
_____ 7) I keep a journal or diary.
_____ 8) I love to work in my garden and I am very successful in helping plants to grow.
_____ 9) When I ask for directions, I need names of streets written down for me.
_____ 10) I add and subtract numbers quickly in my head.
_____ 11) I am good at organizing materials in my environment.
_____ 12) I like to hike and/or ride bicycles.
_____ 13) I listen and respond to music frequently.
_____ 14) I frequently participate in social activities.
_____ 15) I am strong-willed.
_____ 16) I know the names of many different kinds of flowers and trees.
_____ 17) I visit the library and/or book stores often.
_____ 18) I like to visit science centers.
_____ 19) I can follow a map easily.
_____ 20) I like to work with my hands.
_____ 21) I can read music.
_____ 22) I know the names of my neighbors.
_____ 23) I set reasonable goals.
_____ 24) I love to visit the zoo and I can identify and describe most of the animals in the zoo.
_____ 25) I enjoy poetry readings.
_____ 26) I like manipulating numbers and playing number games.
_____ 27) I am good at painting, drawing, working with clay, sewing, needlepoint, crocheting, hammering, drilling, and/or building objects out of wood.
_____ 28) I need to touch and manipulate things to learn about them.
_____ 29) I can sing in tune.
_____ 30) I am often a leader of a group.
_____ 31) I attend personal growth seminars.
_____ 32) I frequently go camping, hiking, fishing, and/or hunting.
_____ 33) I have a large vocabulary.
_____ 34) I can problem solve quickly, sometimes even before the problem can be completely stated.
_____ 35) When rearranging furniture, I can visualize where things should go before moving them.
_____ 36) I use hand gestures when talking to someone else.
_____ 37) I hum and/or sing short pieces of music as I complete a task.
_____ 38) I can easily verbalize what others are thinking and feeling.
_____ 39) I like to meditate and reflect about life experiences.

FIGURE 10.1 | continued

_____ 40) I frequently visit and enjoy natural history museums.
_____ 41) I learn best about things by reading about them.
_____ 42) I like to perform experiments.
_____ 43) I can visualize images when I close my eyes.
_____ 44) When arranging furniture, I have to move things to see where to put them.
_____ 45) I can dance in time to music.
_____ 46) I am comfortable in crowds of people.
_____ 47) I realize what my strengths and weaknesses are.
_____ 48) I know the names of and can identify many constellations.
_____ 49) I am considering or am already involved in one or more of the following careers: author, poet, speaker, journalist, editorialist, or news broadcaster.
_____ 50) I am considering or am already involved in one or more of the following careers: mathematician, accountant, computer programmer, chemist, engineer, or scientist.
_____ 51) I am considering or am already involved in one or more of the following careers: artist, designer, architect, draftsperson, pilot, sailor, navigator, make-up artist, or interior decorator.
_____ 52) I am considering or am already involved in one or more of the following careers: athlete, dancer, craftsperson, or surgeon.
_____ 53) I am considering or am already involved in one or more of the following careers: musician, composer, or instrument maker.
_____ 54) I am considering or am already involved in one or more of the following careers: teacher, social worker, actor, or politician.
_____ 55) I am considering or am already involved in one or more of the following careers: psychologist, philosopher, or theologian.
_____ 56) I am considering or am already involved in one or more of the following careers: gardener, landscaper, astronomer, biologist, botanist, zoologist, or paleontologist.

I was good at and enjoyed the following subjects in school:

_____ 57) Reading

_____ 58) Mathematics, Algebra or Computer class

_____ 59) Art

_____ 60) Physical Education

_____ 61) Music

_____ 62) Lunch

_____ 63) Philosophy

_____ 64) Science

_____ 65) English

_____ 66 Chemistry

_____ 67) Shop

_____ 68) Recess

_____ 69) Band

_____ 70) Psychology

_____ 71) Religion

_____ 72) Horticulture

FIGURE 10.1 | continued

Mark the numbers you checked in each category:

Group A	Group B	Group C	Group D	Group E	Group F	Group G	Group H
1	2	3	4	5	6	7	8
9	10	11	12	13	14	15	16
17	18	19	20	21	22	23	24
25	26	27	28	29	30	31	32
33	34	35	36	37	38	39	40
41	42	43	44	45	46	47	48
49	50	51	52	53	54	55	56
57	58	59	60	61	62	63	64
65	66	67	68	69	70	71	72

Total marks for Group A _____

Total marks for Group B _____

Total marks for Group C _____

Total marks for Group D _____

Total marks for Group E _____

Total marks for Group F _____

Total marks for Group G _____

Total marks for Group H _____

A score of 7–9 may indicate a strength in that intelligence area.
A score of 4–7 may indicate a moderate potential for the particular intelligence.
A score of 1–3 may indicate an intelligence that has proved to be challenging to develop.

Group A: Linguistic
Group B: Logical/Mathematical
Group C: Spatial
Group D: Bodily/Kinesthetic
Group E: Musical
Group F: Interpersonal
Group G. Intrapersonal
Group H. Naturalist

MI adult assessment, developed by Rae Ann Hirsh, 1998.

absolute measure of intelligence potential. Rather, this is a tool that may help you identify your strengths and challenges as an early childhood teacher.

Curricular Implications of the Multiple-Intelligence Theory

The multiple-intelligence theory lends itself to several curricular strategies. Gardner (1999) explains that the multiple-intelligence theory can be used to provide:

1. Multiple key entry points to content.
2. Meaningful and/or relevant analogies.
3. Multiple representations of core concepts.

Key Entry Points

The intelligences allow for multiple ways of presenting information and/or introducing a concept. Approaching topics in unusual, unexpected, or alternative ways can have a powerful effect on retention, acceptance, and utilization of a topic. For example, teaching a reading concept can begin with a bodily/kinesthetic, interpersonal, intrapersonal, musical, or spatial experience. The key entry point can interest and motivate the child to readily embrace a concept and can encourage development in other intelligence areas. Gardner (1999) describes the key entry points as:

1. Narrational (linguistic intelligence),
2. Quantitative/numerical (mathematical intelligence),
3. Logical (logical intelligence),
4. Foundational/existential (existential intelligence),
5. Aesthetic (spatial, musical, naturalist intelligence),
6. Hands-on (bodily/kinesthetic intelligence), and
7. Social (interpersonal/intrapersonal intelligence).

An eighth key entry point can be added, naturalist. Naturalist would involve approaching content through interaction with the natural world.

To illustrate this idea, Table 10.1 shows how linguistic content can be approached through multiple key entry points.

Any content area (science, mathematics, reading, etc.) can be approached from multiple key entry points. Approaching content in this way encourages children to utilize their strengths to address unknown concepts. Table 10.2 provides a list of specific mathematical concepts. Review the key entry points. Plan experiences that approach the mathematical concepts through multiple entry points.

Linguistic Concept	Key Entry Point	Activity/Experience
Story Comprehension	Hands-on	Role-play, Puppetry
	Aesthetic (musical)	Retell the story in song form, use instruments to convey different moods portrayed in the story
	Narrational	Storyboard, miniature life play
	Social	Have the child retell the story, substituting themselves for the main character
	Logical	Retell the story, changing one event. Have the child identify which event was changed.
	Social	Story comprehension game. Have a group of small children retell the story, having each child retell only one line.
Letter Identification	Aesthetic	Create letters out of clay
	Musical	Alphabet songs
	Hands-on	Create different letters using the body, learn sign-language alphabet, touch sand paper letters
	Social	Letter games
	Natural	Find objects in nature that resemble letters (s—snake, t—tree, etc.)
	Numerical	Give the child three sticks and ask what letters the child can create with them—vary the material and the quantity and ask what letters the child can create with them.

TABLE 10.1 | *Approaching Linguistic Content through the Various Key Entry Points*

Meaningful Analogies

In the first chapter of this book, an analogy was made that compared a garden to the education of a child. Someone who has an interest and strength in naturalist intelligence and who enjoys gardening would find the analogy more meaningful then someone who does not have the naturalist interest or strength. Analogies can connect

TABLE 10.2 | *Approaching Mathematical Concepts through Various Key Entry Points*

Math Concept	Key Entry Point	Activity/Experience
Number Recognition	Aesthetic (Spatial)	
	Hands-on	
	Aesthetic (Musical)	
Sequential Ordering	Narrational	
	Numerical	
	Natural	
	Social	
Measurement	Social	
	Hands-on	
	Narrational	
	Aesthetic	

unfamiliar concepts to familiar experiences. The following analogy provides an example.

In the block area, a group of children had been arguing over the placement of several blocks. The teacher tried facilitating conflict resolution. Her attempts were not working. Play time ended and the teacher called the children over for a story. The children had been interested in beavers after a trip to the local zoo.

Once upon a time, there were three beavers. They were very busy building a house. A storm was coming and they had to get their house built before the storm hit. They were worried that they would not get the house built in time. One beaver said, "What's the matter with you, you're not doing it right! That stick goes over here." Another beaver said, "Oh why won't you be quiet, I'll build it the way I want to." The third beaver kicked over part of the house, "The two of you are not doing this right. I'm sick of working with you." The beavers began to argue even more. One beaver started throwing sticks at the other one. Suddenly, a flash of lightning was in the sky. It started to rain, but the house was not done. The water from the storm started to flood the land around the beaver's home. Many of the animals that lived on the land had to climb trees to get away from the storm. Many lost their homes. After the storm, the beavers felt very sad. They apologized to the other animals and finished their home quickly. They decided to help the other animals build new homes. They did not argue while they finished their work.

After the teacher read the story, the children thoughtfully looked at each other. One child jumped up and said, "Oh man, that was just like us. We were trying to finish our building so we could play with it, but we couldn't because we were arguing." Another child said, "Yeah, and we couldn't play at play time because we never finished our building. We won't do that tomorrow." The teacher then asked, "What might you change for tomorrow?" The children responded, "If one of us fights, I'm going to remind them of the story." Another said, "We should draw our building out first and each take a job to do."

The children listening to the story were able to connect the story to their experience. The narrative story provided an entry point into interpersonal content that the children were able to identify.

Multiple Representations of Core Concepts

Varying intelligence strengths will be present in a classroom. A core concept presented once using one intelligence will not reach all children. Multiple representations of core concepts will be necessary to tap

10.2

Journal Activity

After a birthday party, a five-year-old let a balloon go. The children watched it go up into the sky, past the trees. One child asked, "Why does it go up?" The teacher asked the children and they gave some possible reasons. One child stated, "My mom said there's different air in a balloon or something like that. How does the air make the balloon go up?"

Create an analogy that might explain the concept to the children.

10.3
Journal Activity

You are a kindergarten teacher. An unexpected snowstorm closed the school for several days. It is the children's first day back after the snowfall. They are consumed with talk about the snow. Plan one activity in each of the intelligence areas that addresses the concept of snow. Use the activity plan in Box 10.7. Use the core set of operations presented in Chapter 11 if you need help coming up with core concepts and objectives.

into individual intelligence strengths and to make the concept accessible to more children. Multiple representations of a concept can be made in different ways.

1. The teacher can present a concept in multiple ways.
2. The teacher can set up exploration stations for children to investigate a particular concept in multiple ways. The exploration stations would be set up after an initial presentation of the content.
3. Play centers can be set up to address specific content from different perspectives.

PRESENTING A CONCEPT IN MULTIPLE WAYS   The planning phase of this curricular text addressed the creation of developmentally appropriate activities. Activities should be created with the interest, need, and development of the children in the class in mind. Teachers can use various activities to present a concept in different ways. The examples in the key entry point section provide ways of introducing content through varying intelligences. The suggestions in the key entry section of this chapter also address multiple ways of presenting core concepts. Presenting content through the use of many intelligence areas is a powerful curricular tool. The tool allows the teacher to reach more children and take advantage of children's strengths.

EXPLORATION STATIONS   This text's curricular focus is on the child's ability to construct knowledge. Children can construct their own knowledge by using exploration stations and play centers. A teacher can create multiple ways for children to explore content. For example, a number of play centers can be set up to address measurement for seven-year-olds.

Station one could address measurement through linguistic intelligence. Provide the children with a ruler, a large sheet of construction paper with a caterpillar drawn in the middle, and the following story. *A caterpillar is looking for a place to make his chrysalis. He walks three inches to the left. He then walks six inches toward the north. He does not see a good place to stop. He walks four inches to the right. He walks ten inches to the south. Suddenly, he sees a nice tree to the left. He walks seven inches to the left, stops, and decides to build his chrysalis there.*

Station two could address measurement through blocks. Offer the children blocks and ask them to create a building that is twice as high as it is long.

Station three could provide art materials. Ask the children to create a symmetrical art project. (They will need to measure in order to make sure their creation is symmetrical.)

CREATING PLAY CENTERS THAT ADDRESS THE INTELLIGENCES, ENCOURAGE SYMBOL DEVELOPMENT, AND APPROPRIATELY CHALLENGE YOUNG CHILDREN Chapter 8 offered information on how to plan and create play centers in the early childhood classroom. This chapter offers an opportunity to create and/or modify a play center in an early childhood classroom. Make arrangements with a preschool, kindergarten, or first-grade teacher to go into their classroom, evaluate one of their play centers, and implement changes to a play center in the classroom. Box 10.4 includes a sample letter that might be helpful in explaining your role in this project to a director or principal.

Planning for individual play centers is challenging. Materials that foster the development of the intelligences must be included along with materials that encourage all levels of play. The following journal activities will help you review and evaluate a play center in the classroom.

Evaluating a Play Center—Journal Activities

It is important to evaluate existing play centers in your curriculum to see what is working and what needs work.

BOX 10.4 | *Sample Letter*

Dear _____,

Hello, I am an early childhood student at _____. I am currently studying the curricular aspects of the early childhood classroom. Currently, my coursework involves information concerning play in the early childhood classroom. I have been assigned a project entitled "Evaluating a Play Center." My responsibilities include:

- Visiting a school and choosing a specific play center (such as blocks, or dramatic play),
- Evaluating the materials in the play center,
- Evaluating how the children interact in the play center,
- Creating a sketch of the play center,
- Suggesting and gathering play materials,
- Reorganizing the play center, and
- Reevaluating how the children interact in the play center.

I am asking permission to learn more about the early childhood profession through your example and would love a chance to work on one of the play centers in your school. If you have any questions, please contact my supervisor at _____. If permission is granted, please sign below.

Thank you so kindly for your time!

Sincerely,

_____   _____
(student signature/date)   (director signature/date)

A complete evaluation involves the following process:

1. Make an original drawing of the play center. (Only concentrate on one center at a time, do not attempt to change the entire room at once.)

2. Complete an original materials checklist. (What materials do the children have access to?)

3. Do an interaction observation. (How are children interacting with each other and their materials in this center? What play levels do you see? Do the materials and/or presentation of the materials inhibit play levels?)

4. Determine what materials will encourage different levels of play.

5. Determine what intelligence(s) the play center addresses.

6. Decide what changes to make to the play center. (What materials need to be added, taken away, rearranged? How should the physical environment of the center change? What interactions should I facilitate?)

7. Complete a formal observation. (With the changes I made, what is now happening in the center? Are play levels changing?)

8. Present the evaluation and changes to other classmates/staff members to get their input on other possible changes and to let them get ideas from successful changes you made.

Implementation of the Eight-Step Process

This eight-step process we presented in the previous section will challenge you to use your theory and planning information to create a successful play center that respects the development and needs of the children you will teach.

1. Pick a play center in the classroom (such as the art or housekeeping, center). Draw a sketch of what the center looks like. Identify the purpose of the center and the intelligences the center addresses.

2. Complete an inventory of the materials offered in the play center. Box 10.5 offers a sample material inventory.

3. Observe the center you chose on three separate days for three to five minutes each day. Describe exactly what the children are playing with, who they are playing with, how they are using the materials, how many children are in the center, and any other information you observe. Then complete the materials and social interaction questions.

After completing the observation, answer the following questions related to how the children interacted with each other and the materials available.

Were any of the children engaged in sensory play?
    If yes, please give an example:

BOX 10.5 | *Material Inventory*

Name _____

Date _____

Types of Shelving: _____

Furniture: _____

Child Materials: _____

Adult Materials: _____

Were any of the children engaged in motor (functional) play?
  If yes, please give an example:

Were any of the children engaged in cognitive manipulative (constructive) play?
  If yes, please give an example:

Were any of the children engaged in creative/expressive (dramatic) play?
  If yes, please give an example:

Were any of the children engaged in language (games with rules) play?
  If yes, please give an example:

How were the children interacting with each other?

Were any children engaged in onlooker play?
  If yes, please give an example:

Were any children engaged in solitary play?
  If yes, please give an example:

BOX 10.6 | *Observation*

Day 1

Time observation begins: _____
Time observation ends: _____
Observation: _____

_____

_____

_____

Day 2

Time observation begins: _____
Time observation ends: _____
Observation: _____

_____

_____

_____

Day 3

Time observation begins: _____
Time observation ends: _____

Observation: _____

_____

_____

_____

Were any children engaged in parallel play?
    If yes, please give an example:

Were any children engaged in associative play?
    If yes, please give an example:

Were any children engaged in cooperative play?
    If yes, please give an example:

4. Look at the different levels of play. What materials might encourage more sophisticated levels of play? Complete Table 10.3.

5. What intelligences does this play center address? How can you encourage development of other intelligences in this play center? Complete Table 10.4.

6. Plan the changes that are necessary to make in order to improve the play center. Complete the environment plan in Table 10.5.

7. Complete another observation of the center. Refer to the observation format presented in Box 10.6. Answer the following questions after the observation:

Were any of the children engaged in sensory play?
    If yes, please give an example:

Were any of the children engaged in motor (functional) play?
    If yes, please give an example:

Were any of the children engaged in cognitive manipulative (constructive) play?
    If yes, please give an example:

Were any of the children engaged in creative/expressive (dramatic) play?
    If yes, please give an example:

Were any of the children engaged in language (games with rules) play?
    If yes, please give an example:

How were the children interacting with each other?

Were any children engaged in onlooker play?
    If yes, please give an example:

Were any children engaged in solitary play?
    If yes, please give an example:

Were any children engaged in parallel play?
    If yes, please give an example:

Were any children engaged in associative play?
    If yes, please give an example:

Were any children engaged in cooperative play?
    If yes, please give an example:

TABLE 10.3 | *Encouraging Different Levels of Play*

To Encourage This Play Stage:	Provide the Following Materials:	This Is What Play in This Stage Would Look Like:
Sensory		
Motor		
Level I Representation (Cognitive/Manipulative)		
Level II Representation (Creative/Expressive)		
Level III Representation (Language-Mediated)		

TABLE 10.4 | *Addressing the Intelligences through Play*

Which Intelligence(s) Does (Do) the Play Center Address?	How?
Linguistic	
Logical/Mathematical	
Spatial	
Musical	
Naturalist	
Interpersonal	
Intrapersonal	
Bodily/Kinesthetic	

TABLE 10.5	*Changing the Play Center*	
Materials to increase play levels:	Materials to facilitate the development of two or three of the intelligences:	Materials that need to be taken away:

Create a new sketch of the center. How will you rearrange the center?

8. Evaluate the center you prepared. How did the level of symbolic and social play change with the alterations you initiated? Were the changes successful? Are there any additional changes that should be made? Develop a project that communicates to the rest of the class the changes you made.

BOX 10.7 | *Activity Plan*

Activity name:

> Picture or drawing of
> activity if needed

Activity Objective: (What is the generalized expectation of the activity?)

Core Concepts: (What core concepts specific to the intelligence area does the experience address?)

Materials Needed: (What materials are needed to complete the activity? Do any materials need advance preparation?)

Developmental Rationale: (Why is this experience appropriate for this age group? What developmental needs or issues does this activity address? Why should this activity be presented at this time?)

Procedure: (How should this activity be carried out? Is there an appropriate sequence? Time length?)

 Conclusion

The theory and planning strategies in this text offer many implementation strategies. Content can be approached in multiple ways; exploration stations can offer investigation of content using children's interests and strengths; and play centers allow children to construct knowledge with appropriate materials. The implication phase of curriculum development in this text was created to offer a starting point in the facilitation of the multiple-intelligence theory. The implication phase information enables the teacher with the power to create a meaningful and purposeful appropriate learning environment.

 References

Bredekamp, S., & Rosegrant, T. (Eds.) (1999) *Reaching potentials: Transforming early childhood curriculum and assessment.* Washington, DC: NAEYC.

Gardner, H. (1999) *The disciplined mind.* New York: Simon & Schuster.

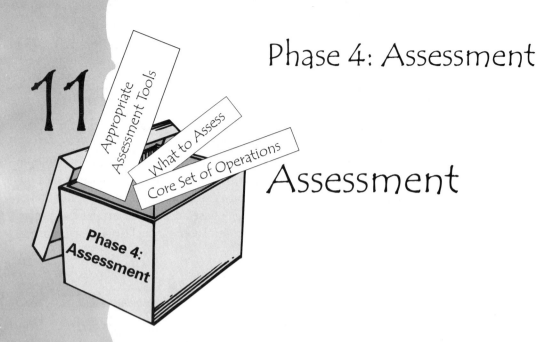

Phase 4: Assessment

Appropriate Assessment Tools

What to Assess

Core Set of Operations

Phase 4: Assessment

Assessment

T his chapter concludes this early childhood curriculum development text with an in-depth look at Phase 4: assessment.
Assessment is a crucial curriculum tool that is "inseparable"
from the rest of the early childhood curriculum (Hills, 1999). Assessment is often not taken as seriously as the rest of the early childhood
curriculum. Hills (1999, p. 43) explains that "assessment has been
underemphasized in early childhood education, not integrated in
most teacher preparation programs, and relatively neglected in many
curricula." The inattention to assessment leads to many inappropriate
assessment strategies. The early childhood teacher must thoroughly
understand what assessment is in order to effectively use it as a curricular tool.

The assessment phase of the curriculum development in this text will provide an opportunity to:

1. Read and respond to a child's portfolio.
2. Create lesson plans based on assessment
   results.
3. Develop strategies for assessing children
   using multiple techniques.

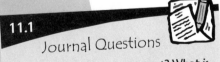

11.1
Journal Questions

How do you define assessment? What is
the purpose of assessment? What are
appropriate assessment tools for young
children?

 Assessment Tools

Assessment is an invaluable component to any curriculum. The National Association for the Education of Young Children and the National Association of Early Childhood Specialists in State Departments of Education (NAEYC AND NAECS/SDE Position Statement, Adopted 1990, p. 10) define assessment as a "process of observing, recording and otherwise documenting the work children do and how they do it, as a basis for a variety of educational decisions that affect the child, including planning for groups and individual children and communicating with parents." It is important to understand that assessment is not a judgment of or value given to a child's finished product. Assessment is a *collection of tools* used to evaluate a child's progress in meeting curriculum goals. It provides the teacher with information on how to change content, strategies, and objectives to meet the needs of each child. Teachers should utilize assessment tools daily. Teachers should observe children, then reflect on their observations, and utilize their knowledge of child development to plan and teach accordingly (Hills, 1999).

Letter Grades

Tools that are used to make a judgment on a child include traditional letter grading and standardized tests. Letter grading judges the child's worth by assigning a value to a finished product. The motivation, effort, and process that are involved in achieving the final product are not considered important. Letter grades in the early childhood years (up to second grade) can interfere with motivation and can result in a negative outlook toward school (Kohn, 2000).

Standardized Tests

Kamii and Kamii (1990, p. 15) warn that standardized tests "are not valid measures of children's learning or of teachers' accountability, and the pressure for higher test scores is resulting in classroom practices that are harmful to young children's development." The tests do not truly reflect the child's abilities and challenges (Gardner, 1999); may interfere with the child's construction of knowledge (Kamii & Kamii, 1990); and may measure what matters the least (Kohn, 2000). Standardized tests focus narrowly on isolated skills limited to logical/mathematical and linguistic intelligence (Gardner, 1999). Standardized tests compare the acquisition of skills to a select group of children. There is no connection between performance and the goals and objectives of the curriculum. The child's culture, process, coordination of skills, application of skills, and other

11.2

Journal Questions

What value do you think standardized tests hold? How did you feel when you took standardized tests in school? Did you think they accurately represented your strengths and challenges?

Interview a kindergarten and first-grade teacher. Ask the teachers if they give standardized tests to their students. Ask why they give the tests, what the tests show, and how the test results affect their curriculum. What changes in their classrooms as a result of the standardized tests?

intelligences are omitted. This limits the educational process and places the emphasis of learning on isolated skill development in noncontextual settings. The tests do not encourage, provide, or reflect any contextual application of the knowledge the child has acquired/ constructed. Standardized tests often become an end to themselves (Kamii & Kamii, 1990). They are used as a judgment, to compare children, and to rate and classify schools/teachers. They are seldom used for curriculum consideration. Kamii and Kamii (1990) suggest eliminating standardized testing altogether during the early childhood years (up to second grade).

Appropriate Early Childhood Assessment Tools

Perhaps the most powerful assessment tool of the early childhood classroom is the teacher's observation skills. Observation and reflection provide insight into children's abilities, strengths, challenges, development, and interests. Observation helps the teacher assess progress and mastery of goals and objectives that may occur at unexpected times in unexpected places.

Recording the observation can take many forms. Hills (1990) suggests recording observations as anecdotal records, specimen descriptions, journal entries, time sampling, event sampling, checklists, rating scales, and shadow or case studies. Anecdotal records are descriptions of a child's behavior during an activity, written after the behavior or experience happens. Anecdotal records can offer insight for planning purposes and teacher conferences (Hills, 1990). A specimen description is a detailed narrative description written while a behavior is occurring. Journal entries allow a teacher to write down the behaviors, accomplishment, or challenges of a group of children after they have participated in a task, activity, or experience (Hills, 1990). Hills (1990, p. 51) describes time sampling as "an observation of what happens within a given period of time, coded with tallies or symbols, while the behavior is occurring." Time sampling provides insight into how many times a specific behavior occurs during a planned part of the day. Event sampling targets a specific activity or time of the day (Hills, 1990). The teacher writes down what happens before and after the event and records the event as it occurs. Checklists allow the teacher to check off specific behaviors as they happen. Checklists can be used to record isolated behaviors or a process. The checklist should outline those steps the child needs to take in order to achieve a specific goal or objective. Rating scales record the frequency of a specific behavior. Shadow or case studies are in-depth studies of one child. Many of the other observation methods may contribute to the information recorded in the shadow or case study.

Other assessment tools include work samples, videos, and photographs. Work samples demonstrate processes and finished products. They include artwork, snapshots of block buildings and other constructions, writing samples, mathematics samples, taped storytellings, music compositions, and journal entries.

Conferencing allows assessment information to be shared with parents and/or other teachers. Conferences with students encourage children to reflect and assess their own work. Conferences with parents can provide important information on noted strengths and challenges discovered at home.

Managing the variety of assessment methods can be an overwhelming task. Portfolios offer a method for organizing assessment tools (Hills, 1990). Portfolios involve more than just housing classwork. Hills (1990, p. 60) explains that "portfolios are not just educational scrapbooks; they are systematic collections of similar products constructed at regular intervals that can be compared to assess children's progress over time." The portfolio should reflect information pertaining to each of the intelligences and can be organized into eight sections reflecting the eight intelligences. Keeping two portfolios for each child can increase the benefit of using a portfolio. One portfolio can be a working portfolio—a large expanding envelope or cubby that houses samples that the child and teacher pick on a daily basis. The second portfolio is the child's permanent portfolio, which can be kept at the school as the child's permanent record. Once a

FIGURE 11.1

PURPLE BY TOP

I love purple,
  it's my favorite color.
I see it on mountains,
  I see it on Gabi's dress.

A purple ball, a purple tea set,
a purple ribbon, a purple puppy,
A purple person.

Purple feels like diamonds,
  like jewelry.
I see it when it's sewn.

Purple is Mel.

Poem dictated to her mother.
Tori wrote the title.
(she copied the word Purple
  from a crayon wrapper.)

month the child and teacher can go through the child's portfolio and pick one sample to demonstrate growth in each intelligence. These samples will be put in the permanent portfolio. The rest of the work will be taken home. Parents can go through these samples with the child and pick something they would like to see added to the permanent portfolio.

Using a portfolio as an assessment tool emphasizes the process a child is involved in and can demonstrate interests and competencies in all intelligences.

 # What to Assess?

It can be difficult to identify exactly what to assess. Young children have incredible potential and many expressions of that potential are possible. Gardner (1993) explains that each intelligence involves a number of core capacities that form a necessary foundation for intelligence development. Foundations for intelligence are laid in the earliest years of life. This text will present a core set of operations for each intelligence. The operations reflect appropriate developmental expectations for the child between the ages of three and eight. It must be stressed that intelligence is viewed as a potential in this text, not as a set of prescribed skills. The core sets of operations do not explain the intelligences, nor do they limit the expression of the intelligences.

The term *core set of operations* is borrowed from Gardner's work (1983, 1993). In Gardner's view, in order to be considered an intelligence, a number of criteria had to met (as discussed in Chapter 2). One of the intelligence-identifying criteria is a core set of operations. The core set of operations demonstrates key abilities that are necessary in order for an intelligence to develop. (Many of the core concepts identified by Gardner have been presented in the earlier chapters on the intelligences.)

This text's list of core operations has been strongly influenced by child development theory, nationally recognized organizations in specific disciplines, and appropriate expectations provided by NAEYC. The core set of operations has been greatly influenced as well by the expectations put forth in *Developmentally Appropriate Practice* by Sue Bredekamp and Carol Copple (1996).

How to Use the Core Set of Operations

It cannot be stressed enough that the core set of operations should not be used to identify the intelligences or limit the potential expression of the intelligences. The multiple-intelligence theory adheres to the belief that all children (and adults) are able to develop a competency in all of the intelligences (except in cases of an extreme disability). This text has examined which concepts and operations are necessary and appropriate for a child to master in order to develop a foundation in each intelligence. The concepts and skills provided in this chapter offer the reader an age-appropriate guide for developing activities, play centers, themes, and lesson plans.

Most of the operations presented are appropriate to begin with a three-year-old and mastery can be expected by the time the child is eight. There are concepts that are more appropriate to facilitate when a child is older. These concepts will be specifically marked.

Some of the core concepts will be listed under more than one intelligence. Many times a particular skill or concept will serve the purpose of helping the child develop in an unexpected intelligence area. This list of concepts is not absolute. The teacher needs to decide if the concepts are appropriate for her individual classroom. It might be necessary to add or delete some of the operations/concepts. The core set of operations also provides a framework useful for assessment and teacher conferences.

The core concepts were inspired by the standards set forth by the following organizations:

> National Association for the Education of Young Children,
> National Council for the Teachers of Mathematics,
> Association for the Advancement of Health Education,
> Music Educators National Conference,
> National Geographic Association,
> National Association for Sport and Physical Education,
> The Consortium of National Arts Education Association,
> The National Dance Association,
> National Art Education Association,
> The American Alliance for Health, Physical Education, Recreation, and Dance, and
> The American Alliance for Theatre and Education.

Intrapersonal Core Set of Operations

> The child will choose to be alone at times.
> The child will accept a routine.
> The child will verbally express feelings.
> The child will be able to manage impulses.
> The child will be interested in his/her environment.
> The child will trust him/her self and his/her environment.
> The child will develop autonomy.
> The child will understand, remember, and respect rules.
> The child will discuss likes and dislikes.
> The child will present accomplishment in a positive way.
> The child will explore the intrapersonal intelligence area through his/her senses.

The child will manipulate materials motorically.

The child will be able to represent personal information through Symbols (Level I Representation).

The child will reflect on his/her experiences.

The child will recognize how he/she is alike and different from other children.

The child will celebrate his/her uniqueness.

The child will discuss changes.

The child will take part in relaxation exercises.

The child will experiment with materials.

The child will ask questions.

The child will express positive feelings toward school and learning.

The child will identify his/her own strengths and challenges.

Appropriate expectations beginning at age four/five:

The child will channel emotions appropriately.

The child will demonstrate initiative.

The child will plan, initiate, and complete tasks independently.

The child will help establish procedures for proper use of materials.

The child will keep a pictorial journal.

The child will accept the privilege that he/she can make a mistake.

The child will be able to represent personal information creatively and expressively (Level II Representation).

The child will use the appropriate language to express personal information (Level III Representation).

The child will recognize when he/she needs to be alone.

The child will identify and cope with a change in routine.

The child will manipulate materials appropriately.

The child will appropriately offer and ask for help.

Appropriate expectations beginning at age six/seven:

The child will keep a written journal.

The child will experience various roles and tools of intrapersonal domains.

The child will interact with and learn the techniques, tools, and roles of a master in an intrapersonal domain.

Interpersonal Core Set of Operations

The child will trust an adult.

The child will notice emotional distinctions and interpret moods.

The child will communicate information about others using symbols.

The child will engage in parallel play.

The child will engage in associative play.

The child will express ideas.

The child will understand a speaker accurately.
The child will express interpersonal intelligence sensorially.
The child will express interpersonal intelligence motorically.
The child will express interpersonal intelligence symbolically (Level I Representation).

Appropriate expectations beginning at age four/five:

The child will engage in cooperative play.
The child will feel powerful.
The child will respect social/cultural diversity.
The child will experience activities from a uniquely challenged child's perspective.
The child will participate in activities that reflect traditions and the culture of the child.
The child will participate in activities that reflect other cultures.
The child will accept ideas.
The child will express interpersonal intelligence creatively and expressively (Level II Representation).
The child will use appropriate and sophisticated language to express interpersonal intelligence (Level III Representation).
The child will respect another child's body and belongings.
The child will communicate information to peers through dramatization.
The child will initiate a play theme.
The child will accept a play theme.
The child will contribute to a common play theme through interactions and dialogue.
The child will define community roles.
The child will understand and communicate familial roles.

Appropriate expectations beginning at age seven/eight:

The child will acknowledge another child's point of view.
The child will respect another child's point of view.
The child will interact with adults and other children empathetically.
The child will experience various roles and tools of interpersonal domains.
The child will interact with and learn the techniques, tools, and roles of a master in an interpersonal domain.
The child will choose to apprentice with a master in an intelligence area the child shows strength and interest in.

Linguistic Core Set of Operations

The child will use verbal language to communicate needs, wants, thoughts, and ideas.
The child will be verbally understood by others.
The child will choose to look at books and ask to be read to.
The child will respond to language motorically.
The child will represent language symbolically (Level I Representation).

Appropriate expectations beginning at age four/five:

The child will represent language creatively/expressively (Level II Representation).
The child will engage in language-mediated play (Level III Representation).
The child will be able to identify similarities and differences between words.
The child will begin to learn a second language.
The child will be able to name all classmates.
The child will predict story outcomes.
The child will use pictures in a book to make up a story.
The child will tell a creative story.
The child will tell a story with a beginning, middle, and end.
The child will be able to repeat familiar text.
The child will develop a large vocabulary.
The child will use adjectives and adverbs in verbal communication.
The child will use language associated with a familial and/or community role.
The child will recall events in sequence.
The child will demonstrate sensitivity to sounds, rhythms, inflections, and meters of words.
The child will represent the written word symbolically through pictures, markings, and symbols (Level I Representation).
The child will use appropriate dialogue when socializing with peers.
The child will demonstrate an understanding that print contains meaning.
The child will express an interest in reading and writing.
The child will be able to recognize his/her name.
The child will be able to identify some uppercase letters.
The child will be able to write some uppercase letters.
The child will verbally construct a poem.
The child will use adjectives/adverbs in speech.
The child will be able to identify the purpose or function a story serves.

Appropriate expectations beginning at age six/seven:

The child will be able to identify upper- and lowercase letters.
The child will be able to write uppercase and lowercase letters.
The child will be able to identify letter sounds.
The child will be able to put phonemes together to make words.
The child will use adjectives/adverbs in stories and sentences.
The child will use invented spelling.
The child will use various strategies to construct meaning from print.
The child will identify main ideas in text and speech.
The child will demonstrate the implied meaning of a text.
The child will be able to listen to a language purposefully.
The child will visually discriminate between letters and words.
The child will experience various roles and tools of linguistic domains.
The child will interact with and learn the techniques, tools, and roles of a master in a linguistic domain (such as a poet, author, motivational speaker).

Appropriate expectations beginning at age seven/eight:

The child will read independently.
The child will write independently.
The child will locate books to find out about something of interest.
The child will write a poem.
The child will write a story.
The child will tell a story with a beginning, middle, end, problem, climax, and resolution.
The child will use metalinguistic analysis.
The child will use conventional syntax.
The child will use the writing process to create a story.

Logical/Mathematical Core Set of Operations

The child will classify by attribute.
The child will seriate.
The child will arrange objects sequentially.
The child will organize objects in the environment.
The child will compare and contrast.
The child will establish a routine.
The child will differentiate sensorial information.
The child will develop strategies for organization of information.
The child will develop problem-solving strategies.
The child will understand the difference between a little and a lot.
The child will ask a question.
The child will identify and compare sets.
The child will set a goal.
The child will represent and communicate ideas through scientific descriptions.
The child will formulate questions and hypotheses.
The child will use generating skills (infer, predict, elaborate).
The child will draw creative/expressive conclusions.
The child will respond to logical/mathematical concepts motorically.
The child will represent logical/mathematical concepts symbolically through play materials (Level I Representation).
The child will verbalize observations.

Appropriate expectations beginning at age four/five:

The child will identify a few numbers from 1 to 10.
The child will represent numbers symbolically.
The child will explore and employ estimation strategies.
The child will creatively explain scientific phenomenon.

The child will plan and organize equipment in the environment.

The child will creatively represent logical/mathematical concepts (Level II Representation).

The child will engage in language-mediated experiences to represent logical/mathematical concepts (Level III Representation).

Appropriate expectations beginning at age six/seven:

The child will justify a solution to a problem.

The child will use integrating skills (restructure, establish criteria, etc.).

The child will explain the life cycle of a plant, animal, and/or insect.

The child will accurately explain scientific phenomenon.

The child will use evaluating skills (summarize, conclude).

The child will draw logical conclusions.

The child will pose a problem.

The child will identify relationships and patterns.

The child will demonstrate knowledge of reversibility.

The child will conserve liquids and solids.

The child will add sets.

The child will use addition symbols.

The child will identify numbers from 1 to 20.

The child will be able to write numbers from 1 to 20.

Appropriate expectations beginning at age seven/eight:

The child will estimate more accurately.

The child will subtract sets.

The child will use subtraction symbols.

The child will understand place value.

The child will be able to identify and write numbers to 100 or more.

The child will begin to understand the concept of multiplication (through an understanding of addition).

The child will begin to understand the concept of division (through an understanding of subtraction).

The child will experience various roles and tools of logical/mathematical domains.

The child will interact with and learn the techniques, tools, and roles of a master in a logical/mathematical domain (such as a scientist or mathematician).

Spatial Core Set of Operations

The child will manipulate objects in his/her environment to recreate or communicate ideas or experiences (Level I Representation).

The child will perceive and interpret the environment through his/her senses.

The child will complete a simple puzzle.

The child will engage in controlled/named scribbling.

The child will create original shapes.

Appropriate expectations beginning at age four/five:

The child will respect body boundaries.
The child will respect materials boundaries.
The child will respect environment boundaries.
The child will identify how objects move.
The child will move purposefully in the environment.
The child will engage in preschematic art representation.
The child will manipulate color and light.
The child will identify shapes in the environment.
The child will draw shapes seen in the environment.
The child will create creative/expressive art representation (Level II Representation).
The child will experiment with gears.
The child will disassemble complex equipment.
The child will critically analyze the spatial details of an object.
The child will arrange objects in the environment for aesthetic purposes.
The child will appropriately classify and arrange a grouping of related objects.

Appropriate expectations beginning at age six/seven:

The child will give simple directions to a familiar destination.
The child will be able to put together complex equipment.
The child will draw a map of the classroom.
The child will engage in schematic art representation.
The child will recognize the adult use of spatial tools.
The child will experience various roles and tools of spatial domains.
The child will interact with and learn the techniques, tools, and roles of a master in a spatial domain (such as an artist, mechanical designer, interior decorator, makeup artist, or navigator).
The child will represent the environment in a map.

Musical Core Set of Operations

The child will respond physically to music.
The child will memorize a fingerplay or short song.
The child will manipulate objects to create sounds.
The child will mimic sounds heard in nature.
The child will identify familiar sounds.
The child will represent music motorically.

Appropriate expectations beginning at age four/five:

The child will imitate a rhythm.
The child will sing in a group.

The child will respond to different tempos and rhythms.

The child will identify different genres of music.

The child will sing independently.

The child will appreciate music of different genres.

The child will represent music symbolically through creative symbols and pictures (Level I Representation).

The child will be able to name a few musical symbols.

The child will engage in creative/expressive music representation (Level II Representation).

The child will communicate feelings and thoughts through music.

The child will create a melody.

The child will create musical symbols.

The child will play an instrument (such as cymbals, bells, rhythm sticks, drums, etc.) creatively.

The child will engage in language-mediated music representation (Level III Representation).

The child will make up his/her song to communicate a thought or feeling.

Appropriate expectations beginning at age six/seven:

The child will be able to name a quarter, half, whole, and sixteenth note.

The child will be able to recognize the length the note represents.

The child will be able to write short pieces of music.

The child will be able to play an instrument such as the pentatonic flute or recorder.

The child will be able to read short pieces of music.

The child will experience various roles and tools of musical domains.

The child will interact with and learn the techniques, tools, and roles of a master in a musical domain (such as a musician, conductor, composer, or singer).

Bodily/Kinesthetic Core Set of Operations

The child will be able to explain the benefits of exercise.

The child will coordinate body movements.

The child will maintain balance.

The child will appropriately manipulate large objects.

The child will appropriately manipulate small objects.

The child will experiment with scissors, hole punchers, tape, and glue.

The child will explore the physical roles and tools of an adult.

Appropriate expectations beginning at age four/five:

The child will move his/her body with purpose and control.

The child will exercise.

The child will give force to the body through space (run, jump, hop, skip, leap).

The child will give force to and from objects (throw, catch, kick, strike, dribble).

The child will move in straight and curved paths.

The child will demonstrate body movements.

The child will manipulate art media to represent an experience or idea.

The child will engage in woodworking tasks (saw, drill, hammer, manipulation of a vice).

The child will manipulate blocks.

The child will represent his/her world physically (Level I Representation).

The child will creatively manipulate the body to: recreate experiences, represent objects in the environment, tell a story, convey feelings, share information (Level II Representation).

The child will participate in and initiate physical games with rules (Level III Representation).

The child will intentionally start and stop body movements according to the will of others.

The child will use a pincer grasp when drawing.

The child will dress him/herself.

The child will zip and snap.

The child will maintain balance (one-foot balancing, beam walking, body rolling, dodging, and landing).

The child will use glue, tape, scissors, and hole punchers appropriately.

Appropriate expectations beginning at age six/seven:

The child will incorporate exercise into his/her daily routine.

The child will tie his/her shoes.

The child will participate in formal dance instruction.

The child will experience various roles and tools of bodily/kinesthetic domains.

The child will interact with and learn the techniques, tools, and roles of a master in a bodily/kinesthetic domain (such as an athlete, dancer, aerobic instructor, surgeon, or artist).

Naturalist Core Set of Operations

The child will exhibit sensory play with natural materials (the child will observe, listen to, touch, taste, and smell the natural world).

The child will exhibit motor play with natural materials.

The child will represent the natural world symbolically (Level I Representation).

The child will classify natural objects.

The child will interact with the natural world through outdoor play, field trips (zoos, botanical gardens, pet stores, museums).

Appropriate expectations beginning at age four/five:

The child will represent the natural world creatively/expressively (Level II Representation).

The child will use language-mediated naturalist representation (Level III Representation).

The child will discuss, interpret, and predict weather patterns.

The child will initiate appropriate changes to the environment.

The child will visit, observe, record, and interpret information gathered from the interaction with the natural world through outdoor play, field trips, and nature walks.

The child will help care for a classroom pet or plant.

The child will be able to identify objects and patterns in space.

The child will use natural materials in functional ways.

The child will identify differences between natural objects and man-made objects.

The child will acquire information gained through experimentation with scientific tools (binoculars, microscopes, magnifying glasses, telescopes, etc.).

The child will grow a plant from a seed.

The child will witness the life cycle of an insect or animal.

Appropriate expectations beginning at age six/seven:

The child will use scientific tools appropriately.

The child will interpret information gathered through the use of scientific tools.

The child will successfully plan and maintain a garden.

The child will identify stages of insect and animal life cycles.

The child will experience various roles and tools of naturalist domains.

The child will interact with and learn the techniques, tools, and roles of a master in a naturalist domain (such as a gardener, botanist, oceanographer, environmentalist, or park ranger).

The child will begin to recognize his/her place in the country, world, and space.

The child will identify the planets.

Portfolio Development

This sample portfolio includes play charts, intelligence checklists, work samples, photographs, audio transcripts, artwork, and anecdotal records for a five-year-old girl, Tori.

The following charts can be included in the child's portfolio to demonstrate her level of play in each of the intelligences. The charts utilize the play stage framework presented by Schomburg. By assessing the play levels of the child in each of the intelligences, the teacher can gain insight into the symbolic development of the child. The intelligence checklists were developed from the age-level expectations presented in the core set of operations section of this chapter.

After reading through the portfolio, journal exercises will be provided. The journal exercises will demonstrate how to interpret the information contained in the portfolio. The exercises also demonstrate how to use the information gained from the portfolio.

TABLE 11.1 | *Linguistic Intelligence Play Assessment*

The Child:	Needs Help	Progressing	Mastered
Explores materials with the senses (Sensory)			X
Manipulates objects motorically (Motor)			X
Moves objects intentionally and begins to use objects to represent ideas (beginning of symbolic thought) (Level I Representation)			X
Elaborates play ideas and develops themes (Level II Representation)			X
Uses words to represent experiences (Level III Representation)			X

FIGURE 11.2 |

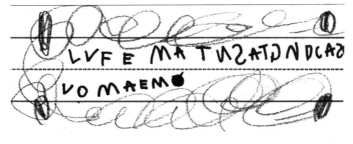

Lovely maidens sit in the castle of the maidens.

By the river sat a lovely maiden

TABLE 11.2 | *Linguistic Intelligence Checklist*

The Child Will Demonstrate the Linguistic Ability to:	Not Interested	Needs Help	Progressing	Mastered
Express an interest in reading and writing				X
Use writing spontaneously				X
Use invented spelling			X	
Draw pictures and use print freely				X
Demonstrate an understanding that print contains meaning				X
Use language-mediated representation			X	
Relate print to pictures				X
Engage in pre-letter writing tasks				X
Use various strategies to construct meaning from print		X		
Use conventional syntax		X		
Use conventional punctuation and sentence structure		X		
Recall events in sequence				X
Identify main ideas in text and speech			X	
Verbally describe projects, creations, and activities that he/she has engaged in				X
Use the language associated with a familial, community, or school role				X
Be able to communicate personal information			X	
Use appropriate dialogue when socializing with peers			X	
Identify similarities and differences between words				X
Be able to name all classmates				X
Be able to be understood by peers				X

TABLE 11.2 | *continued*

The Child Will Demonstrate the Linguistic Ability to:	Not Interested	Needs Help	Progressing	Mastered
Give directions				X
Be able to repeat familiar text				X
Be able to listen purposefully			X	
Use the language that is appropriate to a particular setting			X	
Visually discriminate between letters and sounds				X
Auditorally discriminate between sounds			X	
Demonstrate directionality			X	
Predict story outcomes			X	
Demonstrate the implied meaning of a text			X	
Identify uppercase and lowercase letters				X
Develop a large vocabulary			X	
Learn about the world through reading materials	X			

- Tori writes short stories with pictures and invented spelling. She writes story maps and writes stories using pictures.
- Tori shows a strong interest in listening and writing her own poetry.
- Tori demonstrates knowledge of sound/symbol relationships through her invented spelling.

FIGURE 11.3

FIGURE 11.4

TABLE 11.3	*Logical/Mathematical Intelligence Play Assessment*		
The Child:	**Needs Help**	**Progressing**	**Mastered**
Explores materials with the senses (Sensory)			X
Manipulates objects motorically (Motor)			X
Moves objects intentionally and begins to use objects to represent ideas (beginning of symbolic thought) (Level I Representation)		X	
Elaborates on play ideas and develops themes (Level II Representation)		X	
Uses words to represent experiences (Level III Representation)	X		

TABLE 11.4 | *Logical/Mathematical Intelligence Checklist*

The Child Will Demonstrate the Logical/Mathematical Ability to:	Not Interested	Needs Help	Progressing	Mastered
Classify by attribute			X	
Seriate			X	
Arrange objects sequentially				X
Organize objects in the environment			X	
Compare and contrast			X	
Establish a routine			X	
Measure using various units	X			
Predict logical conclusions for simple experiments	X			
Demonstrate knowledge of reversibility	X			
Demonstrate knowledge of conservation	X			
Differentiate sensorial information			X	
Develop observation skills			X	
Form number concepts			X	
Identify and compare sets	X			
Combine and separate sets	X			
Explain a cause/effect relationship	X			
Define a problem	X			
Set a goal	X			
Identify relationships and patterns			X	
Formulate questions and hypotheses			X	
Use generating skills: infer			X	
Use generating skills: predict			X	
Use generating skills: elaborate			X	
Use integrating skills: restructure	X			

TABLE 11.4 | *continued*

The Child Will Demonstrate the Logical/Mathematical Ability to:	Not Interested	Needs Help	Progressing	Mastered
Use integrating skills: establish criteria		X		
Use evaluating skills: summarize			X	
Use evaluating skills: conclude		X		
Develop and apply strategies to solve a wide variety of problems			X	
Draw logical conclusions		X		
Identify solutions to problems		X		
Help plan and organize equipment in the classroom			X	
Conserve materials		X		
Identify boundaries			X	
Initiate changes to the outside environment		X		

FIGURE 11.5 |

FIGURE 11.6 |

- X rays & EkG readings - made during hospital play theme

FIGURE 11.7

TABLE 11.5	*Bodily/Kinesthetic Intelligence Play Assessment*		
The Child:	Needs Help	Progressing	Mastered
Explores materials with the senses (Sensory)			X
Manipulates objects motorically (Motor)			X
Moves objects intentionally and begins to use objects to represent ideas (beginning of symbolic thought) (Level I Representation)			X
Elaborates on play ideas and develops themes (Level II Representation)			X
Uses words to represent experiences (Level III Representation)		X	

TABLE 11.6 | *Bodily/Kinesthetic Intelligence Checklist*

The Child Will Demonstrate the Bodily/Kinesthetic Ability to:	Not Interested	Needs Help	Progressing	Mastered
Maintain balance: On one foot			X	
Beam walking		X		
Body rolling		X		
Dodging			X	
Landing		X		
Give force to the body through space: Run				X
Jump				X
Hop				X
Skip				X
Leap				X
Give force to and from objects: Throw			X	
Catch		X		
Kick			X	
Strike		X		
Dribble		X		
Move in straight and curved paths			X	
Demonstrate directionality: Right and left		X		
Up and down		X		
Side to side		X		
Use a pincer grasp when writing and drawing				X
Use the body to perform a culturally acceptable role				X
Use scissors				X
Use a hole puncher				X
Use tape				X
Manipulate small objects				X
Manipulate large objects			X	
Incorporate exercise into his/her daily routine			X	
Demonstrate schematic drawing abilities				X
Manipulate art mediums to represent an experience or idea			X	

Tori's interpretation of
Evard Munch's *The Scream.*

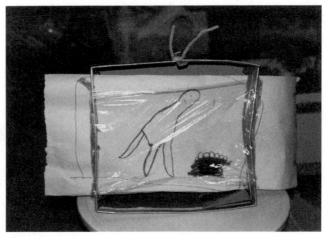

Creating a museum on TV

TABLE 11.7	*Spatial Intelligence Play Assessment*		
The Child:	**Needs Help**	**Progressing**	**Mastered**
Explores materials with the senses (Sensory)			X
Manipulates objects motorically (Motor)			X
Moves objects intentionally and begins to use objects to represent ideas (beginning of symbolic thought) (Level I Representation)			X
Elaborates on play ideas and develops themes (Level II Representation)			X
Uses words to represent experiences (Level III Representation)			X

TABLE 11.8 | *Spatial Intelligence Checklist*

The Child Will Demonstrate the Spatial Ability to:	Not Interested	Needs Help	Progressing	Mastered
Respect body boundaries			X	
Respect environmental boundaries			X	
Respect materials boundaries			X	
Move appropriately in the environment			X	
Identify how objects move				X
Predict how an object would move				X
Complete a simple puzzle				X
Complete a complex puzzle				X
Draw a map				X
Explain simple directions to a familiar destination			X	
Conserve space			X	
Use schematic art representation				X
Use language-mediated art representation				X
Participate in visual art activities from various cultures			X	
Represent him/herself through visual arts			X	
Identify and recreate shapes seen in the environment				X
Create original shapes				X
Represent an experience using a model				X
Identify the function of a map and globe				X
Manipulate light			X	
Manipulate color			X	
Use a mental map to organize information			X	
Organize drawings and materials to communicate a message				X

FIGURE 11.8

Tori the Famous Ballerin

FIGURE 11.9

FIGURE 11.10 | A Summer Day

FIGURE 11.11 |

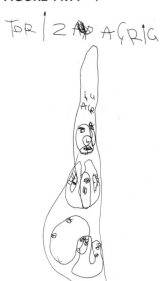

TOR | 2 AD AGRIG

i 4
ACR

FIGURE 11.12 |

All the things
I like to do
with my
family
by Tori

BOX 11.3 | *Spatial Anecdotal Record*

Spatial Intelligence

Anecdotal Record taken on 11/12/02

During a dinosaur project, Tori demonstrated a great strength in representing an experience using a model. After the project ended, Tori gathered clay and a large box in the art area. Tori asked Koni to sit at the table and listen to her tell a story about dinosaurs. Tori made a long green shape that she called Diplodocus. She began to tell a story to the other child,

One day, a zillion years ago, a diplodocus lived in a forest. It was time for her to have her babies. She built a nest in the forest and hid it in weeds. She laid her eggs. (As she said this, she made eggs and a nest out of clay.) *The eggs hatched and a baby dinosaur began to move around.* (She made a baby dinosaur out of the clay.) *The dinosaur grew, and soon was an adult.* (She placed the original dinosaur into the box again.) *Suddenly, a meteor shower began.* (She threw clay balls into the box.) *It killed the dinosaur.* (She placed the dinosaur on its side in the box.) *The world began to change. Many years later, a paleontologist was walking in the forest. He discovered some bones.* (She made bones out of clay and scattered them through the box.) *The paleontologist took the bones back to his lab and put them together.* (She arranged the bones in a small plastic box and placed it into the large box.) *Now, kids can see that same dinosaur.* (She gathered plastic people and placed them inside the box to look at the bones.)

TABLE 11.9	*Intrapersonal Intelligence Play Assessment*		
The Child:	Needs Help	Progressing	Mastered
Explores materials with the senses (Sensory)			X
Manipulates objects motorically (Motor)			X
Moves objects intentionally and begins to use objects to represent ideas (beginning of symbolic thought) (Level I Representation)			X
Elaborates on play ideas and develops themes (Level II Representation)		X	
Uses words to represent experiences (Level III Representation)		X	

Tori evaluating her own work in her portfolio.

TABLE 11.10 | *Intrapersonal Intelligence Checklist*

The Child Will Demonstrate the Intrapersonal Ability to:	Not Interested	Needs Help	Progressing	Mastered
Discuss likes and dislikes			X	
Choose to be alone at times				X
Present accomplishments in a positive way			X	
Accept the privilege that he/she can make a mistake		X		
Create projects that resemble self				X
Present how she/he is alike and different			X	
Follow a routine			X	
Identify and cope with a change in routine		X		
Choose appropriate materials to complete a task			X	
Put materials away after completing a task		X		
Initiate ideas for class and individual projects			X	
Help to establish procedures for proper use of materials			X	
Manipulate materials appropriately			X	
Understand, remember, and respect rules			X	
Use transductive reasoning			X	
Discuss what it feels like to be mad, sad, happy, etc.			X	
Develop strategies to channel emotions appropriately	X			
Use materials to express feelings	X			
Reflect on and evaluate experiences	X			
Discuss changes			X	

FIGURE 11.13

X A P E   S L E P

BOX 11.4 | *Intrapersonal Anecdotal Record*

Intrapersonal Intelligence

Anecdotal Record Taken on 12/02/02

Tori was in the art area working on a picture. Tori has demonstrated great artistic strength with many different art materials. As she was attempting to construct a three-dimensional building, Tori verbalized that her building did not look right. She threw her materials on the ground, stomped on them and said, "I hate this stupid tape."

This experience is typical of the way Tori expresses frustration.

BOX 11.5 | *Intrapersonal Anecdotal Record 2*

Intrapersonal Intelligence

Anecdotal Record Taken 8/02/02

During sharing time, Tori asked if she could share a story she made up about a fairy. Over the past few weeks, news headlines had centered on child abduction cases. The story was recorded. The transcript follows:

Once upon a time, there was a beautiful fairy. She wanted to fly around the whole world. Her mother told her she was too young and could not go. She was so angry and sat in her room. She ran away and explored the world. Suddenly, during her exploration, the fairy met a strange fairy. He was a stranger and started to talk to her. She got very scared and flew home as fast as she could. She cried when she saw her mother and promised never to run away from home again and was never stolen.

Interpretation:

The story communicates her sense of the headlines that have been in the news. It also communicates her fear of being stolen, and perhaps communicates her association between wrongdoings and bad life events.

TABLE 11.11 | *Interpersonal Intelligence Play Assessment*

The Child:	Needs Help	Progressing	Mastered
Explores materials with the senses (Sensory)			X
Manipulates objects motorically (Motor)			X
Moves objects intentionally and begins to use objects to represent ideas (beginning of symbolic thought) (Level I Representation)			X
Elaborates play ideas and develops themes (Level II Representation)		X	
Uses words to represent experiences (Level III Representation)		X	

TABLE 11.12 | *Interpersonal Intelligence Checklist*

The Child Will Demonstrate the Interpersonal Ability to:	Not Interested	Needs Help	Progressing	Mastered
Engage in cooperative play			X	
Participate in activities from a differently abled child's perspective			X	
Initiate and maintain appropriate peer interactions			X	
Participate in activities which reflect various cultures			X	
Be able to solve social conflicts appropriately	X			
Respect another child's body and belongings			X	
Express and accept ideas			X	
Understand a speaker accurately			X	
Determine the mood and intention of another	X			
Be able to express a different point of view appropriately			X	
Respond to another child's actions or projects appropriately			X	
Communicate information to peers through dramatization			X	
Contribute to a common play theme through interactions and dialogue during free play			X	
Accept and/or offer help from/to others when needed		X		
Define community roles				X
Understand and communicate familial roles			X	

TABLE 11.13 | *Musical Intelligence Play Assessment*

The Child:	Needs Help	Progressing	Mastered
Explores materials with the senses (Sensory)			X
Manipulates objects motorically (Motor)			X
Moves objects intentionally and begins to use objects to represent ideas (beginning of symbolic thought) (Level I Representation)			X
Elaborates play ideas and develops themes (Level II Representation)			X
Uses words to represent experiences (Level III Representation)		X	

FIGURE 11.14 |

TABLE 11.14	*Musical Intelligence Checklist*			
The Child Will Demonstrate the Musical Ability to:	**Not Interested**	**Needs Help**	**Progressing**	**Mastered**
Identify a sound pattern			X	
Respond to various types of music			X	
Repeat a simple melody using words and sounds				X
Manipulate objects in the environment to produce sounds				X
Manipulate a single object to produce a variation of sounds			X	
Identify different types of music			X	
Identify differences in tones and pitches			X	
Improvise songs to go along with daily activities				X
Identify the source of common sounds				X
Remember a melody				X
Write or tell a poem				X
Imitate a rhythm				X
Create a rhythm				X
Create a melody				X
Sing independently				X
Sing in a group				X
Describe different types of music				X
Move to a musical beat and change in tempo			X	
Read simple musical selections		X		
Write a short musical selection		X		
Explores materials with the senses (Sensory)				X

BOX 11.6 | *Musical Anecdotal Record*

Musical Intelligence

Anecdotal Record Taken 11/4/02

During play, Tori put on butterfly wings and began to dance and sing on the large carpet in the center of the room. Her song was recorded. The transcript of the cassette follows:

Fairies are beautiful. So beautiful. When the time comes, I love to fly with them. Fairies every day. Flying in the forest, Looking for the flowers. So beautiful. We'll be together forever, flying with the fairies.

Tori typically narrates her play through songs and stories.

TABLE 11.15 | *Naturalist Intelligence Play Assessment*

The Child:	Needs Help	Progressing	Mastered
Manipulates objects motorically (Motor)			
Moves objects intentionally and begins to use objects to represent ideas (beginning of symbolic thought) (Level I Representation)			X X
Elaborates play ideas and develops themes (Level II Representation)			X
Uses words to represent experiences (Level III Representation)			X

TABLE 11.16 | *Naturalist Intelligence Checklist*

The Child Will Demonstrate the Naturalist Ability to:	Not Interested	Needs Help	Progressing	Mastered
Classify natural objects			X	
Participate in field trips				X
Discuss weather patterns			X	
Interpret weather patterns			X	
Predict weather patterns			X	
Initiate positive changes to the environment		X		

Gather information about the natural world through:
    Outdoor play
    Field trips
    Nature walks
			X
			X
			X	

Care for a classroom pet or plant			X	
Identify patterns in nature			X	
Use natural materials in functional ways			X	
Identify characteristics between natural objects and human-made objects			X	
Use tools to learn about the natural world			X	
Grow a plant from a seed			X	
Describe the life cycle of an insect or animal			X	
Interpret information gained through scientific tools			X	
Successfully plan and maintain a garden			X	

11.7

Journal Activity

After reviewing the information contained in the portfolio, complete an intelligence profile for Tori. What strengths do you notice? What challenges do you notice? A sample challenge has been provided. (You might not have information for each square on the following chart.)

Intelligence Profile

Intelligence	Strengths	Challenges
Interpersonal		
Intrapersonal		Tori has a great strength in aesthetic expression; however, she has a difficult time expressing and dealing with frustration. She also has difficulty asking for and accepting help.
Musical		
Spatial		
Linguistic		
Bodily/ Kinesthetic		
Logical/ Mathematical		
Naturalist		

11.8

Journal Activity

After completing the profile, what goals might be appropriate to set for Tori?

Intelligence Profile

Intelligence	To Encourage Strengths:	To Address Challenges:
Interpersonal		
Intrapersonal		
Musical		
Spatial		
Linguistic		
Bodily/ Kinesthetic		
Logical/ Mathematical		
Naturalist		

11.9

Journal Activity

Choose one of the intelligences from the previous chart and look at the challenges. Pick one challenge and plan one activity that might help Tori deal with the challenge.

Intelligence: _____

Activity:

> Drawing of the activity if needed.

Activity Objective:

Core Concepts:

Materials:

Developmental Rationale: (Why did you pick this activity for Tori? How will this help her address her challenge?)

Procedure:

11.10
Journal Questions

In reading through Tori's bodily/kines-thetic portfolio material, what do you notice about her gross-motor and fine-motor abilities?

Tori has demonstrated challenges in gross-motor aspects of bodily/kinesthetic development. How could you use her strengths to help her deal with gross-motor challenges?

For example, how would you use music to encourage gross-motor development?

How could you use her spatial strength to encourage gross-motor development?

FIGURE 11.15

11.11
Journal Question

What materials could you include in the musical center of the classroom to encourage Tori's interest and strength in musical intelligence?

11.12
Journal Question

Look at Figure 11.4 and a typical page from a phonics workbook. Figure 11.4 is a sample of Tori's linguistic development. What do you think tells more about Tori's knowledge of the connection between sounds and symbols?

Curricular Implications of Assessment and Multiple-Intelligence Theory

The sample portfolio demonstrated examples that were organized into the eight intelligence areas. The intelligences can also be used to develop assessment strategies. After a particular concept has been presented, children can demonstrate mastery in a variety of different ways. Children can be asked to come up with presentation methods on their own, or teachers can provide different experiences for children to choose from. The children can pick one activity that will demonstrate mastery of a particular concept.

For example, after the children have had experience constructing measurement concepts, the teacher can set up a number of assessment stations. The children can choose a station to express their knowledge of measurement.

Station 1 can be used to assess measurement through linguistic intelligence. Provide the children with a ruler, a large sheet of construction paper with a caterpillar drawn in the middle, and the following story.

A caterpillar is looking for a place to make his chrysalis. He walks three inches to the left. He then walks six inches towards the north. He does not see a good place to stop. He walks four inches to the right. He walks ten inches to the south. Suddenly, he sees a nice tree to the left. He walks seven inches to the left, stops, and decides to build his chrysalis there.

The children can be asked to draw the path the caterpillar took, as the story is told.

Station 2 can be used to assess measurement through spatial intelligence using blocks. The children can be offered blocks and asked to create a building that is twice as high as it is long.

Station 3 can be used to assess measurement through art materials. The children can be asked to create a symmetrical art project. They will need to measure in order to make sure their creation is symmetrical.

11.13 Journal Activity

Congratulations! You have finished the text! Think back to the box that was talked about at the beginning of this text. Look back at the contents of the box you identified in Journal Question 1.2. Add to that box, based on your interactions with this text. Have your ideas concerning curriculum, pedagogy, intelligence, assessment, activities, developmentally appropriate practice, and play changed? Stayed the same? Added to? Remember, the contents of that box will stay with you throughout your early childhood education career.

Write your final 1 to 2 page philosophy of early childhood education. Use your philosophy created in response to Journal Question 1.7 as a starting point. This philosophy will guide you as you create, prepare, and utilize early childhood education curricula.

Remember, you are a powerful individual. You have the power to influence and touch the lives of many children. What you say and what you do with children today will have a lasting impact on society. Treat this responsibility with great care and consideration.

Station 4 can be used to assess measurement through bodily/kinesthetic intelligence. Children can predict and measure how far they can jump or hop.

Station 5 can be used to assess measurement through naturalist intelligence. Children can be asked to create a bird house out of sticks. The bird house must be built to specific dimensions.

 # Conclusion

A variety of assessment strategies exist and can be organized using a portfolio. Portfolio assessment strategies allow the teacher and the child to create the assessment process together.

Approaching assessment through the multiple-intelligence theory provides more useful information than a standard pencil and paper task. The above assessment methods assess the child's application of knowledge and skills in contextual settings, where the knowledge/skills really matter.

References

Bredekamp, S., & Copple, C. (eds.) (1996) *Developmentally appropriate practice in early childhood programs* (Revised Ed.). Washington, DC: NAEYC.

Gardner, H. (1999) *The disciplined mind.* New York: Simon & Schuster.

Gardner, H. (1983) *Frames of mind.* New York: Basic Books.

Gardner, H. (1993) *Frames of mind.* New York: Basic Books.

Hills, T. (1999) "Reaching potentials through appropriate assessment." *Reaching potentials: Appropriate early childhood curriculum and assessment for young children.* Washington, DC: NAEYC.

Kamii, C., & Kamii, M. (1990) "Why achievement testing should stop." *Achievement testing in the early grades.* Washington, DC: NAEYC.

Kohn, A. (2000) *The case against standardized testing: Raising the scores, ruining the schools.* Portsmouth, NH: Heinemann.

National Association for the Education of Young Children and National Association of Early Childhood Specialists in State Departments of Education Position Statement. (1991) "Guidelines for appropriate curriculum content and assessment in programs serving children ages 3 through 8." *Young Children,* 46(3), 21–38.

Index